Radical Hospitality for a Prophetic Church

Radical Hospitality for a Prophetic Church

Amanda D. Quantz

Foreword by Roger Schroeder, SVD

LEXINGTON BOOKS/FORTRESS ACADEMIC
Lanham • Boulder • New York • London

Published by Lexington Books/Fortress Academic
Lexington Books is an imprint of The Rowman & Littlefield Publishing Group, Inc.
4501 Forbes Boulevard, Suite 200, Lanham, Maryland 20706
www.rowman.com

6 Tinworth Street, London SE11 5AL, United Kingdom

British Library Cataloguing in Publication Information Available

Library of Congress Control Number: 2019914247

Contents

Foreword

Just after she finished her doctorate and joined our faculty, Amanda Quantz and I some fifteen years ago designed a course that we would team-teach in a newly designed interdisciplinary curriculum at Catholic Theological Union. One of the primary goals of the course, entitled "Foundations: Understanding Christian Tradition," was intended to introduce first-year master-level theology and ministry students to the nature, breadth, and pluriformity of the Christian tradition, from a global and contextual perspective. The latter represented a move away from a primarily Eurocentric, "mainstream," male perspective to one in which varied expressions of Christianity in multiple contexts across time and space would begin to find a voice at the table. This course provided Quantz and me a "launching pad" into new fields of discovering and exploring theology, history, and ministry. *Radical Hospitality for a Prophetic Church* is the rich fruit of the development and maturation of her thought and reflection since those early years of graduate teaching.

The terms "inculturation" and "contextualization" were initially associated with grounding Christian faith with the former "mission lands" of Asia, Africa, Latin America, and Oceania. Scholars and others now recognize that this necessary dynamic is not geographically bound. Rather the "West" is in just as, and perhaps more of, a need of such inculturation. The groundbreaking contribution by Amanda Quantz is her bold attempt to offer alternative avenues for understanding and engaging the opportunities for contextualizing the Christian life among the Millennial generation of North America. Furthermore, while a number of theologians and church ministers are addressing this urgent issue with new but more traditional Christian categories and perspectives, Quantz is using a much more radical avant-garde approach. This may be shocking for some readers, but she is moving beyond the "normal" margins of describing Christian expressions. This is similar to including the first

Chinese Christian writings of the seventh century, the lay women's Beguine movement of the Middle Ages, and the African Independent Churches in "mainstream" Christian history and theology. Furthermore, the significance of Quantz's work is that she is not only describing the current phenomena of Millennials' spiritual and life experience, but in the process, she is proposing an emerging contextual theology by drawing upon both comparative and practical theologies.

The past occasional tendency of Christianity to label cultures, religions, and peoples as "pagan" and "heathen" has unfortunately continued to be cast upon Millennials, "Nones," and others of secular society or marginalized groups. Quantz is tapping the radically inclusive reign-of-God vision and mission of Jesus Christ to appreciate and dialogue with several expressions of the spiritual yearnings of young people in Western society today. While this proposal is deeply dialogical, it is just as deeply prophetic. In both cases it is radical. In both cases it is deeply Catholic.

The 2018 World Youth Day in Panama City, the Synod on Youth, and the follow-up 2019 Apostolic Exhortation by Pope Francis on "Young People, the Faith, and Vocational Discernment" points to the church's shared concern to find a way to listen to the Millennials and "Nones" of today. Quantz is likewise striving to engage in a mutually enriching and challenging conversation. May the readers of *Radical Hospitality for a Prophetic Church* be able to discover in the words of the African American ex-slave Sojourner Truth: "Oh God, I did not know you were so big!"[1]

Dr. Roger Schroeder
Louis J. Luzbetak, SVD Professor of Mission and Culture
Catholic Theological Union at Chicago

NOTE

1. Sojourner Truth, "Document 3, Sojourner Truth: The Conversion of a Female Slave," in *In Their Own Voices: Four Centuries of American Women's Religious Writing*, ed. Rosemary Radford Ruether and Rosemary Skinner Keller (San Francisco: HarperCollins, 1995), 173.

Acknowledgments

This book was very much a joint effort. It was molded by the curiosity and spiritual longings of undergraduates at the University of Saint Mary. Several of these gifted ministers who have since finished graduate school poked holes in early drafts: Preston Becker, Mary Kate Becker, Connolly Huddleston, and Shana Moriarty. Robert Mundle, a longtime *anam cara*, provided encouragement and insight as we accompanied one another through our individual projects. Colleagues and sojourners who helped me sort out dangling threads include Rosie Kolich, SCL; Steve Bevans, SVD; Roger Schroeder, SVD; Masa Watanabe; Max Hetherington; Angela Paviglianiti; and Mary Kallman. An unusually talented polyglot Mark Bowers helped me probe the essence of a dozen or so ancient languages. Jenny Tan provided guidance in my search for the etymologies of Chinese characters.

Several institutions and communities offered their own contributions to this book. The University of Saint Mary graciously provided a sabbatical. Travel support to Burning Man was provided by Bill Krusemark, Sister Mary Janet McGilley Endowed Chair in Liberal Arts as well as Karenbeth Zacharias, Liberal Arts and Humanities Division Chair. The University of San Francisco hosted numerous outstanding writing retreats. The staff at the Linda Hall Library and the women and men of Guardian Angels Catholic Church in Kansas City encouraged my exploration from beginning to end. The guests, volunteers, and unflappable staff at The Gubbio Project, especially John Brett, Christina Alvarez, and Laura Slattery, boldly evoke and witness to the gospel daily. The New Skellig Celtic Christian community and St. Columba's Episcopal Church provided kinship through hospitality and prayer, especially Vincent Pizzuto, Fernando Esponda, Monica Doblado, Anna Haight, and George Rangitsch. In their creative efforts to support young adults through MercyWorks and their celebration of prayer in the tradition of

Taizé, Patsy Harney, Jean Evans, Suzanne Toolan, and other Sisters of Mercy have provided companionship for many years. Fr. Brian Baker's courage and imagination inspired me to follow him down the rabbit hole to Black Rock City, NV, for an inimitable experience of church outside the walls.

I am indebted to two people for the cover photos: Fernando Esponda took the picture of the altar in the vicarage at St. Columba's Episcopal Church in Inverness, CA. With great enthusiasm, Annie Doherty captured the picture of Rev. Baker at Burning Man. Chapter 4 includes a drawing of the interior of the Episcopal Church of St. John the Evangelist by a Gubbio Project guest I call "Johnny."

This book is dedicated to Micky Powell, the teacher whose acrobatics provided a formative, upside-down glimpse of the world, and to Bob Powell (1937–2018), who modeled graciousness and joy for generations. In gratitude for their generosity, wisdom, friendship, and many decades of laughter.

Introduction

A Prophetic Endeavor—Mutuality, Plurality, Transformation

AUDIENCE AND METHOD

When I graduated from college in 1995, the hopeful mood of the Second Vatican Council (1962–1965) still permeated Roman Catholicism both in ecclesial and in academic spheres. My peers and I were trained by theologians who could not have foreseen the rapid changes that would impact the council's reforming trajectory. By the time I finished my PhD in 2003, some ecclesial regions were experiencing a rapid climate change. I was teaching courses in church history from a global perspective at a progressive Catholic U.S. institution. As with many institutions of higher education, there was a strident minority consisting of U.S. members of religious communities who envisioned as normative a church that I did not recognize: rigid, self-assured, reactionary, anti-intellectual. That small group held an uncritical view of the Roman Catholic tradition, projecting onto it a pristine past as well as a present that was unaffected by the ambiguities of postmodernity. Often wrong but never in doubt, they argued their positions by conjuring narratives that collectively formed what they saw as the "authentic" Catholic tradition. It was as if they saw the church as a giant flawless diamond: housed in a museum, protected by bullet-proof glass, and guaranteed to dazzle the viewer. Naïve and unaware of the dehumanizing potential of a rigid ecclesiology, they supported a model that reinforced the patriarchal, heterosexist prejudices that have kept the church from living the gospel as fully as possible. Then, as now, I saw the history of Christianity as a yearbook filled with the thoughtful, unfinished contributions of curious, well-meaning, eccentric historical figures.

More than fifty years since the conclusion of the Second Vatican Council (1962–1965), most committed U.S. Catholics are aware that for obvious reasons, radical traditionalists have gained momentum in our increasingly chaotic era. They are not the majority voice in the U.S. church, nor do I believe that their views will become normative. Though I find their intellectual outlook to be superficial, their organizations tend to be well funded by people who reject any suggestion that Jesus as portrayed in the gospels lived according to what today we call socialist values. I will not try to persuade those who see themselves as radical traditionalists who they are misinformed. However, I am hopeful that some who currently see only a narrow theological spectrum might be drawn to the surprising, grace-filled ecclesial realities that fill a wide historical vector. Mindful of traditionalists but not addressing them specifically, I am writing for those whose work and spiritual lives will be fed by the stories, wisdom, key figures, and ministries, past and present, that can help propel the church into an uncertain future.

As my primary audience I have in mind North American graduate students in theology, or those who plan to serve in North America and need a deeper understanding of the U.S. mission field. I believe that the ministries and resources included in this volume will appeal to those who identify with any number of Christian denominations. I am also writing for seasoned ministers who are on the lookout for alternative ways to draw on the church's history and mission. I hope this serves as an academic resource to help both groups respond more creatively and boldly to the gospel. Kindred spirits in this conversation are colleagues who received their academic formation in the twentieth century and want to ensure that the future church will thrive on the solid food of spiritual sustenance and intellectual nourishment. My hope for all of us is that we will adapt and change faithfully and creatively in order to serve the church and its future ministers effectively well into the third millennium. My own reference points are primarily Roman Catholic, but I draw on resources beyond the boundaries of that tradition.

Though I was sure at first that he was joking, a Presbyterian colleague once told me about a Protestant seminary in which the course on early Christianity began with the sixteenth century. Since many Protestant churches grew out of Roman Catholicism, I intentionally weave in and out of Christian denominations. I have structured the book in a way that parallels my teaching method, which requires a bit of patience and elasticity on the part of participants. Students have described it using the image of concentric circles: I draw on historical narratives, theological concepts, and pastoral endeavors to form distinct Venn diagrams that collectively depict an interactive model of the Christian tradition. In this book I have been guided by the image of the church as an array of constellations. In the actual sky some stars are older than others, which is also true of ecclesial movements and ministries, as well as other religious traditions. Both the span of Christian history and the night sky are too vast to process in looking up at the "dome." Planetariums design exhibits to highlight specific features. As mesmerizing as the individual features are, if we do not occasionally scan the entire night sky while star gazing, we will fail to appreciate the unique location and relative size of each constellation. Neither lens enables us to perceive every aspect of what we are seeing. As with the night sky, the backdrop for our ecclesial constellations is the universe that was created and is sustained by a loving, generous God who is "something greater than which cannot be thought."[1]

Because God knows no limits there is enough room in the universe for all of creation, both among and beyond the constellations that make up the church. I am offering the reader one exhibit from the vast array of constellations that belong to the church. The assortment I have chosen is unique but is no more or less significant than the assortment chosen by colleagues. Since I have written a book rather than a program for stargazing, a conventional way to think of this contribution is as just one volume in a library of faith-filled resources.

Other scholars who teach at the intersection of missiology, historical theology, and pastoral ministry would draw on a different variety of narratives and theological points, creating additional "exhibits." Reaching into our own social locations and interests, our theological vocation compels us to encourage both the academy and the church to focus on three primary, humanizing, Trinitarian emanations: goodness, truth, and beauty. Through the influence of the Holy Spirit, these emerge most effusively as complex, untidy, often fraught conversations, and endeavors. As a friend once described our communion as "the church of the great unwashed," to which I replied: "Thanks be to God."

With regard to the future of academic theology in the U.S. Catholic context, an article in *Commonweal Magazine* named some of the dangers of complacency and denial within theology departments about impending curricular changes.[2] They offer two main points: So that we do not end up in a Catholic ghetto, theologians need to continue to find ways to engage deliberately with the ecclesial establishment. Also, we do not know what form or function academic theology will have in the second wave of the New Education,[3] but it will surely be different than what those of us trained in the twentieth century long believed we could count on. Given these two premises I am hopeful that this book will help my Catholic colleagues who are mid-career or beyond find ways to continue the reforming, impactful work of Vatican II. Perhaps together we can encourage younger colleagues to join us in that Spirit-filled commitment. Given our shared theological heritage, I believe that most of what I have written will be equally helpful to Protestant colleagues and students when applied to their unique ecclesial contexts.

A Prophetic Endeavor

While today there are exemplary ministries that occupy the margins, the church's twenty-first-century way of loving seems at times a dim reflection of Jesus' radically inclusive mission. Since it is tempting to choose another, less controversial path, in every era the church must revisit St. Paul's "gift of love" (1 Cor. 13). It would be romantic to suggest that the church was consistently better at navigating the pilgrims' path in earlier eras and distant places. However, I believe that when the church reaches deep into its history, it can find what it needs in order to make its way along the journey: to be more prophetic, "to speak on behalf of" (*pro + phanai*); to advocate for people's needs. To be prophetic is to choose action over apathy. If the Protestant Reformations demonstrated anything, it was that if the church is not continually in a process of self-reformation, rather than be an agent of change, it will be changed from without. Prophetic action and dialogue are hallmarks of "a still more excellent way." It precludes meandering timidly through life.[4]

Fr. Greg Boyle, SJ, the founder of Homeboy Industries, has spent several prophetic decades practicing a ministry of kinship in his work with former gang members. His commitment to people who have been alienated from themselves and their families has inspired ministers, philanthropists, community organizers, and social workers to reframe their understanding of the power of street ministry. In a lecture given at the University of San Francisco in 2018, Boyle highlighted something that he had not explored in the earlier presentations I had attended. Quoting Jeremiah, he reflected on the unmistakable power of God to transform all things, even the places we deem most contaminated: "In this place of which you say, 'It is a waste without human beings or animals,' in the towns of Judah and the streets of Jerusalem that are desolate, without inhabitants, human or animal, there shall once more be heard the voice of mirth and the voice of gladness."[5] Deeply aware of the connection between harmful behavior and spiritual malaise, he notes that "the God we have is different than the partial, puny God we've settled for."[6] He hopes that the church hears in Jeremiah an exhortation to redirect the people of God whenever we begin down a path toward a false, puny god.

Informed by flourishing ministries that remind the church of the transformative power of God, this book bridges pastoral theory and practice, illustrating its potential to live into its conviction that God is greater than our greatest imaginings. Just as the energy of falling water is converted by a turbine into hydraulic power, the energy for this study was generated through the interspiritual work of creative theologians, especially Raimón Panikkar, Anthony de Mello and Wayne Teasdale. The hydraulic energy we use in our daily endeavors can be released both in huge waves that fuel high-intensity projects involving power tools and at the lower, more gradual rate that keeps the lights on at home. Both come from clean sources and serve good and useful purposes. Powerful and life giving, water has miraculous properties. No matter how seemingly insignificant the condensation on a thin membrane of glass, when gathered into a pool, even a tiny amount of standing water can fuel a clock that keeps us on task. Different and necessary for the life of the church, I will illustrate high-voltage projects, such as street ministries, as well as slow-burning contemplative practices. Both encourage the church to continue to spend its energy at the margins, where diverse expressions of faith can invigorate its mission and identity.

Mutuality

An intuition that drives this project is a biblical-cosmological concept of what the church can look like when human beings are in right relationship with God and one another. In the Genesis narrative, God commissions human beings to care for and enjoy the world God has made. In that pre-incarnational spiritual age, humanity served as God's bridge between heaven and earth.[7] In John's Gospel, we learn from the incarnate Word about what human love ought to look like. Through the Christ event, divinity reaches out to humanity, reinforcing the bridge between earth and heaven and clearing the path to God. Making all things new, wherever there is self-absorption and complacency, Jesus calls humanity to establish generosity of spirit and justice. Our cosmotheandric scriptures tell the story of God's desire for real relationship and reconciliation.[8] In collating the work of visionary Christian theologians, as well as historical examples and contemporary ministries that illustrate success at the institutional level, I am inviting the church to emphasize mutuality as a model of justice-centered work. The book is not intended to confront the institutional church about what many Catholics, particularly loosely affiliated U.S. Millennials, believe are areas in which the church fails to live the gospel as radically as Jesus intended. There are several recent, excellent studies that explore the root causes of shrinking numbers of institutionally affiliated Catholics and other Christians.[9] Rather, by celebrating what it has done and continues to do well at the margins, I am inviting the whole church to be transformed by faithful fringe movements. If done with integrity and optimism, what is currently marginal can become mainstream.

An Educational *Aggiornamento*

With each passing year, institutional religion becomes less attractive to the majority of North Americans. Roughly 36 percent of U.S. American Millennials (born 1981–1996) are religiously unaffiliated "Nones," yet 80 percent are attracted to emerging spiritual communities and practices. Millennials are 13 percent more likely to reject institutional Christianity than members of Generation X (born 1965–1980).[10] Ministers and religious educators have been unable or unwilling to teach Christian doctrine in a way that enables believers to maintain enthusiasm over the course of their lives, in part for fear of losing the nexus of the gospel. Since little has been done to translate the symbols, metaphors, and worldview within the narratives of the most widely read and least understood book in history, the stories can be perceived as flat, especially as Christians move into young adulthood. The problem lies not with the biblical texts, but rather, with the narrow criteria that have traditionally been used to determine which extra-biblical resources are suitable for illuminating the teachings of Jesus. Marginally Christian Millennials who received stale catechesis are often receptive when Christian principles such as humility and non-judgment are presented through the wisdom stories of other religious traditions. In chapter 2, I explore a way to illuminate the Christian scriptures by drawing on those resources.

Along with E. J. Dionne, I believe that "religion has a strong case to make for itself—to the young and to everyone else—given its historical role as a prod to personal and social change and the ways in which movements for justice have been inspired through the centuries by the words of Exodus, Micah, Isaiah, Amos and Jesus."[11] This book is an alternative resource for those who are open to drawing on global wisdom as well as the church's own best practices, in order to help Millennials and others discover new ways to enter into and live out the teachings of Jesus.

The church has many tools for revivifying the Christian message. One of the great resources for creative theological reflection is the Franciscan Intellectual Tradition, which had a strong impact on my own faith development and therefore on this book. An abiding love for creation and creativity are among the many gifts that the Franciscan imagination has imparted to the church. These values have enabled Franciscans to help move the church forward in its awareness of God's diffusive love throughout the cosmos, from the smallest ant to the widest ocean to the most off-putting human beings whom society tries to ignore. When I described this book to a Franciscan sister who I interviewed for one of the chapters on street ministry, she reflected back to me that what I am advocating for in theological terms is something that permaculture gardeners understand: growth begins at the margins and moves inward.[12] She explained that the first principle of biointensive gardening is that native plants and those that grow without too much intervention make the best candidates. Another best practice is to choose individual organisms that will naturally work well together, including plants that are diverse enough to support one another. In planting a healthy, low-maintenance garden those who tend to it must understand essential aspects of the environment, such as soil, light, and temperature variations. Citrus trees are difficult to grow in the Midwest and can only be cultivated in a carefully controlled environment. They can survive with pampering but are not candidates for biointensive gardening in that region and are likely to remain ornamental.

As with permaculture gardens, ministries that have been planted at the margins can provide nourishment for the whole church if the landscape architects are willing to introduce species that are uncultivated instead of those that require a lot of fuss. With time and space, wild species will influence tidy plants. This is not to say that tidy gardens are useless. In fact, the intensity of their colors and fragrances naturally attract birds and bees without which there would be no propagation. The design of medieval and early modern ornamental gardens such as those that cover most of Vatican Hill and Hampton Court put into perspective why the church must attend to ornamental beauty. The expansive Vatican Gardens can help the popes and other church leaders find respite in a chaotic world, reminding them to cultivate a life of prayer. The Maze Garden at Hampton Court demonstrates the divinely infused gift of the imagination. Rituals, traditions, and institutions are good and necessary for the church, but just as they influence ecclesial life, messy, bold encounters, and ministries are vital reminders to the institutional church that Jesus is present not only in the tabernacle and the palace garden, but also in the streets and community gardens.

Pope Francis took a bold step toward integrating the contemplative and radical roots of the church when he installed showers and shelters at the Vatican for those who are unhoused. Reporting on Pope Francis' 2015 visit to the United States one *Washington Post* reporter noted that "to go from some of the most powerful to the least reflects his view of the world and the church and economics."[13] There is global wisdom and a prophetic call in the pope's recognition that a benevolent society ensures that powerful institutions are attentive to the gifts and needs of those who are seeking to live with integrity while struggling spiritually, financially, psychologically, and/or socially. He especially recognizes the struggle of young people to make sense of "the social dimensions of global change."[14] In speaking with the youth of Brescia, Italy, on April 7, 2018, Pope Francis indicated that the October Synod of Bishops would address "Youth, faith and vocational discernment." This was in response to a question from a young man: "Do the bishops really believe that young people can help the church to change?" His reply: "It is very important to me that the next Synod of Bishops . . . be prepared by a *true listening* to young people. And I can testify that this is being done. . . . And when I say 'true listening' I also mean the willingness to change something, to walk together, to share dreams, as that young man said."[15] Pope Francis' 2019 post-synodal apostolic exhortation, *Christus vivit*, is part theological reflection, part after-action report.[16] There he recognizes young peoples' questions and concerns. However, whether in the long term the "willingness to change something" manifests as prophetic, life-giving change initiated by the institutional church remains to be seen. This will test the hierarchy's willingness and ability to undertake a spiritual application of organic farming, a radical idea for administrators who value an ancient, carefully cultivated infrastructure.

Throughout most of Christian history, learning was believed to flow in one direction: from the hierarchy and other teachers to students, both lay and religious. The Catholic intellectual tradition has always encouraged the faithful to temper with love what we learn through reason. One of the most learned popes Gregory the Great (590–604) noted that love itself is a form of knowledge. He also believed that the higher a person's office, the lower she or he must bend in mercy in order to be worthy of it. If Pope Gregory were engaged in active ministry today, he would probably agree that the clergy and theologians have at least as much to learn from acts of love that unfold in the lives of faithful nonspecialists as they can from theological resources and humble clerics. By illustrating the success of street ministries and contemplative prayer groups that function horizontally rather than hierarchically, I am drawing attention to the potential of love and mutual learning to inform and transform the church. In the case of a Franciscan ministry discussed in chapter 4, the language and administrative model used, as well as the relational nature of the ministry itself, demonstrate that the guests who use the shelters are as valued and respected by the staff and volunteers as these servants are by one another. In that form of outreach there is no question that God's house has room for all.

Interspirituality

The authors of *The New Monasticism: An Interspiritual Manifesto for Contemplative Living* define interspirituality as "a contemporary movement that looks beyond any one form to the sharing of wisdom that lies at the root of all religions, to the 'mystic heart.'"[17] Decontextualizing core Christian beliefs and practices by reaching into the wisdom of non-Christian and extracanonical Christian sources, a substantial focus of the book is the needs of people who are underwhelmed by the traditional modes of teaching and living Christianity, including patterns of worship that they believe are behind the times. It is designed to help people who are still somewhat interested in Christianity find new metaphors, symbols, stories, and insights that make sense of Christian faith.

Sources in world Christian history are especially helpful in illustrating why metaphors matter. For example, from the field of missiology, we have the *Masai Creed*, written in 1960 as a collaborative effort by the Masai people of East Africa and the Spiritans, a congregation of Roman Catholic missioners. A catechetical lightning rod, it frames the Nicene-Constantinopolitan Creed in a way that is faithful to both the Masai culture and the theological insights of the patristic era: "He was crucified for us under Pontius Pilate and suffered and was buried, and the third day he rose again" becomes: "He was rejected by his people, tortured, nailed hands and feet to a cross, and died. He lay buried in the grave but the hyenas did not touch him, and on the third day he rose from the grave." The Creed is not compromised by this adaptation. Rather, it is made accessible to a specific community. The reception of the gospel is always contextual, and the contexts grow more challenging as global networks become more intricate and immediate. U.S. Millennials, for whom globalization is a lived reality, need relevant ways to understand the core tenets of Christianity. This book offers a starting point for the challenging work of cultivating a faithful, relevant church.

I should note that this book will not explore the beliefs of individuals and groups (terrorists) who bastardize the faith traditions they claim to exemplify. Their violent acts reveal irrationality and heartlessness. The insanity of violence committed in the name of religion does not have a place in a book that spotlights the beauty and shared wisdom of major faith traditions. That said, I would like to challenge the reader to seek to understand the contexts and worldviews of those who would do harm to others, testing the premise of the bumper sticker that reads: "Love trumps hate." In puzzling over heartlessness and sectarian violence it is helpful to keep in mind that anger is sadness turned inside-out and compassion has a way of cutting through our most solid defenses.

In a world in which it is a standard practice to video conference with friends and strangers on the other side of the world, the church, too, must do its part to cultivate intimacy with our distant neighbors, with whom we have more in common than not. This was one of the greatest contributions of the Second Vatican Council, which continues to impact hopeful ecclesial communities. As events that have unfolded since the 2016 U.S. elections made clear, a commitment to understanding our neighbors cannot be a leisure activity confined to academic conversations and the celebration of one another's holidays. Our neighbors are our health-care providers, supervisors, refugees in need of compassion and material assistance, and sometimes, unfortunately, political opponents.

The book shares its roots with studies in comparative theology, yet my primary goal, to reanimate people's faith lives, falls within the scope of practical theology. An intertheological study, the book provides tools for rediscovering Christian faith not only from sources within the church but by respectfully borrowing from the wisdom of other traditions. Most of the people I interviewed for this book are unaffiliated Millennial seekers who were to some extent raised as Christians but have a felt need for greater nourishment through "interspiritual" principles and practices. Some see themselves as "radical" while others see themselves as more mainline. The greatest concentration of that demographic interviewed for this book consisted of "Burners" as well as contemplative seekers who practice Taizé prayer.[18] Overall, the Millennials I interviewed are college-educated professionals. They include visual artists, educators, financial managers, computer tech specialists, social workers, street ministers, parish ministers, seminarians, construction project managers, lobbyists, administrative assistants, and one bartender-model-reality television contestant. Some use recreational drugs. A few have considered priesthood or religious life. A handful have spent time in prison. To assist ministers in guiding Millennials through big questions, such as whether to jettison the Christian tradition, chapter 2 focuses on recontextualizing the teachings of Jesus in order to present them anew for people who crave a transcendent experience that they might struggle to articulate. Five interlinear tables present and engage with multireligious teachings on themes that feature prominently in the gospel: humility, non-judgment, faith, friendship, and wisdom. It offers a sharper pitch for those who are prepared to feed their communities' imagination through innovative teaching and preaching.

Plurality

This study probes the work of Panikkar and Teasdale, developing their conviction that religious plurality is a sign of God's creativity and a starting point for healing and humanizing interpersonal relationships. In fact, Wayne Teasdale invented the word "interspirituality," which I borrow throughout this book. Teasdale passed away in 2004 however, through an interview with Fr. Thomas Matus, a Camaldolese monk in Big Sur, CA, who lived with both Bede Griffiths and Wayne Teasdale, I learned more about Teasdale's understanding of this term. Matus summarized it this way: "Interspirituality is a dialogue in which we realize that we are moving in a similar spiritual environment."[19] Here it is important to underscore the word "similar." None of the comparisons I make in this book between people of different religions, or even between individuals who belong to the same religious tradition, is meant to indicate a one-to-one correlation. At every turn I draw on analogical language which enables a person to celebrate similarities while recognizing differences. Evolving practices develop at the intersection of the two.

In an era in which we are increasingly overwhelmed by the rallying cries of neo-nationalism, this book is a resource for cultivating understanding and respect for our neighbors' faith and values. The title was inspired by the *Prologue* and first chapter of the *Book of Sirach*, which proclaim that wisdom precedes everything else in the universe, and that the teachings of sacred scriptures: the Law, the prophets, and the other books that follow them are "many and great."[20] I would like to help Roman Catholic leaders dial down our church's emphasis on its role among other ancient churches, as *primus inter pares* (first among equals), as well as its fairly limited view of the truth claims of non-Christian religions. Above all, the book takes seriously the implications of the conviction that divine wisdom is an animating and unifying reality for all who seek it.

Anthony de Mello was an Indian Jesuit who founded the *Sadhana* ("Way to God") *Institute*. He drew on a wide variety of proverbs and precepts from Eastern religions as a starting point for exploring Christian principles. His enduring contribution to Christian theology is his way of modeling his own teaching style after Jesus' use of metaphors and analogies. I imagine that during his earthly ministry, Jesus would have appreciated these insights about human beings' longing for spiritual sustenance: "When the pond dries up and the fish are lying on the parched earth, to moisten them with one's breath or damp them with spittle is no substitute for flinging them back into the lake. Don't enliven people with doctrines; throw them back into Reality. For the secret of life is to be found in life itself—not in doctrines about it."[21] Similarly, "By blowing on the thermometer you got it to register higher, but you did not warm the room."[22]

In the Vatican's *Notification Concerning the Writings of Father Anthony de Mello, S.J.*, published after de Mello's death, Cardinal Joseph Ratzinger (Pope Benedict XVI) and Archbishop Tarcisio Bertone, both of the congregation for the Doctrine of the Faith, stated that some of de Mello's "positions are incompatible with the Catholic faith and can cause great harm." Their assessment seems to suggest an unwillingness to step inside de Mello's analogical imagination, wherein God is seen as a *holos*, simultaneously a whole and a part, just as ice and vapor are water in different states. Though de Mello's sudden death at the age of fifty-two prematurely ended his inter-spiritual work, this study celebrates his agility in stretching his own and the church's analogical imaginations.

Calling to mind the various theologians who have received unwanted (and, as has been suggested of some, unwarranted) attention from Vatican overseers, I believe that theology is a work in progress for as long as we are on this side of life. In the wayfaring state we necessarily see through a mirror dimly. I do not know of a single theologian who believes at the end of life that she or he has spilled that last bit of ink in a summary statement on a given topic. There are only experimental works, developing theses, and partial insights. In this book I give primacy of place to the contributions of several innovators who I believe were both faithful and poorly understood. Since no person of good will knowingly adheres to the wrong thing, the concept of heresy (*adhaerere*) is a slippery thing. Integrity leads theologians, both lay and professional, to explore and critique ideas with a spirit of curiosity and generosity, keeping only a loose grip on most analogies, models, and conclusions.

Distinguishing between the relativism of new age eclecticism and the true plurality that provides a deeper understanding of our neighbors' gifts and sharpens our perceptions about our own tradition's truth claims, the book begins and ends with Panikkar's images of the rainbow, the window, and the harmony of many discordant voices. From various angles, including a critique of analogical language, in chapter 2 I confront what is at issue when twenty-first-century Christians argue that certain principles and prayer practices as articulated by other major religious traditions are incompatible with Christianity. I make the case that, even without a doctrinal one-to-one correlation, iterations of Jesus' teachings as expressed by other traditions can challenge the church to move creatively beyond the boundaries of traditional Christian spirituality, while remaining faithful to Scripture and liturgy. Such an effort provides a starting point for religious leaders, whether academic, clerical, or those who work in lay ecclesial ministry, to reach young adult seekers by celebrating global wisdom that enhances Christian faith and practice. It is a response to the invitation extended by Pope John XXIII at the inception of Vatican II to open the doors and windows of the church in order to let in some light and air.

In an essay on interreligious dialogue, Paul Knitter acknowledges that for many years he had "too hastily hoisted the banner of 'pluralism,' before sufficiently recognizing the reality of 'plurality.'"[23] Not an abstract idea dreamed up in an ivory tower, plurality is a fact that has shaped cultures for millennia. While sectarian violence is real, and always has been, it is not a given. For example, Palestinian Christians and Muslims who lived in the Holy Land before the creation of the State of Israel, recall a time in which they lived peacefully with one another and with their Sephardic Jewish neighbors.[24] The core tenets of Judaism, Christianity, and Islam have not changed though the political situations governing daily life in Israel and Palestine have. When in 1917 the British took control of Ottoman Jerusalem they did so without bloodshed. Menachem Klein notes the layered intricacies represented by the transition of power: "Did anyone reflect on the historical irony that the Christian British Empire was taking control of the city from the Muslim Ottomans on Hanukah, the Jewish holiday that commemorates the ancient Jewish conquest of Jerusalem and the liberation of the Holy Temple?"[25] Reflecting on his experience of life in a mixed Jewish-Muslim community in Jerusalem before World War I, Ya'akov Yehoshua noted: "We were like one family, we were all friends. Our mothers poured out their hearts to Muslim women and they poured out their hearts to our mothers."[26] Communities across time and around the world have witnessed to the fact that living well with our neighbors whose beliefs and practices are different from our own cultivates solidarity and brings joy.

Another example of religious plurality is from Southeast Asia, where it is common to have a lived experience of multiple belongings.[27] If one parent is Muslim and the other Christian, a child will often attend both the mosque on Friday and the church on Sunday. The substance of the child's interspiritual *praxis* unfolds through an expression of love when, for example, the Muslim parent encourages the bi-religious child to pray to Jesus, recognizing where she or he ends, and the child begins. In such situations, the Muslim parent reaches into his or her own tradition's reverence for Jesus, and sometimes stretches beyond it for the sake of the child, encouraging him or her to pray as a Christian. She or he does so knowing full well that the child might view Jesus as divine, a departure from the Muslim doctrine that portrays Jesus as a prophet. In such situations, openness to the fluidity of diverse traditions stems from the parent's recognition of the ineffable truth of religious diversity within his or her community, as well as an implied understanding of the ambiguity of language. It is also a sign of a right-sized ego and the subsequent willingness to put the good of the other ahead of one's own.

Transformation

While I was visiting a religious house on the Feast of the Transfiguration, one of the priests mentioned that he had said his morning homily: "We are better at promoting disfiguration than we are at seeking to understand transfiguration." Power struggles between bishops and theologians, and within faith communities, perpetuate this toxic habit. At the core of these, as well as global interspiritual conflicts, is a fear of loss of identity, of our distinctive expressions of faith being collapsed into or diluted by the assertion of others' concerns and creeds. However, our better selves know that plurality is a sign of God's creativity and is therefore a starting point for healing and humanizing interpersonal relationships. There is perhaps no better moment in history to test this theory than our own day, a time in which reification is normalized and U.S. nationalism is promoted through fear-inducing hate speech. Churches have a prime opportunity to organize and promote interspirituality and yet they, too, are in a strange moment in history. Panikkar noted that universities and their faculties are in a privileged, if also challenging, position to reassert the spirit of the surprisingly radical early charter by which Emperor Frederick Barbarosa granted *sui iuris* status to the University of Bologna in 1158: "Since the beginning universities did challenge the *sacerdotium* and *imperium*, the prevailing *mythoi* of that period, as today they have to withstand the pressures of money, the *mythoi* of our time."[28] I am inviting people in positions of power and privilege, especially in the church and academy, but potentially also those who work in government and other administrations, to give primacy of place to our neighbors' experiences and insights.

Serendipity

In his early life St. Francis was known as a great prankster who enjoyed playing practical jokes on his friends. In fact, one of his nicknames is God's Fool. I have difficulty believing that he fully abandoned that habit after his conversion. Perhaps the reader will agree; my first home was on Francisco Street in the U.S. city named for St. Francis of Assisi. Led by curiosity and faith, I wrote my dissertation about the theology of a painting in a Franciscan convent that was based on a Franciscan book. I did a Clinical Pastoral Education residency at St. Francis Memorial Hospital in San Francisco. Early in my career the Franciscan academic community welcomed me and my lay colleagues by playfully inventing a "Fourth Order" for the Franciscan scholars. Unprompted, Lexington Books requested that I deliver my manuscript on April Fools' Day. In addition to these serendipities, I imagine that God's Fool is amused by the fact that I wrote this book in the dance studio in San Francisco where I learned to do cartwheels as a toddler. The office has a partition made from the same beads that my teacher Micky Powell used forty years ago as a "magic wand" (more as a blessing than a charm) at the end of each class. It turned out that writing this book and doing cartwheels had more in common than I could have imagined: both required flexibility, discipline, and a willingness to try something new. These mysterious, orienting experiences provided an incubator from which this Franciscan-inspired book emerged. As a theologian rather than a cartwheeling toddler, I will replace the word "magic" with "mystery." If this romp through church history, ministry, and interspiritual fluidity feed your imagination as it has mine, I believe that we will have a little bit more of what we need in order to live the church into a new way of being.

NOTES

1. This is the premise of Anselm of Canterbury's *Proslogion.*
2. Massimo Faggioli and Michael Hollerich, "The Future of Academic Theology: An Exchange," *Commonweal Magazine* (May 18, 2018): 7–11.
3. The first wave of the "New Education" was initiated by Charles W. Eliot (1834–1926) with his two-part article by the same title in February and March 1869 issues of *The Atlantic Monthly.* In October of that year he began his forty-year presidency of Harvard University. He was instrumental in developing and propagating the "open curriculum" that gave students the skills they would need in order to make

discerning decisions throughout life. As with all other U.S. institutions of higher education, it had previously followed a vocational model.

4. 1 Cor. 12:31. All biblical references are from the New Revised Standard Version.

5. Jer. 33:10–11.

6. Gregory Boyle, SJ, "The Religious Roots of Working with Gangs in Los Angeles" (Lecture, University of San Francisco, San Francisco, CA, April 16, 2018).

7. In *Today's Word*, Skip Moen offers a helpful description of the responsibility of human beings to serve as a bridge between heaven and earth, and of the Hebrew concepts of "image" and "likeness." "Identity Theft (5)" (blog), March 5, 2012. https://www.skipmoen.com/2012/03/identity-theft-5/. As a bookend to his insight I envision the Gospel of John as completing the circuit: in Genesis we are the bridge between heaven and earth. In John, Jesus is the bridge between earth and heaven.

8. The term "cosmotheandric" was created by Panikkar: "There are not two realities: God *and* [man] (or the world); but neither is there one: God *or* [man] (or the world). . . . Reality itself is theandric; it is our own way of looking that makes reality appear to us sometimes under one aspect and sometimes under another because our own vision shares in both. God and [man] are, so to speak, in close constitutive collaboration for the building-up of reality, the unfolding of history and the continuation of creation." The Trinity and the Religious Experience of Man (New York: Orbis Books 1973), 75. (Brackets mine).

9. See Robert J. McCarty and John M. Vitek, *Going, Going, Gone: The Dynamics of Disaffiliation in Young Catholics*. A Study by Saint Mary's Press of Minnesota, Inc. (Winona, MN: Saint Mary's Press, 2017); Kaya Oakes, *The Nones Are Alright* (Maryknoll, NY: Orbis Books, 2016); Patricia Wittberg, *Catholic Cultures: How Parishes Can Respond to the Changing Face of Catholicism* (Collegeville: Liturgical Press, 2016); Patricia Wittberg, *Not Your Grandparents' Church* (Chicago: Acta Publications, 2017).

10. "America's Changing Religious Landscape," http://www.pewforum.org/2015/05/12/americas-changing-religious-landscape/ (accessed March 31, 2019).

11. E. J. Dionne Jr., "No Wonder there's an Exodus from Religion," https://www.washingtonpost.com/opinions/no-wonder-theres-an-exodus-from-religion/2018/05/06/4ad8c33a-4feb-11e8-84a0-458a1aa9ac0a_story.html?utm_term=.a4628a02d37a. (accessed May 6, 2018).

12. Interview with Sister Mary Litell, OSF, Provincial Minister, Sisters of St. Francis, St. Francis Province on April 7, 2018.

13. John Carr, Director of the Initiative on Catholic Social Thought and Public Life at Georgetown University quoted in Terrence McCoy's article "In Pope Francis' Outreach to the Poor, His Deeds Speak Louder than His Words," *The Washington Post* (September 24, 2015), https://www.washingtonpost.com/local/social-issues/in-pope-franciss-outreach-to-the-poor-his-deeds-speak-louder-than-his-words/2015/09/24/4824a930-62ed-11e5-b38e-06883aacba64_story.html?noredirect=on&utm_term=.64a36429d293. (accessed October 12, 2019).

14. Pope Francis, *Laudato si: On Care for Our Common Home* (Washington, DC: United States Conference of Catholic Bishops, 2015), 4.46.

15. "Address to the Young People of Brescia," April 7, 2018. http://w2.vatican.va/content/francesco/it/speeches/2018/april/documents/papa-francesco_20180407_ragazzi-diocesi-brescia.html (translation mine).

16. http://w2.vatican.va/content/francesco/en/apost_exhortations/documents/papa-francesco_esortazione-ap_20190325_christus-vivit.html.

17. Adam Bucko and Rory McEntee, *The New Monasticism: An Interspiritual Manifesto for Contemplative Living* (Maryknoll, NY, 2015), xi.

18. "Burners" is the name given to those who have attended the Burning Man event in the Nevada Desert.

19. Interview with Fr. Thomas Matus, OSB, Cam on February 27, 2018.

20. I was inspired to explore this biblical reference by the song *Many and Great* by Fr. Ricky Manalo, CSP. *Be Still and Know I'm Here with Mass of Christ the Inner Light* (Portland: Oregon Catholic Press, 2018).

21. De Mello, *Taking Flight: A Book of Story Meditations* (New York: Image Books, 1988), 68.

22. De Mello, *Taking Flight*, 69.

23. Paul Knitter, "Interreligious Dialogue: What? Why? How?" in *Interreligious Dialogue: An Anthology of Voices Bridging Cultural and Religious Divides*, ed. Christoffer H. Grundmann (Winona, MN: Anselm Academic, 2015), 27.

24. Menachem Klein, *Lives in Common: Arabs and Jews in Jerusalem, Jaffa and Hebron* (Oxford University Press), 2001.

25. Klein, *Lives in Common*, 11.

26. Ibid., 21.

27. In chapter 2, I will probe important distinctions between syncretism and religious pluralism.

28. Raimón Panikkar, *Christianity: Opera Omnia, Vol. III.2, A Christophany*, ed. Milena Carrara Pavan (Maryknoll, NY: Orbis Books, 2016), 45.

Chapter 1

Welcoming the Stranger

Courage, Curiosity, Generosity

UNITY IN DIVERSITY

The thirteenth-century Sufi poet Jalaluddin Rumi had what I would describe as a mystical awareness of the wisdom of a unitive vision of faith and relationships. He believed that in and through our differences, we discover that we are standing on common ground: "Out beyond ideas of wrongdoing and rightdoing there is a field. I'll meet you there. When the soul lies down in that grass . . . ideas, language, even the phrase *each other* doesn't make any sense."[1]

Plato, whose work shaped the dominant, Western hierarchical view of knowledge, had an opposite perspective: that the world of ideas about things like rightdoing and wrongdoing is the world of the "really real." Rabbi Jonathan Sacks challenges Plato's claim that since the senses cannot describe an essence, they are unreliable. He recognizes that Plato's belief in a universal truth has had a devastating impact on humanity's ability to embrace the goodness of difference among cultures and between individuals. For Sacks, Plato's view "suggests that all differences lead to tribalism and then to war, and that the best alternative therefore is to eliminate differences and impose on the world a single, universal truth."[2] The implications of Plato's binary perspective justified for much of Christian history a pattern of rooting out religious differences rather than celebrating them as sources of wisdom that support harmonious relationships and greater self-understanding. Eastern sages such as Rumi celebrate the creative potential of plurality.

One of the oldest sources of wisdom literature, the Vedic tradition offers a nondualistic understanding of difference. The Vedas celebrate the form of knowledge that is experienced intuitively, and which is above both reason and the senses. Unlike Plato's concept of reality, the Vedas do not fall into

1

the trap of dualistic thinking. In a way that echoes the Trinity, in the Hindu tradition *saccidananda* is the form of knowing in which "the knower, the known, and the act of knowing are all one."[3] As with Rumi's insight, here the emphasis is not on knowing things rightly or wrongly, but on experiencing harmony through shared understanding. The fact of knowing manifests in bliss (*ananda*) and signals the integration of our shared knowledge into our ways of being in the world. The Vedic understanding of universal truth does not impose on the other a single, universal truth, but rather, consists of a unitive vision. It recognizes that universal truth makes itself known differently in every being (*sat*) because our experiences of universal consciousness vary.[4] This core principle can be discerned throughout the Hindu vignettes in the tables at the end of the next chapter.

The Catholic-Hindu theologian Raimón Panikkar used two analogies that can help us understand the lens through which each individual experiences the Vedic unitive reality: the window and the rainbow. The window frames and therefore limits each person's perspective. He believes that because we are looking through a window, we do not notice the window and the glass, but become fixated on what we see. We need our neighbors to tell us that we are looking through a particular window, and we can do the same for our neighbor. The first step, therefore, is listening. Because we care about one another, we then compare notes rather than argue about the merits of what we see through our respective windows. By sharing our views of the landscape, we are enriched by one another's vision of reality.[5] This said, he also believes that we must first understand our own religion before we can truly understand other religions. The tables in the next chapter demonstrate that this is a cyclical rather than linear process, and that people of faith can also understand their own religion more deeply by peering at their own beliefs through the windows of other religious traditions.

Reflecting on the criteria for effective ministry, Heije Faber notes that "it is when the minister thinks that [his] belief is a possession, to be handed out at will, that [his] ministry becomes routine."[6] Whether or not one is a minister in a formal sense, a respectful sharing of faith is a ministry to those we host. It requires vulnerability, mutuality, and creativity. It begins with a *habitus* of humility, of an awareness that we cannot understand as much alone as we can together, and that our dialogue partners have a wider view of the very thing we perceive. Learning about one another's view of the landscape provides a starting point for the dialogue that follows and helps us climb out of the ruts we fall into when we rely only on the authority and perceptions of our own communities. A provincial view of spirituality is necessarily limited in scope. Just as we cannot thrive without enough oxygen, those who live with a narrow worldview are constricted by it. Spiritual leaders who struggle to meet seekers in a multicultural, interreligious society can learn from Panikkar's metaphor of the window. Perhaps Pope John XXIII had in mind the importance of external influences in describing the Second Vatican Council as an opportunity "to throw open the windows and let in the fresh air."

Another metaphor Panikkar uses to depict the impact of dialogue is the rainbow, in which it is never clear where one color ends and the next begins.[7] In this process, because reality itself is a rainbow, we can choose to interpret contrasting colors in terms of harmonious distinctions:

> Each religion and ultimately each human being stands within the rainbow of reality and sees it as white light—precisely because of seeing through the entire rainbow. From the outside, as an intellectual abstraction, I see you in the green area and you see me in the orange one. I call you green and you call me orange, because, when we look at each other, we do not look at the totality—what we believe—but we evaluate and judge each other. And though it is true that I am in the orange strip with all the limitations of a saffron spirituality, if you ask my color, I say "white"![8]

Panikkar encourages people to be aware of what they bring to inter- and intrareligious dialogue. In exploring his metaphor of the rainbow, it is helpful to note that there are only three primary colors: red, yellow, and blue. From these, all the other colors of the rainbow are derived. Therefore, when the orange person approaches the green person and vice versa, perhaps thinking that she or he has a place of primacy in the dialogue, it can be helpful to recognize that both are derived from other colors. There is no orange without red and yellow and no green without blue and yellow. Orange and green have yellow in common, though they look very different. When Panikkar says that we see ourselves as white, which is true of any object that reflects all the colors of the rainbow, we are unaware that we are only reflecting orange or green. In order to see truly the colors that make up white light, we need a prism, which separates white light into its various components. The prism distinguishes between what we see as white light, and what the white light is in its essence. The margin of error calls for humility in that what we see through the prism is an imprecise interpretation of the rainbow because the nerve cells of each person's retina differ according to nutrition and overall health. Therefore, in describing orangeness and greenness to one another, we can never know exactly what the other sees. The starting point of dialogue, however, of shining the white light through a prism means that we have agreed to discuss our differences in perception and hope to discover a shared essential component. Infrared has the lowest energy and ultraviolet has the highest. They are as far apart in the rainbow as any two colors. Yellow is in the middle of the rainbow, has medium energy, and is a key component of the secondary colors. Both infrared and ultraviolet can be made visible with devices to enable human beings to see beyond what is within our normal field of vision, and are, therefore, essential for real insight. Both the orange person and the green person need infrared and ultraviolet if they want to see the world as fully as possible. Though infrared and ultraviolet are opposites, they are part of the rainbow. Together, the colors of the rainbow make up the white light upon which every human being is dependent in order to see anything at all.[9]

At the end of chapter 2, I will demonstrate that a process that leads us to recontextualize Jesus' wisdom can lead to a deeper understanding of the values and lessons he conveys, and the faith of others. Honoring the wisdom of others can have profound implications for the global community, for example, issuing a direct challenge to nationalism. For the good of the church I will make the case that the stories of interspiritual encounters and practices that are nestled in the history of world Christianity can encourage a shift toward faith formation that engages in creative, cross-cultural reflection. Some of the sources for revivifying Christian doctrine portray the intercultural, and/or interreligious encounters that Christians have experienced across time. Others are contemporary interspiritual practices and ways of life that provide seekers with the sustenance and inspiration needed for meaning making.

A historical paradigm for dynamic, illuminating encounters can be discovered in the cross-cultural medieval narratives that attest to various ways in which hosts paid attention to guests along the Silk Road and the European trade routes to which it connected. On average, the ruins of caravansaries are found every twenty to thirty miles, about a day's journey, along the trade route that ran through modern-day Turkey.[10] Until the thirteenth century, trade along the Silk Road extended between East Asia and West Asia and therefore involved Orthodox and "Nestorians," who I will refer to in this book as East Syrian Christians.[11] Until the thirteenth century, textiles and other goods being imported to Europe were transported by mercantile liaisons rather than Latin Catholic merchants. Their East Syrian predecessors were considered "keen men of business."[12] Along with the East Syrian clergy, the lay merchants were flexible in their interactions with people of other faiths, possibly because their own Christological vision had been judged inadequate by the majority. For example, the East Syrians did not condemn the polygamous custom of the Mongols, even welcoming the secondary wives who wanted to convert to Christianity.[13] In the thirteenth century the circle of communication was expanding, bringing Europeans and East Asians face to face. When the first Christian missionaries from China set out for Europe along the southern Silk Road, north of India, in a town called Miran, they came upon "a second-century Buddhist shrine decorated with Greco-Indian designs and a Tibetan fort from the T'ang era," revealing Miran's cross-cultural richness and interreligious setting.[14] In some of the most challenging, frightening encounters with the other, courageous people of faith have found goodness, dignity, and greater self-awareness by probing their neighbors' beliefs. Their worldviews and understanding of the limits of their own field of vision have yielded even greater courage, humility, and receptivity. What follows is one such example.

Courage and Hospitality as a Model for Mission

Christian mission history can be characterized according to two opposite models: *tabula rasa* (blank slate) and *il modo soave* (the gentle way). Using the *tabula rasa* approach, Christians engaged those they sought to evangelize through a reifying lens: language, customs, beliefs, lifestyle, and other cultural features were obstacles to overcome. The missionaries saw their norms and customs as superior to those of indigenous peoples. They also believed that what they were offering was a pristine form of Christianity that could simply be lifted out of one context and dropped into another. It was not until the seventeenth century that the newly formed Congregation for the Propagation of the Faith (*Propaganda Fide*)[15] issued a directive to all Roman Catholic missionaries in China and Indochina that included an explicit commitment to inculturation: "Make no effort and use no influence to make these people change their rites, habits, and customs, unless they are in evident contradiction to faith and morals."[16] *Il modo soave*, sometimes called the accommodation model, required humility: those who embraced it were aware that the dominant party had power over the other, and therefore had a responsibility to engage in respectful dialogue. Cautious missioners were aware of their social location and cultivated curiosity about, and respect for, the other.

Because *il modo soave* required sensitivity, careful deliberation, and real relationship, it was more difficult and therefore less common than the *tabula rasa* approach. That said, there is evidence of exemplary encounters with the religious other. These can serve as models for welcoming the stranger in the twenty-first century. One of these stories is found in the travel journal of Rabban Sauma (c. 1220–1294), a Uyghur East Syrian monk from Mongolian China. Sauma had been sent on a diplomatic mission for the Mongol Il-Khan, who was hoping that because Sauma was a Christian, the European heads of state, including the pope, would receive him warmly, and grant the Il-Khan's request for assistance against the threat of invading Muslim armies. In the following account, it is helpful to keep in mind Panikkar's observation about genuine dialogue: it "does not primarily mean study, consultation, examination, preaching, proclamation, learning, etc. . . . it listens and observes, but it also speaks, corrects, and is corrected."[17]

In spring 1289, the Franciscan pope Nicholas IV (1288–1292) offered a model of pontifical humility and graciousness toward a non-Latin Christian. What seems to have occurred in his meeting with an East Syrian monk goes beyond fraternal welcome, resulting instead, in a poignant cross-cultural dialogue between Christians from opposite sides of the world. The joyful encounter is described by a chronicler from the East rather than by a member of the papal party, and there is no hint of a pro-Roman bias that might have been included had Sauma intended to use his travel journal subsequently to curry favor with the pope. Instead, their visit seems to have been mutually gratifying, authentic encounter.

Jerome of Ascoli (1227–1292), who in 1288 became Pope Nicholas IV, is believed to have been the son of a scribe.[18] He joined the Franciscan Order as a young man in the 1240s.[19] Beginning in 1255, while still in his twenties, he was likely a member of the papal *curia*.[20] By 1272 he was working in the area of Sclavonia, modern-day Bosnia, where it seems that he became proficient in Greek.[21] He eventually became Provincial Minister.[22] The chronicler Giovanni Villani notes that Jerome was renowned for his goodness and knowledge.[23] When Pope Gregory X called on him in 1274 to serve at the Council of Lyons, he was seen as an exceptional candidate for a sensitive diplomatic mission aimed at reuniting the Latins and the Greeks.

Through nuncios sent to Constantinople, Pope Gregory asked the Greeks to acknowledge the primacy of the Roman pope. A successful mission would require a skilled diplomat to spearhead the dialogue. In the end the experience served as an important training mission for the future pope. In 1274, he was part of a delegation to Constantinople who met with Emperor Michael Paleologos to discuss reunification.[24] Among the members of this envoy, Jerome was one of only two diplomats who knew Greek.

While in Constantinople, Jerome sent Pope Gregory a message about Greek religious practices.[25] His mission required skill and sensitivity given the damage done by the schism of 1054 in which the Latins and Greeks had excommunicated one another. In addition, the sack of Constantinople in 1204 established the Latin kingdom of Constantinople. That period of occupation had ended only thirteen years before the Council of Lyons. Jerome was sensitive to the Greek customs, which perhaps impacted Michael Paleologos' willingness to accept the Roman confession.[26] Another indication of Jerome's effectiveness is that, while at Lyons, Jerome also led some Tatar nuncios to receive baptism from Pope Gregory X. Despite Jerome's skillful interventions, given the lack of episcopal support in Constantinople, the union declared at Lyons was fragile from its inception. It is important to keep in mind that there he was only functioning as nuncio, not as pope and therefore was limited in his ability to shape the terms of the reunification. By 1278 Jerome had become the Franciscan Minister General and continued his peacemaking work. When he became Pope Nicholas IV ten years later, he brought with him diplomatic experience with Greek orthodox Christians, as well as Mongol non-Christians.

A Case Study in Intraspiritual Dialogue: A Chinese Christian Monk on a Mission to Europe

Beginning in the middle of the thirteenth century the Mongolian khans began to take an interest in Christianity. In 1287 King Arghon sent Sauma to persuade the pope, as well as the leaders of France and England, to join forces and thwart the spread of Islam by the Mameluks. Sauma seemed to be the right person for the job. His mentee, Mark, who had become patriarch of Baghdad, called him "the wise man capable of undertaking [such] an embassy."[27] Sauma was already well traveled, having made the difficult and dangerous journey from Tai-Tu, near modern-day Peking, to Tabriz, in Iran.[28] It seems that the spoken languages Sauma knew included Turkic, Chinese, Persian, and probably Mongol.

In 1287 Sauma arrived in Constantinople, where he was met by Emperor Andronicus II (r. 1282–1328). Sauma was enthusiastic about the opportunity to see religious artifacts in Constantinople, including the tombs of the patriarchs and the relics of the saints.[29] By July 1287 he arrived in Rome, where Pope Honorius had recently died. He was invited by the cardinals to their meeting place, where they inquired about Sauma's homeland and the purpose of his visit.[30] They questioned him about who had evangelized his part of the world. The theological quiz presented by the Roman Curia indicates that the cardinals were only minimally familiar with the history of missionary activity along the Silk Road.[31] Sauma explained that his was an apostolic church founded in the first century by St. Thomas and the Galilean Christian saints, Mari and Addai. He said that his *Catholicus*, or patriarch, was in Baghdad and he identified himself as a deacon. The cardinals gave Sauma a tour of their local churches and showed off their relics. Since they had yet to elect a new pope, Sauma traveled north to Tuscany, Genoa, and eventually Paris, where he met with King Philip IV of France.[32] He visited the University of Paris, where he saw the relics of the crown of thorns and the cross, which Philip proudly admitted to having taken during the sack of Constantinople. He then proceeded to England, where he was received by Edward I.

When Sauma finally returned to Rome in February 1288, he found that Jerome of Ascoli had recently been elected Pope Nicholas IV, having refused the honor a week earlier. Whether or not it was due to the coaching Sauma had received about protocol for meeting with Western ecclesiastical dignitaries, he greeted the pope, whom he addressed as Mar (Holy) Papa, by bowing to the ground and kissing his hands and feet. In order to avoid turning his back to the pope, he reverently walked backward, his hands clasped against his chest. Acknowledging the pope's position above all kings and nations, he wished him a long life. Pope Nicholas was certainly within his rights to stay within the boundaries of medieval etiquette, however, at least temporarily, he seems to have stepped down from the throne in an act of humility. The monk from the East presented Pope Nicholas with gifts and letters from King Arghon as well as Sauma's friend, the patriarch of Baghdad. As a man with considerable experience in diplomacy, international travel, and ecumenical dialogue, Pope Nicholas seems to have been impressed with Rabban Sauma, not only because he had traveled from a land that was mysterious even to the cosmopolitan pope, but also because his guest had personally met with the great and powerful Kublai Khan (1260–1294). Pope Nicholas was aware of the importance of the Tatar king and wrote him at least a dozen letters between 1288 and 1291. He not only encouraged Arghon to be baptized but also implored his help in attaining freedom for the church in the Holy Land. As one would expect from a committed Christian leader who was formed by a mendicant order, Nicholas immediately sent the missionary that Arghon had requested. In 1289 he chose for the task John of Montecorvino, a fellow Franciscan, hoping that John would baptize and convert the Mongols. It seems that Arghon was serious about Christianity, as indicated by the fact that some of his children were baptized. By 1305, long after Nicholas had died, John of Montecorvino had been to Persia, Mylapore, and Beijing, and had baptized about 6,000 people.

Since the Romans on both the eastern and the western sides of the Empire had long been concerned about the spread of Islam, it was reasonable for Arghon and Sauma to assume that the pope would be receptive to the suggestion of a political alliance. Even though Nicholas side-stepped that issue in the short term, he received with warmth and openness a monk from the East Syrian tradition. This was a risk since that church identified with Patriarch Nestorius, whose teachings had been condemned at the Council of Ephesus in 431. Given the West's animosity toward what it (mistakenly) understood of East Syrian Christianity, the encounter could easily have ended in spiritual and political disappointment for Sauma and Arghon. However, by Easter 1288, though a political alliance was tenuous, a positive dialogue was about to occur. Depending on how one interprets the theological differences between the East Syrian and the Latin Catholic traditions, it can be seen either as an intra- or interspiritual encounter.

The chronicler remarked that Pope Nicholas paid more honor to Rabban Sauma than was customary, even inviting him to remain as his guest so that they might share the mid-Lenten observance. On the fifth Sunday of Lent Sauma indicated to the pope that he wanted to celebrate the Eucharist in the Syriac tradition in Nicholas' presence. This was an exciting prospect for the newly elected pope, whose curiosity and wanderlust had prepared him to be an enthusiastic participant in Sauma's foreign rite. The Persian chronicler notes that Sauma and Nicholas rejoiced at the celebration. The pope's simple remark following the liturgy seems to reveal genuine awe and respect for the Syriac rite: "The language is different, but the use is the same."[33] Sauma increased his blessing by confessing his sins to Pope Nicholas. He also received Communion from the pope's own hands, possibly a gesture to affirm Nicholas' spiritual primacy as heir to the See of Peter, an ancient tradition among the churches of the East.

An important precondition for what I would call an intraspiritual encounter was Nicholas' curiosity about the Syriac liturgy. His openness and respect can be attributed to his missionary experience as a friar-diplomat. Given the inflated power that the thirteenth-century Latin Church enjoyed in the global arena, he could easily have told Sauma that he would have the opportunity to experience a Latin liturgy, rather than encourage his guest to take the lead. The chronicler reports that Pope Nicholas was so moved by the experiences he shared with his visitor that he invited him to remain with him in Rome indefinitely. Sauma instead excused himself, noting that he would better serve the church by returning to the East. There he could entertain and encourage the Mongolian church and state with the good news of the hospitality and fellowship he received in Europe, especially the blessing he received from Pope Nicholas. According to the chronicler, before his departure Sauma informed the pope of his desire to bring to the East Syrian church some of the very special relics that he had seen in Rome. Sauma did not remark on the annoyance that Pope Nicholas must have felt at that request. Instead, he recorded a measured and gracious response: "If we had been in the habit of giving away these relics to the people who come in myriads, even though the relics were as large as mountains, they would have come to an end long ago. But since you have come from a far country, we will give you a few."[34] In mid-April Nicholas sent his visitor back to China with a piece of Christ's robe, a small fragment of Mary's clothing and several relics of the saints.[35] He also sent gifts for Arghon, a crown for Mar Yahbhallah, liturgical vestments, and a bull authorizing the patriarch to exercise dominion over all of the Eastern churches. He also honored Sauma by authorizing him to act as Visitor General over all Christians. Distracted by pressing issues with the Angevins and Aragonese, it took three years for Pope Nicholas to begin to form an alliance with King Arghon. Any agreement that might have been in progress ended when both men died within a year of one another, but not before Arghon had his eleven-year-old son Oljeitu, baptized and named Nikolya in honor of the pope.

Given that Pope Nicholas had spent the early part of his career in diplomatic service, he might have had multiple motivations in extending fraternal hospitality to Rabban Sauma. For example, his experience as a legate in Byzantium and as Franciscan Minister General would have made him acutely aware of the threat facing the church due to Muslim expansion. He was also sensitive to the plight of the Christians living in Muslim territory and made several appeals on their behalf.[36] What Nicholas understood of East Syrian

Christianity is unclear. It is possible that he was familiar with the "Book of the Union" by the sixth-century East Syrian theologian Babai the Great (551–628), which clarifies the teachings of Nestorius, but this has not been proven. He could also have seen Sauma as a deeply devout individual whose Christology simply needed some fine-tuning. It is just as likely that when Nicholas invited Sauma to stay in Rome, it was so that they could learn more about one other's spirituality. Whatever theological and/or political ambiguities existed between Nicholas and Rabban Sauma, the pope clearly saw the foreign monk's faith as falling within the bounds of orthodoxy. He would not have sent precious religious relics away with someone whose creed was suspect. The relaxed atmosphere of their meeting and the graciousness that both showed one another is a reminder of what can happen when leaders begin by recognizing that they are standing on common ground.

Curiosity and Community

When I was a doctoral student in Toronto, I belonged to a Jesuit parish that was in a large, primarily Hindu Tamil community. Throughout the day, even during Mass, people would enter the church through the side door near the altar to access the large holy water dispenser. Our Tamil neighbors would cup their hands beneath the spout to catch the water and drink it. I often wondered if they were Catholic and whether drinking holy water was a custom in the church of Southeast Asia. I was taken aback when a classmate who was a priest in that parish said that he often had to ask people not to drink the holy water. I thought he meant that he was annoyed by the practice because the people who were drinking the water were not Catholic; however, that was not the reason for his frustration. It was because the dispensers were not cleaned often enough for the water to be safe for drinking. It seems that the Tamil visitors were engaged in the Hindu practice *jalānjali*, an offering of holy water made during prayer.[37] My classmate and the other Jesuits were, in fact, glad to welcome non-Catholic visitors whose beliefs enabled them to reach into the wealth of Catholic symbols in a way that witnessed to their lived experience of multiple belongings. Christians can develop a deeper understanding of the possibility of religious plurality by learning from Hindus about the meaning they experience through this and other interspiritual practices. In the case of the holy water, which is a sacramental to Catholics, through the devotion of our Hindu neighbors, I and other parishioners appreciated more fully the efficacy of water to cleanse not only our own souls, but the souls of those whose faithful intuitions skirt conventional boundaries. These practices can serve as resources for imagining spiritual cross-pollination, as can the values and visions of other belief systems, but first we must recognize, engage, and respect what is taking place all around us.

"Religious" people who oppose mutuality become hardened. The *Tao Te Ching* is full of proverbs that illustrate how rigid things tend to break.[38] When communities become wooden in their reading of their own spirit-filled scriptures and practices, they marginalize seekers who need room to ask open-ended questions, to find new ways to live out eternal truths, to make sense of their faith in constantly evolving contexts. Openness can be a challenge for people who, for various reasons, are afraid that cross-pollination will lead to pollution of their own doctrines, values, and/or practices that are integral to their identity. This is where relationships become essential for understanding our neighbors.

A Case Study in Interspiritual Dialogue: St. Francis and the Sultan

Henri Nouwen makes an inspired point about what makes it possible to draw near to others whom we perceive as a threat: the word "generosity" stems from the Greek word *genos* meaning "of the same kind" and that "generosity creates the family it believes in."[39] When we recognize that we are "kin" connected as kindred spirits, we emulate generosity of the spirit. The Franciscan intellectual tradition witnesses to this self-emptying generosity in a story about Francis' courageous, enthusiastic meeting with the sultan of Egypt, Malik al-Kamil in 1219. Since the encounter took place during the period of the Crusades, Francis very clearly communicated that he was not there as a soldier. He persistently but patiently sought to meet with the sultan, whose advisors simply wanted to kill Francis, as had been the fate of the friars in Morocco. An important difference there was that the friars in North Africa did not accept "no" for an answer to their preaching of the gospel. In their persistence, they made the mistake of preaching against Islam. Francis knew that stubbornness can end tragically when a person relies on his or her own strength rather than on Providence.[40] Though there is no known transcript of the dialogue that unfolded between Francis and the sultan, the values that led him through that encounter can perhaps be detected in the early edition of his *Rule of Life* (1221).[41] He wanted the brothers to develop a habit of prayer and to practice what we would call a ministry of presence. They were to be humble, take initiatives toward dialogue, have faith in the good will of others, and work closely with them: to try to understand rather than to be understood.

The sultan provided medical care, food, and lodging to Francis, who remained at court with him for three weeks. Though Malik al-Kamil did not convert to Christianity as Francis had hoped he would, there is an intriguing story in Islamic oral tradition in which the sultan tells Francis that he would like to convert but cannot because of inevitable retribution from his subjects. Keeping his eye on the cross that also symbolizes the intersection of heaven and earth, Francis realized that on this side of life, on the horizontal plane, we do not have to agree with or fully understand those we engage in order to have a respectful, authentic encounter with another. This is true whether we are encountering a wolf, a sultan or, as we will explore in a later chapter, human outcasts. Francis' sincerity and gentleness had an enduring impact on his community. In fact, his motto, "Peace and All Good," is still a common greeting used in Assisi after eight centuries. Francis gave everyone the benefit of the doubt, including a vulnerable wolf that was attacking villagers out of fear. His vision of the fundamental desire for relationships and a presumption of good will among all creatures has had a lasting impact on the Franciscan charism.

Curiosity and Generosity

In trying to help overscheduled undergraduates appreciate the importance both of stillness and spiritual fluidity, in the summer of 2016 I requested a meeting with Swami Vedananda of the Vedanta Society of Northern California. What began as a conversation about a Hindu perspective on prayer ended with a gift in the form of an insight into the value of interspirituality. His model has been a rich resource for my students, many of whom are culturally Christian, and most of whom have not have the benefit of cross-cultural experiences. What follows is a narrative I developed based on the brief parable he shared.

In Hawaii there is a 6,000-foot mountain. One side of the mountain faces the Pacific Ocean and the other side faces inland. The inland side is on a gentle slope, at the base of which is a field with a banana farm. At the base of the Pacific side is a rainforest. There are two women who live on opposite sides of the mountain, who have never met one another, but find themselves engaged in a cell phone conversation. They each identify themselves as residents of that mountain and describe their neighborhoods, which creates confusion. They wonder how they could possibly be living on the same mountain. The banana farmer describes the view from her home: a bright and cloudless sky, a gentle wind that continuously rustles the leaves of the fruit trees. The whole field has the distinctive smell of fruit and sunlight. Mornings on the gentle slope are still except for the quiet rustle of leaves in the cool breeze. She describes her home and her family, as well as the fruits and vegetables in the garden that they enjoy daily. Sometimes it gets so hot on their land that the family sleeps on the roof of their wooden plantation home, where the evening wind provides relief after the dusty daylight hours. Her family does well in the fields. They can farm for hours in the heat and their skin is well-suited to the long hours of work and play in the sun. The family has lived in that place, used the same recipes, and has had the same Hawaiian dialect for as long as anyone can remember. Every member of the family, and most of the people they know share a distinctive skin tone and body type. They have also gone to the same church for generations, where their Hawaiian language songs are interlaced with the music and English lyrics that they inherited from the missioners who brought Christianity to their land in the 1820s.

The woman who lives at the base of the mountain describes the abundance of rain and the persistent wind that beats against the face of the mountain that they call home. She depicts the landscape as a vibrant, wet jungle with colorful birds and exotic fruits that the other woman has never seen. They begin to wonder if there are two mountains with the same name in the chain of Hawaiian Islands. The neighbor who lives just 100 feet above sea level explains that her family lives in a bamboo house with a thatched roof and shutters on the windows that have no glass because of the wind. The structure is naturally resistant to microbes that thrive in the rainforest. As many generations of her family as she can recall have lived in the rainforest and have adapted to the wet environment. Their ancestors were hunters whose skin and lungs adjusted to the daily rain. She describes the sound of the waves crashing against the rocks on the beach that is a few hundred feet from her home. She explains that their close neighbors live in what used to be a "leper colony" where, a century earlier, the Hawaiian government isolated anyone who had even the slightest skin blemish, for fear of leprosy. Even with the discovery of sulfone drugs that stopped the spread of Hansen's disease, the residents stayed in the valley that they had called home for decades. The rainforest dwellers worship with them at the church established by missionaries who came from halfway around the world to care for the "lepers." As a result, the worship service includes songs that celebrate God's love for the outcast. The wooden floors still have holes made by the newcomers who had contracted tuberculosis. They discovered that they could use tubes made from the long leaves of tropical plants and spit into them during the service. This made it possible to stay for the entire liturgy rather than having to exit the building periodically.[42] None of these facets of daily life are familiar to the woman who lives topside on the sunny, dry slope.

Having listened to one another's stories about home, one day they decided to meet, and to bring pictures of their homes and a dish to share. They settled on a meeting place halfway up what each woman knew as her mountain. As she began to climb, the rainforest dweller caught her first glimpse of the ocean from high above the beach. She continued to climb high enough to see the bright blue sky that the farmer had described. As they got closer to the same elevation and moved around toward the same side of the mountain, the phone reception became clearer. They kept talking in order to make sure that they did not miss one another on the mutually unfamiliar terrain. When, finally they met, they each stood facing the other in amazement. In listening to one another's description of her world, and then finally stand-ing face to face, they realized that they had indeed been living on the same mountain the whole time. Because of their curiosity they left their comfort zones and learned through a new relationship that there is much more to the mountain than they had ever imagined. By sharing a meal of new ingredients grown in their mutual zip code, each woman tasted the goodness of a unique community.

The goal of this chapter has been to demonstrate that inter- and intrare-ligious exchanges require patience, openness, courage, and humility. Pope Nicholas IV and Rabban Sauma; the Jesuit community that welcomed the Tamil Hindus; a fruitful exchange between St. Francis and Sultan Malik al-Kamil; the women whose curiosity compelled them to meet in person all have in common a willingness both to teach and to be taught; an awareness that what we see through our own window is only a partial view; a willing-ness to be flexible and courageous. Depending on one's commitment level, these types of exchanges might end in mutual enrichment. Over time, they can develop into an experience of mutuality, in which one seeks to understand the other for the good of the other. Through faith, these examples convey an appreciation of the good that can come from subjecting to the scrutiny of a prism, the white light that contains a full spectrum of experiences.

NOTES

1. Mevlana Jalaluddin Rumi, "The Great Wagon," ch. 4 in *The Essential Rumi*, trans. Coleman Barks (New York: HarperCollins, 1995), 36.

2. Jonathan Sacks, "The Dignity of Difference: Avoiding the Clash of Civiliza-tions," https://www.fpri.org/article/2013/06/the-dignity-of-difference-avoiding-the -clash-of-civilizations/ (accessed March 31, 2019).

3. *Saccidananda* is comprised of three words: *sat* (being), *cit* (the pure act of knowing), and *ananda* (bliss). Bede Griffiths, *The Marriage of East and West* (Springfield: Templegate Publishers, 1982), 91.

4. Griffiths, *The Marriage of East and West*, 90–91.

5. The interview with Panikkar discussing the metaphor of the window is avail-able online. Accessed March 31, 2019. https://www.youtube.com/watch?v=iNl KDGKhofw.

6. Heije Faber, "The Circus Clown," in *Images of Pastoral Care*, ed. Robert C. Dykstra (St. Louis: Chalice Press, 2005), 85–93, 89–90.

7. Henri Tincq, "Eruption of Truth: An Interview with Raimon Panikkar: On Inter- and Intrareligious Dialogue," trans. Joseph Cunneen *The Christian Century* 117 (23) (August 16–23, 2000), 835.

8. Raimón Panikkar, *The Unknown Christ of Hinduism* (Maryknoll: Orbis Books, 1964), 29–30.

9. I am grateful to Dr. Gerard Lozada, OD, in Overland Park, KS, for his expertise in optometry, especially his explanation of the physics of colors and their role in perception. And in appreciation of God's sense of humor, I should note that a year after explaining this phenomenon, Dr. Lozada found it necessary to add something called "prism" to my new lenses to address an issue with my eye muscle.

10. Morris Rossabi, *Voyager from Xanadu: Rabban Sauma and the First Journey from China to the West* (Tokyo: Kodansha International, 1992). The author notes that "the so-called Pax Mongolica extended across Eurasia, and, although it was not as peaceful as its name implies, it enabled craftsmen, merchants, and missionaries to travel from Italy and France to China," 3.

11. The label "Nestorian" was imposed on East Syrian Christians by the Latin West and Greek East. It resulted from a misreading of Nestorius' Christology. Nestorius of Antioch, who was patriarch of Constantinople from 428 to 431, did not, in fact, believe that Christ is two separate "persons," as he was accused of by his fellow bishops.

12. Wallis E. A. Budge, trans. *The Monks of Kûblâi Khân, Emperor of China* (London: Religious Tract Society, 1928), 32.

13. *Voyager from Xanadu*, 27.

14. Ibid., 52.

15. After 1982 *Propaganda Fide* was renamed *Congregation for the Evangelization of Peoples*.

16. *Collectanea S. Congregationis de Propaganda Fide* (Rome, 1907), I, 130–141. For a summary of important achievements in the last 400 years, see no. 2: accessed March 31, 2019, http://www.vatican.va/roman_curia/congregations/cevang/docum ents/rc_con_cevang_20100524_profile_en.html.

17. Raimón Panikkar, *The Intrareligious Dialogue* (New York: Paulist Press, 1978), 50.

18. Giulia Barone, *Enciclopedia dei Papi* (Rome: Treccani, 2000), 455.

19. Antonino Franchi, *Nicolaus Papa IV: 1288–92: Girolamo d'Ascoli* (Assisi: Edizioni Porziuncola, 1990), 25ff.

20. Franchi, *Nicolaus Papa IV*, 33.

21. Bernard of Besse, the author of the fourteenth-century *Flores Historiarum* said that Jerome was an expert (*peritus*) in Greek and Latin equally (Franchi, *Nicolaus Papa IV*, 37).

22. *Enciclopedia dei Papi*, 455.

23. Giovanni Villani, *Historie fiorentine* vol. 13 in *Rerum Italicarum scriptores* (Milan: Ex Typographia Societatis Palatinae in Regia Curia, 1728), Book 7, chapter 118, 317–318.

24. Deno John Geanakoplos, *Constantinople and the West: Essays on the Late Byzantine (Palaeologan) and Italian Renaissances and the Byzantine and Roman Churches* (Madison: University of Wisconsin Press, 1989), 196.

25. Geanakoplos, *Constantinople and the West*, 201–202.

26. From the Greek perspective, it is important to note that the emperor had few options in accepting the Roman confession, fearing both an invasion by Charles of Anjou and a Turkish advance. In the *Constitutions* of the council, called *Zelus fidei*,

the blame for the schism of 1054 is forced upon the Greeks: "Proudly striving to divide in some way the Lord's seamless tunic, they withdrew from devotion and obedience to the apostolic see." See *Enciclopedia dei Papi*, 455, and "The Second Council of Lyons" (1274), http://www.papalencyclicals.net/councils/ecum14.htm.

27. *Voyager from Xanadu*, 100.

28. Ibid., 99.

29. Sebastian P. Brock, "Rabban Ṣauma à Constantinople (1287)," in *Mémorial Mgr Gabriel Khouri-Sarkis (1898–1968), fondateur et directeur de L'Orient Syrien, 1956–1967*, ed. F. Graffin (Louvain: Imprimerie orientaliste, 1969), 246.

30. *Voyager from Xanadu*, 119.

31. Enrico Menestò, ed., *Niccolò IV: un pontificato tra oriente ed occidente: atti del convegno internazionale di studi in occasione del VII centenario del pontificato di Niccolò IV* (Ascoli Piceno dicembre 14–17, 1989), 149.

32. Kenneth Setton, *The Papacy and the Levant, 1204–1271* (Philadelphia, American Philosophical Society, 1976), 146–147.

33. John Coakley and Andrea Sterk, eds., "The Lives of Mâr Yahbh-Allâhâ and Rabban Ṣâwmâ" in *Readings in World Christianity* vol. 1 *Earliest Christianity to 1453* (Maryknoll: Orbis, 2004), 376.

34. Ibid., 377.

35. Setton, *The Papacy and the Levant*, 147.

36. Ibid., n. 23.

37. E. Nageswara Rao, *Makers of Indian Literature: Aburri Ramakrishna Rau* (New Delhi: Sahitya Akademi, 2002), 25.

38. The title means *Book of the Way of Virtue*.

39. Henri Nouwen, *The Return of the Prodigal Son* (New York: Image Books, 1992), 131–132.

40. In 2 Cel. 4 Francis foretells the massacre of the friars in Egypt. *Francis of Assisi: Early Documents*. Vol. 2, ed. Regis Armstrong et al. (New York: New City Press, 2000), 265–266.

41. See the *Regula Non Bullata* XVI as well as Pasquale and Mahamed, "San Francesco e il Sultano. Un modello per il dialogo," *Città di Vita* 73 (January–February 2018), 69–70.

42. The area I describe here, especially the church, is based on a tour I took of the "leper" colony in the Kaluapapa peninsula on the island of Molokai. The name of the church is St. Philomena.

Chapter 2

Interspirituality

Similarity-in-Difference

OWNING OUR BIASES

In a poem imaginatively attributed to St. Peter, the Lebanese Christian author Kahlil Gibran wrote: "Your neighbor is your other self, dwelling behind a wall. In understanding, all walls shall fall down."[1] As discussed in chapter 1, Panikkar envisions "understanding" as a reality that refracts according to different "colors" (spiritualities, religions, experiences, eras). Our perception of colors varies according to the objects that reflect the light, as well as the unique properties of our eyes. The process of receiving light is both literally and figuratively "particular": made up of particles. Through the prism of the Christian tradition, Jesus reveals the fullness of Truth. Nothing true is outside of Jesus, though his sociohistorical location necessarily means that many facets of Truth were not and could not have been manifested by him. The socio-historical reality of each Christian further refracts, enriches, or perhaps impoverishes her or his interpretation of the Christ event. Impoverishment can result from choosing to embrace an uncritical, narrow view of the implications of the Paschal Mystery. A Jesus who is seen as being "with" and "for" a select group of people excludes neighbors who are unlike the members of our club. In such cases, differences are viewed as liabilities.

Critical engagement with sacred scripture is needed in order to remain faithful to the Christian tradition and so that it retains its currency. Careful theological reflection requires that we seek truth even, or perhaps especially, when it is vexing. For example, today many faithful Christians support marriage equality, asserting that a loving God must be in favor of loving relationships. They would be more contented if the New Testament conveyed even a tenuous approbation of consensual homosexual relationships from Jesus.

However, the community from which Jesus inherited his worldview had no concept of consensual same-sex relationships, making it impossible to interpret Jesus' views on the subject using scripture. Those who object to marriage equality tether the term "abomination" to biblical references to homosexuality, failing to recognize that they fall into the trap of proof-texting. I offer the following example: scripture does not rank the practices and objects considered to be "abominations" by Jesus' community.[2] According to Leviticus eating shellfish (11:9–10), wearing blended textiles (19:19) and getting a tattoo (19:28) are prohibited practices. These are counted as abominations to no greater or lesser extent than homosexual practices (18:22 and 20:13). Today eating shellfish is usually not a life-threatening decision and therefore is not opposed by most people who view the Bible as divinely inspired. Blended fabrics, too, are no longer prohibited by most Jewish and Christian religious leaders. However, some choose to condemn homosexual practices as if the Bible issued an eternally binding blanket condemnation of that "abomination" but not the others. This is an example of proof-texting. Religious people who choose to judge those who are physically and emotionally intimate with members of the same sex are free to do so, but they cannot look to the Bible as their authoritative reference point.[3] Even more importantly, beyond same-sex practices, Jesus and his ancestors simply had no concept of consensual same-sex partnerships.

Because people of faith are bound to fill in the blanks where scripture is silent, we should be intellectually honest about our experiences and our biases. Having been raised in San Francisco, I do not recall the moment in which I became aware of same-sex relationships. LGBTQ individuals and couples were simply part of the community, just as I experienced other forms of diversity as normative because my elementary school classes included children from all over the globe. Today, ethnically, politically, and/or ideologically homogenous communities strike me as odd and, though I cannot explain it, friends and acquaintances in same-sex partnerships continue to witness to the most enduring intimate relationships among all my friends. In terms of percentages, I know far more divorced heterosexuals than LGBTQ individuals. In my experience, people who believe that God *IS* love are gifted at cultivating relationships that witness to love.

My own Christological thought aligns with the orthodox view that in God's kenotic gift of self to humanity in Jesus, God voluntarily relinquished the fullness of God's knowledge so that, as a human being who is like us in all ways except sin, Jesus could truly grow in wisdom with age.[4] Furthermore, Jesus' fellow wisdom figures, such as mystics and prophets, envision and point to the Truth in ways that Jesus never sought to do. To greater or lesser extents, all wisdom figures apprehend rather than comprehend the fullness of Truth, leaving faithful communities to discern what is truly good.

Syncretism versus Dual Systems

In reflecting on the encounter between St. Francis and Sultan Malik-al-Kamil, Gianluigi Pasquale and Hamad Mahamed note that Venice, the world's first-known republic, welcomed Jews, along with their five synagogues, as well as Muslims, in the building designated to house Turkish traders.[5] They offer the blueprint of a bridge as a symbol of interreligious dialogue, in that the integrity of each pillar creates structural integrity. If a piece of a Catholic pillar were joined with a piece of the Muslim pillar, the bridge would crumble. Only unalloyed pillars can provide the support needed for a bridge to serve as a meeting place for members of different faith traditions.[6] Composite structures cannot sustain pilgrims who meet on the deck for dialogue. As we will see, the lack of structural integrity is one problem with syncretism.

St. Francis' approach to the sultan conveyed respect for his dialogue partner. Francis' perspective was not a given but it was occasionally practiced by other medieval Christians, as with the delegation of sixty Byzantine Christians from Najrān[7] who went to Medina to meet with the Prophet Mohammed.[8] They discussed doctrine and disagreed with one another, however they were careful not to affront one another's beliefs. Rather than simply calling a truce out of politeness, Mohammed went a step further, promising to protect the Christians, as well as their property, and allowing them to pray in the mosque. As we learned in chapter 1, many centuries later, St. Francis invited the sultan to hear the gospel. Although Malik-al-Kamil politely refused to convert, according to St. Bonaventure, "the Sultan, perceiving in the man of God a fervor of spirit and a courage that had to be admired, willingly listened to him and invited him to stay longer with him."[9] Francis did not prod the sultan to accept the gospel. Even though he would have welcomed martyrdom, Francis held lightly to his missionary agenda out of respect for his dialogue partner. Because Francis recognized where his agency ended and Malik Al-Kamil's began, the freedom of the "religious other" truly mattered.

Though separated from St. Francis by 800 years, the Jesuit philosopher-physicist Teilhard de Chardin recognized that however fascinating and practical they may be, ideas and arguments will not lead to the fulfillment of humanity. Like Francis, Teilhard knew that only love ignites the human spirit, and that there can be no Christianity without loving our neighbors. Teilhard writes: "The day will come when, after harnessing the ether, the winds, the tides, gravitation, we shall harness for God the energies of love. And, on that day, for the second time in the history of the world, [man] will have discovered fire."[10] Panikkar's metaphor of the window and the rainbow are present as the shard of an idea in Teilhard's slightly earlier cosmology: "Providence is pluralized when in contact with us—just as a ray of sunlight takes on color or loses itself in the depths of the body which it strikes."[11]As a symbol and emanation of God, the ray of sunlight *is* the fullness of all that exists: it transmits every color of the rainbow, producing a different effect for each beneficiary. The impact varies according to a wide range of factors such as one's faith tradition, race, gender, sexual orientation, age, culture, socio-economic status, and geographical location. Together, people of faith must work out the implications of receiving pluralized providence/sunlight. A function of dialogue is to articulate areas of compatibility (shared primary colors) and differences (secondary and complementary colors) regarding what is received. Only then can interspirituality become a lived experience.

Before we explore how interspirituality differs from syncretism, it is important to note the potential of analogical language to expand our understanding as well as its limitations. Reflecting on the use of symbols in analogical language, David Tracy notes that "each theologian is obliged to develop criteria of internal coherence for [a] symbol system and is usually content to achieve some 'rough coherence' among major symbols. That coherence will basically be forged by a theologian's correlation of some personal interpretation of the core symbolism of the tradition . . . and some interpretation of the situation."[12] The function of analogies is to convey "similarity-in-difference."

A lived experience of interspirituality hinges on the function of analogical language as opposed to univocal or equivocal language. When a person says "I love ice cream" the statement does not mirror the affection one feels for a person. The (univocal) meaning of the statement "I love ice cream" is clear. More complex is equivocal language, which involves more than one meaning for a word or phrase. The word "present" signifies a gift, a time period, or an action. Its multiple meanings are obvious in a sentence like: "At present I am going to present her with a present." Analogical language is still more complex, as with the statement: "I love God." One loves God not in the way that one loves ice cream, yet the feeling of satisfaction one experiences from the release of endorphins while eating ice cream can bear a trace resemblance to the experience of loving God. As the Gospel of John teaches, God's very being is love. When we say that we love God, with all our mixed intentions and human misfires, our love for God is miniscule compared with God's love for us. Human beings' love for God and God's love for us are characterized by affection and a desire to be together, yet God loves humanity in ways that are beyond our capacity to understand and reciprocate. God's love can spur us to anger at the injustices that human beings perpetrate but we do not harness our anger as fully or as appropriately God does. Analogical language is necessarily ambiguous and misalignments between intent and impact with our dialogue partners compel all parties to be patient and generous with forgiveness.

In his seminal work *Constructing Local Theologies*, Robert Schreiter explores three varieties of syncretism and three of dual religious systems.[13] By clarifying what falls under the umbrella of syncretism, we can begin to see why it does not apply to interspiritual engagement. His exploration of syncretism with regard to Christianity, which can also be applied to other religious traditions, can be summarized as follows: (1) An amalgamation, rather than a hybridization of belief systems, such as those developed by the enslaved peoples of South America and the Caribbean in which West African religions borrow elements from other traditions. Examples include the ways in which practitioners of Afro-Brazilian Candomblé and Haitian Vaudun (Voodoo) appropriated Christians' views of God and the saints. (2) Religious organizations that model themselves after Christianity and borrow some of its symbols but practice non-Christian rituals. An example is the monotheistic belief system of the Afro-Jamacian Rastafarians. They worship one God (Jah), celebrate Ethiopian Christmas (Genna) on January 7, but also smoke marijuana to stimulate spiritual awareness and reject Eurocentric Christianity. (3) The third form involves selective borrowing from Christianity. Schreiter notes that in Japan, where Christianity is a very small minority, it is common for couples to be baptized in order to have a Christian wedding ceremony, with no intention of practicing Christianity.

In contrast to syncretism, what Schreiter calls "dual systems" is a helpful anchor for interspirituality. I offer a synthesis of his three "dual systems" models, as well as my own analyses of each: (1) A situation in which Christianity and another tradition are both practiced in their fullest expressions. This was true of Christians from the inception of the church. Early texts, such as Paul's letter to the Galatians, convey that the Jews who followed Jesus practiced their faith as fully as non-Jewish Christians, while continuing to practice Jewish rituals and customs.[14] Judaism did not contradict their faith in Jesus. If anything, it enhanced their understanding of Jesus' references and symbols. (2) A Christian who is fully committed to Christianity also embraces practices seen as belonging to another religious tradition. In the examples Schreiter offers, the "selected elements from another system" are culturally mediated. For example, Christians might seek spiritual care from priests as well as practitioners of indigenous medicine. Here I will challenge the implied contradictions he cites by making the case that this form of dualism is often not what it seems. For example, a Christian who practices meditation is reaching into ancient Christian spirituality, and not necessarily into the Eastern religions that have popularized this practice. Centering Prayer is one such practice. It was used by the desert mothers and fathers, yet contemporary Christians are often exposed to it not in Christian settings but through Eastern meditation practices. However, when a Christian meditates using Eastern techniques, choosing for example, the name of Jesus as a mantra, she or he has crossed into the realm of Christian spirituality. Similarly, though Christians might criticize the use of indigenous healers to intercede on behalf of someone possessed with an unclean spirit, we must reconcile our judgment not only with the fact that each Roman Catholic diocese has an exorcist, but that the practice of casting out unclean spirits was part of Jesus' own healing ministry. (3) A culturally rooted experience of double-belonging. Catholicism in Italy is interwoven with Italian culture. Even when an Italian chooses to identify with a religion other than Catholic Christianity, he or she never ceases to be culturally Catholic. Feast days, saints' days, and superstitions such as not walking under a ladder out of respect for the Holy Trinity are ancient expressions of cultural Catholicism that remain embedded in the lived experience of an Italian who converts to a tradition that is very different, such as Hinduism.

In this book, interspirituality refers to diverse understandings of "Truth" either within or among religious traditions. As Rory McEntee and Adam Bucko note, "Each wisdom tradition may hold a puzzle piece as to the ultimate flowering of humanity."[15] On a global level, Roman Catholic leaders and a wide range of guests who gathered at Vatican II were more committed to interreligious encounters than they had been in previous eras. More than fifty years later, those who engage in dialogue through interspiritual communities maintain that life is richer and fuller precisely because our neighbors frame many of our spiritual commitments in surprising ways.

Jorge Ferrer affirms the viability of Wayne Teasdale's interspiritual mysticism as a vision grounded in "the sharing of ultimate experiences across traditions."[16] Ferrer makes a slight distinction between this integrative approach to faith and a model in which religions are mutually transformative through sustained interaction. Teasdale's interpretation of "the sharing of ultimate experiences" precludes syncretism because through relationships cultivated between members of different religions, each moves closer to the fulfillment of itself. Arvind Sharma calls this "reciprocal illumination," which leads to an expansion of diversity rather than its disappearance.[17]

Brother Emile of the community at Taizé has noted that ecumenism is not about negotiation, but fullness.[18] I believe that this also applies to inter- and intraspiritual engagement. For example, imagine a panoramic vista of a mountain range using two pictures taken from neighboring windows. One uses a wide-angle lens and the other, a close-up lens. By placing Wayne Teasdale's macrocosmic vision of the divine mind alongside the microcosmic vision of a hazelnut revealed to the English mystic Julian of Norwich (1342–1416) as a manifestation of all that is made by the divine mind, a more textured diorama of the mysterious divine mind emerges. Whether one considers the result to be a deeper or wider vision is a matter of perspective. Though Julian predates Teasdale by 600 years, together their experiences provide layers of insight into God's density (Julian) and expansiveness (Teasdale). Their mutually illuminating visions of God model what is possible if we can learn from people within our own faith tradition, whose spiritual sensibilities we might find even more unsettling than those professed by members of other traditions.

During a guest lecture in my Feminist Theology course Sister Constance Phelps, Community Director of the Sisters of Charity of Leavenworth, shared with the students the process and goals of active listening as interpreted by her community. Perhaps most importantly, the guidelines include a commitment not to formulate what one is going to say while the other person is speaking. The practice quells the sense of urgency to respond and cultivates the ability to hear clearly what the dialogue partner is saying. I envision the good that this would do for the secular world as well as interspiritual circles. The community's *Dialogue Guidelines* states three goals of this mode of listening: "1) To share in such a way that we achieve new understandings that transcend what any of us previously knew. 2) To reach down and grasp the truth beneath our words, the complex truth that underlies what each of us is able to understand. 3) To learn not only from our certainties but also from our inconsistencies and questions." Contemplative listening involves several components, of which speaking in order to be understood is only one. The others include learning something new about our assumptions, as well as our dialogue partners' perspectives, and developing a shared understanding.[19]

In 1949 the University of Chicago philologist Carl Darling Buck wrote *A Dictionary of Selected Synonyms in the Principal Indo-European Languages.* An expert on Greek dialects, his research into the word *"krisis"* sheds light on what is involved with elevating a challenge, which one might encounter in dialogue, to the level of a crisis. The Greek term signals a decision or judgment. In Old Norse, Danish, Swedish, Old and Middle English, and Old German, the word for judgment implies an outcome that is related to the word "doom." In a way that varies between languages, the concept of judgment is linked to the idea of an agreement or a pronouncement: to what is established as a law according to norms and customs. If we recognize the fluid nature of the judgments we make in particular moments, and within unique cultures, we can grant ourselves the freedom to establish new paradigms. Laws are constructed according to values, desires, and practical needs. The root of the Irish word for judgment *breth* is to "bear, carry or bring." A judgment, therefore, is determined according to "what is brought." Whether we choose to exercise hospitality or disdain, human beings are free to choose what we bring to relationships. Sanskrit has additional ways of seeing judgment: *samdha* is a "union, agreement, or compact." *Nirnaya* means "to decide" or "to discern." Embedded in both concepts is the freedom to determine the outcome. Judgments are decisions we make; they are not our taskmasters.

Table 4 collates insights about what non-judgment might look like according to the world's major religious traditions. In my conclusion I will explore a potential paradigm shift should the church make an earnest effort to learn from these traditions, cultivating a *habitus* in which assumptions that lead us to judge one another are supplanted by discernment processes. The idea is that our felt need to be right can give way to mutual illumination and respect through a commitment to dialogue. We can break the habit of treating things that do not have ultimate importance as if they did and of escalating issues to crisis level where we could instead make a lateral move to work through challenges.[20]

Similarity-in-Difference

As I explored in chapter 1, two people with different experiences who are looking through the same window perceive variations in the landscape. Each can learn about that vista through the description of the color scheme, symbolism, or contours witnessed by his or her dialogue partner. For example, let's imagine that a Buddhist and a Christian take a trip to Palestine. Each has a unique symbolic understanding of the Jordan River. The Christian can be enriched by the description of the Buddhist who is struck by the power of a river to cleanse the body and refresh the spirit. From the Christian's interpretation of ritualized drowning that leads to new life in Christ through baptism, the Buddhist can develop a deeper understanding of the fragility of life and greater insight into the wisdom of nonattachment. This is mutual enrichment. In using analogical language, it is just as important to recognize that "the dissimilarities between God and world are as great as the similarities."[21] By being attentive to the easy slippage from similarities-in-difference to likenesses, we avoid "the sterility of a relaxed univocity and a facilely affirmative harmony."[22]

A careful approach to interspiritual practice can yield an authentic, integral experience of what the Hindu tradition calls *advaita*: similarity-in-difference; unity of belief without syncretism. Mother Teresa is a good example of a Christian who understood this insight. According to Fr. Thomas Matus, "Mother Teresa was asked why the people of India love her. She said it was because she had not converted anyone but worked to serve everyone in need. Many Hindus saw her as one who had realized nonduality. She had a state funeral in India in addition to a funeral Mass."[23]

The process of being transformed by one another's insights is gradual, just as patience is required in making bread. It takes time for the yeast to metabolize the sugar in flour, which releases carbon dioxide and allows the ingredients that yield the dough to mature. The type of yeast, liquid, salt, and sugar used, as well as the time allotted for expansion, the room temperature, and the temperature at which the bread is baked, will produce food that is both unique and nourishing. Interspiritual growth is also a gradual process that requires patience and flexibility. As a habit of the soul, astute active listening cultivates the ability to respond rather than react to what one hears, and a genuine desire to be fed by the bread that is offered, regardless of whether it is the bread that was anticipated.

Panikkar, de Mello, and Teasdale maintain that we receive revelation in ways that are compatible with our belief systems. According to Panikkar, "It simply is an unwarranted overstatement to affirm that the Trinitarian concept of the Ultimate, and with it the whole of reality, is an exclusive Christian insight or revelation."[24] For Teilhard de Chardin, the divine mind is in all and through all, "sur-animating" people of faith according to "pluralized Providence."[25] This insight asserts that divine illumination has no horizon line and offers an alternative to the freeloading syncretism that fills new age bookstores and relativizes religious traditions. McEntee and Bucko reflect on the "New Age pitfalls of walking a shallow spiritual path that comforts rather than transforms the ego."[26] The goal of interspiritual living is to discover God beyond our known vistas: to learn about who and how God is for others, not to pick and choose what makes us feel good. This approach does not flatten the contours of Christianity but recognizes that Christian teachings refract differently through the prism of each tradition (and vice versa).

Michael Amaladoss distinguishes between "difference" as an enhancement to diversity rather than a source of division.[27] I had a challenging but powerful lived experience of this during my year of Clinical Pastoral Education (CPE). In gathering a cohort, it is common for CPE supervisors to select individuals who are likely to have interpersonal tensions with one another, so that students will confront and exorcise their demons. My supervisor was especially gifted in discerning how best to facilitate the group's learning. Observing a squabble between two members of our peer group, he calmly noted that "just because someone wants something different from you doesn't mean that there has to be conflict."[28] Amaladoss reflects on this awareness through a Hindu lens, which is a tradition and worldview that bears witness to the value of holding in creative tension a wide range of sacred ideas, images, and experiences: "The vision of the *advaita*, the One-in-the-many, integrates and unifies Reality." This can only come to fruition where there is trust and good will, even without consensus. Without starting from a commitment to friendship, without an appreciation for the goodness of our core differences, relationships calcify and crumble into heaps of distrust and resentment. Not only is it impossible to polish away core differences that would create the illusion of harmony, the effort itself defaces the unique and beautiful contours of the world's religions. When a desire to "win" is part of a conversation the exchange is inevitably marked by dehumanizing, childish behavior.

The Trump Card

I like to think that if there were a tonic that could instill a generous spirit in adults who fear or resent their neighbors, it would be sold by the barrel. A Presbyterian minister, Fred Rogers, developed a television show called *The Children's Corner*, which later became *Mr. Roger's Neighborhood*. He knew that this habit of the soul either begins in childhood or is likely never to develop. He sought to cultivate in children a healthy sense of self, both in their image of themselves and in relationship to their neighbors. For nearly four decades Rev. Rogers' weekday show focused on building soft skills, in episodes that exhibited the values he hoped children would internalize. Among them are "Alike and Different"; "Be Yourself: That's the Best"; "Conflict"; "Curiosity"; "Giving and Receiving"; "Kindness and Unkindness"; "Sharing"; "When Things Get Broken"; "You and I Together" to name just a few.[29] These foundational values instill a commitment to the vision of genuine dialogue embraced by Panikkar as well as the Sisters of Charity of Leavenworth, in which each person "listens and observes . . . speaks, corrects, and is corrected."[30] Rogers credited Dr. Margaret McFarland, a child psychologist and advisor to his program, with the statement: "Anything that's human is mentionable and whatever is mentionable is manageable." With surgical precision Rev. Fred Rogers excised shame by helping children explore topics that, if left unexamined, would metastasize into their adult selves' deepest fears.[31]

In an episode from 1972, a sunny, even-tempered character named X Owl wants to be alone in order to write poetry.[32] The mischievous Lady Elaine Fairchilde becomes suspicious about his behavior. She wants to satisfy her curiosity and does not respect X Owl's desire for privacy. Whether motivated by a desire to control X Owl, or perhaps fear of the unknown or even envy, she reacts out of the assumption that he is doing something wrong. X Owl neither succumbs to her incessant knocking on his treehouse door, nor lashes out at her. He is occupied with his poetry and maintains his focus. The good-natured mailman Mr. McFeely asks X Owl's neighbor, Henrietta Pussycat, to take responsibility for X Owl's special delivery, which she is glad to do. In the meanwhile, Lady Elaine asks King Friday XIII to grant her permission to spy on X Owl since he refuses to come out of his tree. Using his authority responsibly, his answer is a firm "No." Assuming the worst about his elusiveness, Lady Elaine is fixated on forcing X Owl to reveal the content of the poems. Modeling wisdom and respect, King Friday tells Lady Elaine that he will extend an invitation to X Owl: "I shall not demand to see X's poems, but I would like to invite him to share them with us." Lady Elaine finally names her insecurity: "I just don't like secrecy." Having learned about the gifts and challenges of spending time alone, X Owl welcomes the invitation to share his poetry. The episode introduces two concepts: While curiosity is a great value, it is morally wrong to manipulate or bully people into satisfying our desires. It also illustrates how our demons will manage us if we don't manage them.

Because the show aired on public television, Rev. Rogers could not reference scripture directly. However, I imagine that he trusted that the adults who overheard the dialogue would be moved by the ease with which his sensible young audience internalized what were for him gospel lessons. Perhaps his approach reminded some parents and teachers of Jesus' admonition: "Truly I tell you, unless you change and become like children, you will never enter the kingdom of heaven."[33] They might have recognized a piece of his metanarrative: that operating from a position of certitude is not an act of self-assertion but of self-sabotage, which we practice regularly in inane ways. Without the help of a formal sermon Rev. Rogers invited adults to join the little ones in humbly sitting on the ground (*humus*).

The Neighborhood of Make-Believe welcomes people, at whatever stage of life, to live our way into a new way of thinking and being, leaving behind the ego's need to defend itself. Rev. Rogers' discreet catechism, which is available on DVD, continues to offer a primer for the soft skills that many people learned as children but gradually forgot.[34] By relearning those skills, in listening authentically to our neighbors, we recognize that the most important voice in the room is the one that is not our own. By listening not only to those we naturally like or agree with, but to those we judge or would like to dismiss, we learn to build peaceful neighborhoods in which everyone is respected and received. Rev. Rogers understood that neighborhoods are the foundation of cities, which exist for the common good. In a unique way, the work of Rev. Baker and the Christian camp at Burning Man in Black Rock City, NV, which I will explore at length in chapter 3, is a twenty-first-century expression of Mr. Rogers' view of a good and just society. Both Burning Man and *Mr. Rogers' Neighborhood* are examples of Aristotle's *polis*: an urban environment designed for the enjoyment of each resident. Some readers will find themselves stretching in order not to pass judgment on the values and approach to ministry embraced by members of the camp. The case study offers an ideal opportunity to test their mettle in looking through their neighbors' window.

With the recent normalizing of incivility and intolerance in public discourse, the gentle way of Mr. Rogers, with his decades-long lived celebration of diversity, is a simple but powerful reminder of the importance of cultivating a spirit of generosity. That Rogers, a lifelong member of the Republican Party, maintained his gentle tone throughout his career is a testimony to his spiritual maturity. His way of mitigating conflict is an especially important lesson given the vitriolic one-upmanship of our own era. He compels us to hold lightly to

our own experiences and truth claims, which are not paramount. Like Lady
Elaine Fairchild, we make poor decisions when we are not at our best.

Even when we are functioning well, we do not have all the facts even about
our own beliefs. Panikkar recognizes that in looking at the world through our
neighbor's window, not only do we learn something about the view from his
or her house, but we also develop a fuller picture of what lies beyond our own
window. The effort clarifies for us where we end, and another begins. Being
a respectful guest in another's home cultivates a *habitus* of generosity both in
the guest and in the host. A polite guest respects the host's space, while the
host offers the guest the best of what she or he has. If we take Jesus' second
great commandment seriously, when we give priority to our neighbors we are
witnessing to their dignity and the goodness of the God who made them. That
itself is a prayer. At the journey's end what we believe manifests in what we
did rather than in what we espoused, so how we treat one another has ultimate
importance.

In a parable about righteousness in Matthew 25, Jesus underscores the
importance of greeting and serving Christ in our neighbor. The "me first"
attitude that drives imperialism as well as individual self-centeredness reveals
humanity's narcissism and blocks our ability to live the gospel with our
whole hearts. How much effort has been wasted by prosperity evangelists
who edit the gospel so that it serves the ego needs of the elite?[35] A government that claims a Christian heritage but rejects the aspects of the gospel that
challenge its own agenda patently misrepresents Jesus' mission. When we
check the charity box through a donation by serving breakfast at a shelter or
going to church because we feel pressure to be seen, but secretly put our own
needs above those of others, we undermine humanity and marginalize divinity. Pope Francis put into perspective what should be an obvious connection
between orthodoxy and orthopraxis: "You pray for the hungry, then you feed
them. That is how prayer works."[36]

In the subterranean world of the mind, we mask our inconsistencies with
rationalizations and half-truths, forgetting that light, especially divine light,
reveals what is hidden in darkness. Closing our eyes in the darkness does not
keep light from revealing to God and others what we are trying to hide in plain
sight. Dorothy Day recognized the fact that humanity wants to reach out toward
divinity: we all desire "to build that kind of society where it is easier to be
good."[37] In stumbling toward the *eschaton*, courage makes it possible to suspend
our preferences so that we might attend to the basic needs of others. Sustained
spiritual development is impossible until we become tired of the way things are.
In a simple phrase, the sociologist Brené Brown noted what is necessary for
growth: "Our capacity to be wholehearted can never be greater than our willingness to be broken-hearted."[38] Broken-heartedness leaves us vulnerable, but the
alternative is worse: a constricted heart that cannot sustain life.

The spiritually and emotionally rigid "us first" politico-religious ethos in the United States calls for a critical reappraisal of the mistaken belief that Christian faith conflicts with the core beliefs of other traditions. That stance has set the United States on a collision course even with our allies around the globe. The vignettes found in the tables at the end of this chapter demonstrate that Christians have as much to learn from beauty and truth as interpreted by non-Christian traditions as those traditions can learn about beauty and truth from the mystery of the incarnation and the ministry of Jesus. In fact, had Jesus of Nazareth lived in any of those cultures when their wisdom was conceived, he might well have spoken those words himself. The vignettes are resources for people who have grown weary of "talking about talking about" interspiritual dialogue. Those who view Christianity (or other traditions) in binary terms such as good/evil; right/wrong; true/false will reject models that call for mutual illumination. As the psychologist and interspiritual teacher David Richo noted, "An adult-oriented church loves change because it is a sign that a Spirit, a mighty unpredictable wind and uncontrollable tongues of fire, is at work. Such a church is not afraid of the new directions into which it might be led."[39] This exploration of inter- and intraspiritual engagement invites the church to grow into a more mature version of itself.

Church leaders have the capacity to guide or misguide the church. An effective bishop's pastoral functioning is shaped by the needs and characteristics of the community she or he serves. Awareness of these considerations is a hallmark of an attentive leader, and one who will likely continue to have followers. In his book on preaching Bishop Ken Untener provided a valuable reminder that the homilist is addressing real people: that she or he is not preaching in order to feel smart, proud of a clever turn of phrase or morally right. He emphasized the need to receive feedback from the people in the pews and to respond to the needs they express.[40] When the church loses sight of people who are disenfranchised, sometimes due to its own policies (*polis*), and sometimes because it loses focus, it is morally obligated to regroup courageously, rethink its mission, practice active listening, and respond accordingly. Faithful leadership is a high wire act.

Scaling the Fence around the Torah

I used to live in a diocese in which the bishop had forbidden the parishes to sing the popular liturgical song "All Are Welcome" by Jesse Manibusan. He declined an opportunity to embrace the song's unitive vision. Those who knew the bishop well suggested that the line that bothered him was: "Here the love of Christ shall end divisions." The lyrics do not say that the love of Christ will collapse differences. Rather, they imply that love will end the resentment that smolders under a refusal to gather together *with*, and in celebration *of*, our differences. In a rigid system, orthopraxis is sacrificed on the gleaming altar of orthodoxy. Preferring a messy rather than meticulous approach to faith, Jesus challenged several of the sabbath laws in the Jewish *Mishnah* (oral tradition) because he recognized that his contemporaries' interpretation of the laws undermined a central goal of the Torah: to give rest to the weary. He violated *muktzeh*, which prohibits faithful Jews from gathering food, such as wheat, or anything that must be cooked, as well as the law against carrying something from outdoors (*reshut ha-rabim*) into a dwelling place on the sabbath. Some of the specific items on the list of prohibited activities are reaping, binding, sifting, grinding, and kneading, all of which are required to make bread.[41]

The divisions implied in the contemporary song "All Are Welcome" would include political views, positions on marriage equality, the ordination of women, and intercommunion. These are very real points of creative tension within the church. We do not know how or even whether Jesus resolved his disagreements with the religious authorities of his day, but we know that he continued throughout his public ministry to challenge the individual scribes and Pharisees "who lock people out of the kingdom of heaven" (Mt: 23:13). Even the most well-meaning church leaders will occasionally miss the mark in pastoral affairs. Though perfection is unattainable on this side of life, humility, by which we rightsize our outsize egos, provides opportunities to try again. The rejection of binary, finite terms, such as the rigid interpretation of the Jewish law that resulted in Jesus' death, is the beginning of the end of divisions and brings us closer to unity: *communio*. Jesus welcomed to the Communion table all who looked to him for something more. He did not invite them for conversation only then to refuse their company when it came time to share the bread.[42]

Radical Hospitality

Henri Nouwen defines hospitality as "the ability to pay attention to the guest"[43] (*hospes*). He understands that generosity of spirit is a disposition. A host who lives generously (*genos* = of the same kind) is open to the needs, gifts, and differences of the guest because she or he recognizes that we are kin. A generous host welcomes whoever comes to dinner and whatever they might bring, even if what they are carrying is a burden. The first principle of Burning Man and the sixth principle of The Gubbio Project, which are the ministries discussed in chapters 3 and 4 testify to these organizations' commitments to an unconditional welcome for anyone who enters the camp or walks through the church door. Those who specialize in hospitality recognize fearful hearts through people's body language. When we are cold, we instinctively turn in on ourselves, believing that it is the best way to get warm.[44] Avoiding eye contact, we retreat into a world with a population of one. A courageous host seeks out guests whose values, beliefs, demeanor, and appearance, including hygiene, might differ from his or her own. In fact, at Burning Man as well as at both Gubbio Project locations, neon signs proclaiming non-judgment about personal hygiene would be well-placed. Both populations sleep outdoors at least some of the time.[45] Some refuse conventional hygiene practices, some seek it but have difficulty managing it, and some are unaware that it is a social issue. Individuals have various ways of managing human contact, as well as a range of reasons for their habits. If we believe, as the Christian tradition teaches, that God is not only in Christ, but also in one another, we have no right to reject a neighbor with whom we feel uncomfortable.

Attentiveness to the guest can be expressed through dialogue, and in shared celebrations, including liturgical events. The Entrance Rite in the New Skellig Celtic Liturgy discussed in chapter 5 begins with the priest saying: "Let us stand and greet Christ who comes to us in one another." All members of the community then bow to one another, saying: "Beannaim Chríost ionat!" ("I greet Christ in you!"). Given the inevitability of interpersonal conflicts in any community, St. Paul recognized that new life in Christ has far-reaching implications. In Col. 3:8–11 he writes:

> But now you must get rid of all such things—anger, wrath, malice, slander, and abusive language from your mouth. Do not lie to one another, seeing that you have stripped off the old self with its practices and have clothed yourselves with the new self, which is being renewed in knowledge according to the image of its creator. In that renewal there is no longer Greek and Jew, circumcised and uncircumcised, barbarian, Scythian, slave and free; but Christ is all and in all![46]

Because Christ is present in all, in his name we must establish a place where all are welcome.

From his own interspiritual context, Panikkar said it this way: "God is the transcendent mystery immanent in us."[47] By "us" Panikkar means all of us. God cannot be understood fully by one being or one religious tradition because there are always new people and perspectives to engage. While necessary for a full life, a commitment to cultivating unity is fraught with obstacles, as are most fulfilling endeavors. The Christological debates of the fourth and fifth centuries remind us that the most minute linguistic or conceptual differences rooted in culture can create misunderstandings about core ideas, leading to unnecessary strife. For example, whether a Christological formula describes Jesus as being *of* two natures in the one nature of the incarnate Word or *in* two natures in the incarnate Word is a matter of emphasis and the orientation of the Christian imagination. What mattered for St. Paul was that one recognizes *that* Christ is the human being whom God "puts on."[48] Christians in the early stage of the church were not yet preoccupied with precisely *how* the two natures coexist in Christ. Faith in the incarnate Word was essential, while explanations for it were fluid and even optional. As I will discuss in chapter 3, Heisenberg's Uncertainty Principle strongly suggests that there are aspects of the Really Real, of things as they really are, that *cannot* be fully known. Since understanding and communication are inherently ambiguous, communion, which is an elastic epistemological reality, can exist between two people who have very different Christological lexicons and images. Whether in meditating on the incarnation one envisions Christ as the divine essence clothed in humanity, or as grace-filled humanity wrapped in divinity, the point is that there is a shared understanding that Christ is both divine and human. This extends to Eucharistic celebrations in which, for example, a Christocentric Hindu will participate wholeheartedly in the celebration, deeply aware of what she or he is doing in receiving the Eucharist. Augustine said in a sermon delivered to catechumens in the Easter season sometime between 405 and 411 CE: "Be what you see. Receive what you are."[49] In the same sermon he says that he does not feel the need to explain how Christ is present in the Eucharist. Instead he encourages catechumens to rejoice in becoming members of the one body of Christ. Bread is not made from a single grain, but many, and just as wine is made from the juice of many grapes. A single grain cannot produce the bread of life, and the juice of a single grape would evaporate before ever becoming wine. Augustine continues: "If you, therefore, are Christ's body and members, it is your own mystery that is placed on the Lord's table! It is your own mystery that you are receiving! You are saying 'Amen' to what you are: your response is a personal signature, affirming your faith. When you hear 'The body of Christ,' you reply 'Amen.'"

Global Wisdom for the Church

A well-known saying by Anthony de Mello is "the shortest distance between the human heart and truth is a story."[50] The simple truths of Jesus' parables are found in other wisdom traditions because they point to pluralized Truth. My work with undergraduates has provided insight about the need for a new approach to theological reflection. Students who are numb to the gospel stories because of inadequate catechesis or poor modeling by their churches are often receptive to the parables when presented alongside comparable wisdom of traditions that preceded and followed the New Testament period. In other words, when they are presented in their proper historical and cultural context, and translated with twenty-first-century Millennials in mind, the lessons of Jesus are clearer and more vibrant. The heart of the gospel remains and is magnified through new imagery and varied contexts, invigorating those who need to hear it differently because of their life experiences. The prophets and wisdom figures of Taoism, Confucianism, Hinduism, Buddhism, Judaism, and Islam join their voices with Jesus' own provident message, each contributing a unique voice, forming a harmonized polyphonic composition. Each voice is lovely but together they are enchanting.

Many years ago, in Chicago I attended an open-air *Sama* (listening) ceremony, the sacred dance of the Whirling Dervishes. The Sufi mystics practice this unique form of *dhikr*, a concept similar to the Greek idea of *anamnesis* (remembrance) in which one enters conscious awareness of the divine presence in the Eucharist. Though the divine presence is continual, worldly distractions hinder our awareness of it. *Anamnesis* facilitates an "unforgetting" in which Christians enter *Kairos*, the fullness of time: time as it is meant to be experienced. Through the *Sama* ceremony the Sufi enter *wajd*, a trance in which the practitioners experience self-transcendence. While the ritual differs from the pattern of centering prayer in the Christian tradition, Christians share the self-transcendent aim of *dhikr*. With centering prayer and Eucharist as my own reference points I was able to witness the transcendent prayer of the Muslim friend with whom I attended the ceremony. She described the ritual as a path to the heart of God through the remembrance of death, which is symbolized by the clothing worn by the Dervishes: the white gown signifies death, the black cloak evokes the image of the grave, and the hat is in the shape of a tombstone. Her description reminded me of some of the Good Friday devotional practices.

I asked my friend to tell me about her view of the Prophet Mohammed, whom she described in terms of love. I probed a bit further: Did she mean the type of love between friends? Parents and children? Leaders and disciples? I should not have been surprised when she described it as divine love poured out through Mohammed, whom she sees as God's preeminent conduit to humanity. She was careful to distinguish this love from the Christian view of Jesus as God in human form, noting that Mohammed is seen only as human, albeit the closest one to God ever to have lived. I tried to bracket off for a moment my view of the divinity of Jesus and his perfectly-oriented human will.

As I grappled with my friend's description, what came to mind was a lesser-known treatise by the twelfth-century mystical theologian Hugh of St. Victor. In his exploration of the will of Christ, he concludes that in his humanity, Christ loved God as fully as any human being ever could because he possessed the full goodness of human nature.[51] Since normative (Chalcedonian) Christology does not conceptually separate out the human and divine natures, Jesus' perfect humanity is, in part, due to his full divinity. For Muslims, who recognize the goodness and wisdom of Jesus, but not his divinity, the concept of perfect humanity is excessive. By entering as fully as possible into my friend's understanding of the goodness of Mohammed as God's prophet, but not as God in human form, I understood, if only fleetingly, why she describes her love of Mohammed in a way that bears a resemblance to Christians' language about their love for Jesus. Since Muslims do not profess faith in the divinity of Jesus, they cannot be expected to articulate love for Jesus in the way that Christians do. Returning to the metaphor of a polyphonic composition, my Muslim companion's image of Mohammed as a friend of the ineffable God and as a model of human love is the musical note that bridges the First and Second Commandments. The affection that Muslims express for Jesus stems from their belief that in his own exemplary human life, Jesus connected these divine laws so thoroughly through his teaching that there was no daylight between them: to love the One is to love others.

In an interview with Krista Tippet, the San Francisco–based Rabbi Lawrence Kushner offered a Jewish mystical view of divine immanence through an endearing story:

> I was leading a tour of the sanctuary, of the prayer hall, with the children in the congregation's preschool. And then I figured, as a pièce de résistance, I'd have them come onto the *bima*, or the little prayer stage up in front of the room, where there was an ark where we kept the scroll of the Torah. It was accessible via a big floor-to-ceiling curtain. And I got them up on the stage, and I was about to call them—"Open the ark," but I saw the teacher at the back tapping her wristwatch, which, as you may know, is an old Talmudic gesture, which means "Your time is about up, bucko." So, I said, "I tell you what, boys and girls. We'll come back when we get together again in a couple of weeks. We'll come back here and I'm going to open that curtain there and show you what's behind it. It's very special." And so they all say, "Shalom, Rabbi," and like little ducklings, follow the teacher back to the class.
>
> Well, the next day, the teacher shows up at my office with the following story. Apparently the preceding day's hastily-concluded lesson has occasioned a fierce debate among the little people as to what is behind the curtain. They didn't know. And the following four answers are given, which is I think pretty interesting. One kid, obviously destined to become a professor of nihilistic philosophy at a great university, opined that behind that curtain was absolutely nothing. Another kid, less imaginative, thought it had a Jewish holy thing in there. A third kid, obviously a devotee of American game show television subculture, guessed that behind that curtain was a brand new car. And the fourth kid—and that's what brings us back to Gershom Scholem and Kabbalah—said, "No, you're all wrong. Next week when that rabbi man comes and opens that curtain, behind it, there will be a giant mirror." From a four-year-old. Somehow, that little soul knew that through looking at the words of sacred scripture, he would encounter himself in a new and a heightened and revealing way.[52]

Though wisdom stories told from an explicitly religious perspective can be very inspiring, occasionally the church can also learn about courage, vulnerability, and integrity from the vision of for-profit corporations. One of the world's largest producers of wine, spirits, and whiskey barrels, the U.S.-owned Brown-Forman Company asks their 4,400 employees around the world 4 questions that reflect the importance of expressing the courage of one's conviction: (1) Do you think for yourself? (2) Do you say what you think? (3) Do you do what you say? (4) Are you true to yourself?[53] If the church as a whole were to internalize the value of these questions it would be well-positioned to respond radically to the realization that "in a country that is dividing by economic prospects, by years of education, by the look and feel of what constitutes a family, and by political persuasion, we continue to believe there might be a more important message we all need to hear. The message people living in a democracy must understand, more than any other message, is that there are Americans who aren't just like you. They don't live like you, they don't have families like yours, and they don't think like you. They may not live in your neighborhood, but this is their country too."[54] Though the church does not see itself as a democracy, it embraces some democratic principles such as the dignity of each person, the value of community, honesty, and fidelity to one's conscience.

In keeping with this chapter's focus on interspirituality and hospitality, in the next section I am inviting the reader to imagine Jesus, as well as Christians, from the apostles through their twenty-first-century successors, having conversations with the spiritual masters of the world's major religious traditions. The tables include some of the parables, vignettes, and tales told by wisdom figures such as Lao Tzu, Rumi, the Hasidic masters, Gandhi, and Pope Francis. Imagine early Christian missioners meeting the religious other as they carried the gospel from Jerusalem to Kerala, India, and Alexandria, Egypt; to Baghdad via Persia and on to Xian, China. Instead of depicting Mohammed split from chin to groin as a sower of schism, imagine what Dante Alighieri, the thirteenth-century author of the *Divine Comedy*, might have contributed to interfaith relations if he had lived in a society that valued religious plurality. He might have been able to offer a respectful challenge to the Islamic theology of his day. Instead he condemns its founder as a heretic, placing him in the sixth circle of Hell.[55] Establishing mutuality between people of different faiths should not include an expectation of shared theology, metaphors, symbols, or worldviews. Such efforts enhance our understanding of others' values and perspectives and create the necessary conditions for appreciating what we can learn about our own views through our neighbors' windows. For example, though there is no reason to suggest that Jesus loved widows and children less than Gandhi, in his one hundred volume *Complete Works*, the latter devoted far more attention to writing about the suffering of, and justice for, widows and children than is conveyed by the Gospel. Gandhi therefore offers Christians additional material for exploring God's love for those who are vulnerable. Since in all things Jesus points to divine love, Gandhi's many pages devoted to social justice as acts of love are also sources for Christians who want to understand more fully God's Preferential Option for the Poor.

Prophetic Hospitality: Engaging Global Wisdom

In chapter 1, I noted that, for Panikkar, we must first understand our own religion before we can truly understand other religions. This involves a cyclical process rather than linear one. By cyclical I mean two things: that there are various avenues for investigating and connecting the vignettes of wisdom traditions and that the process is never complete because evolving contexts as well as each person's experience shape new insights. In this approach to interspirituality, I would like to invite Christians to probe the gospel passages included with each table by imagining a dialogue between Jesus and the authors of the assorted vignettes. It is important to keep in mind that the Christian tradition teaches that in his earthly life Jesus was able to learn new things.[56] That was part of the condition that God placed on Godself in order to live a genuinely human life. The tradition also maintains that the preincarnate Logos contains the fullness of divine wisdom as a co-equal member of the Trinity. Since our lives are meant to be passages through Jesus' life and his actions are for us to imitate, the exercise that follows can help us practice openness and hospitality toward our neighbors. By extension we can also imagine what is possible in relating to other Christians whose theological interests differ significantly from our own. By exploring wisdom from sources that coincide with gospel wisdom, we can deepen our understanding of our own sacred scripture. As noted in the Introduction, the vignettes are not intended to be read as one-to-one correlations. Rather, in unique ways they can help us understand the spirit of the gospel passages. It is an exegetical practice that follows a circuitous path into catechesis, providing a deeper understanding of the wisdom of Jesus without distorting or forcing the vignettes to conform to the gospel. I should note that the examples I provide are just a handful of the countless possibilities for exploring the gospels through the wisdom of non-Christian traditions. Further work in this area would be an enlightening exercise for small groups in parishes, graduate students in theology, ministers who would like to move more deeply into interspiritual awareness, and undergraduate faculty who teach at the intersection of Christianity and other world religions. While it would be possible to fill a book with the fruits of additional exercises, that is not my objective here.

I have provided multilingual etymological information for the terms that pertain to what I see as core concepts in the gospel passages that accompany the tables. The languages represented vary somewhat across the five tables. They were selected for their potential to convey additional perspectives on a word. The etymologies are intended to deepen our appreciation for the ways in which each term is culturally mediated and therefore differ widely. For example, in the table pertaining to non-judgment, I have included Taoist and Buddhist vignettes, and therefore provide a Chinese etymology for the concept of judgment. The characters used to convey the idea include representations of a house, a living animal, and a knife. The house introduces the sense of searching for clues where we live. The fact that the animal is living indicates that she or he is a subject. There is danger or threat to an animal due to the knife. The question of which animal is threatened is determined by the judge. By contrast, the Greek term for judgment is linked to the idea of a crisis (*krisis*) whereas the Irish concept is connected to a sense of doom. Embedded in these etymologies is a warning about the *gravitas* of judging. For the Greek terms, the origins found below are both the biblical words and those that predate them. In several cases, Hebrew has more than one word for the term, so I chose the one that illuminates the spirit of the gospel passage. Whether you work in adult faith formation, seminary education or with undergraduates, what follows are some suggestions for thinking in broader terms about the gospel message. I recommend reading the vignettes in the appropriate table either before or with the reflections below.

Matthew 11:29: "Take my yoke upon you and learn from me; for I am gentle and humble in heart, and you will find rest for your souls."

Table 1. Humble/Humility: Lat. *humilis* (on the ground); Gk. *chamai* (on the ground); *chamai-genes* (earth-born), *praus* (in the New Testament, an obedient domestic animal); 谦卑 Chinese qiān bei (modest, unassuming, low, submissive); Heb. *anav* עָנָו (in the Hebrew Bible, it implies reliance on God).

Hinduism	1. Behavior is the mirror in which we can display our image.
	2. Inborn humility can never remain hidden, and yet the possessor is unaware of its existence.
	3. Bow down and worship where others kneel, for where so many have been paying tribute of adoration the kind Lord must manifest [himself], for [he] is all mercy.
Buddhism	4. Who can know that far off in the misty waves another yet more excellent realm of thought exists?
	5. The flute without holes is the most difficult to blow.
	6. The good merchant hides his possessions well and appears to have nothing.
	7. I do not emulate the sages; I do not esteem my own spirit.
Taoism and Confucianism	8. It is easier to carry an empty cup then one that is filled to the brim.
	9. The highest good is not to seek to do good but to allow yourself to become it.
	10. Because the *Tao* does not seek greatness it is able to do great things.
	11. One may move so well that a footprint never shows, speak so well that the tongue never slips, reckon so well that no counter is needed.

(Continued)

Table 1. Humble/Humility: Lat. *humilis* (on the ground); Gk. *chamai* (on the ground); *chamai-genes* (earth-born), *praus* (in the New Testament, an obedient domestic animal); 谦卑 Chinese qiān bei (modest, unassuming, low, submissive); Heb. *anav* עָנָו (in the Hebrew Bible, it implies reliance on God). *(Continued)*

Judaism	12. Poor Man and Rich Man: Rabbi Shmelke said: "The poor man gives the rich man more than the rich gives the poor. More than the poor man needs the rich man, the rich is in need of the poor."
	13. The Baal Shem said: "I let the sinners come close to me, if they are not proud. I keep the scholars and the sinless away from me if they are proud. For the sinner who knows that he is a sinner, and therefore, considers himself base—God is with him, for He 'dwelleth with them in the midst of their uncleannesses.' But concerning him who prides himself on the fact that he is unburdened by sin, God says, as we know from the Gemara: 'There is not enough room in the world for myself and him."
	14. The rabbi of Lublin said: "I love the wicked man who knows he is wicked more than the righteous man who knows he is righteous. But concerning the wicked who consider themselves righteous, it is said: 'They do not turn even on the threshold of Hell.' For they think they are being sent to Hell to redeem the souls of others."
Islam	15. When the world pushes you to your knees you're in the perfect position to pray.
	16. Sell your cleverness and buy bewilderment
	17. Very little grows on jagged rock. Be ground. Be crumbled, so wildflowers will come up where you are.
	18. The quieter you become the more you are able to hear.
Unknown, miscellaneous	19. The local priest was often seen talking to a comely woman of bad repute—and in public places too—to the great scandal of his congregation. He was summoned by his bishop for a dressing-down. When the bishop had done, the priest said, "Your Excellency, I have always held that it is better to talk to a pretty woman with one's thoughts set on God than to pray to God with one's thoughts fixed on a pretty woman."
	20. A woman dreamed she walked into a brand-new shop in the marketplace and, to her surprise, found God behind the counter. "What do you sell here?" she asked. "Everything your heart desires," said God. Hardly daring to believe what she was hearing, the woman decided to ask for the best things a human being could wish for. "I want peace of mind and love and happiness and wisdom and freedom from fear, for everyone on earth." God smiled, "I think you've got me wrong, my dear," He said. "We don't sell fruits here. Only seeds."
	21. If it is peace you want, seek to change yourself, not other people. It is easier to protect your feet with slippers than to carpet the whole earth.

Drawing on the etymologies for table 1, there are two Greek terms for humility: one from the New Testament and one from the pre-Christian Greek context. The New Testament term evokes the image of a domesticated animal. Given the ubiquity of Greek in the ancient Mediterranean, this could reflect the author's understanding of Jesus' message in Mt. 11:29. Jesus' Hebrew understanding points to God as the one to whom we are meant to be obedient. Since the church maintains that Jesus is God, in Matthew's Gospel we learn that God is a humble shepherd rather than one to be feared. Obedience is meant to be a gentle experience of being led (yoked) by God. In 1.1, the Hindu vignette indicates that obedience, a close cousin of humility, should be visible in our actions first, and only subsequently in our self-understanding. From this Jesus might offer an example of the fruits of obedience. From the Buddhist vignette in 1.5 we are reminded that vulnerability (the holes in the flute) is an essential part of humility, and therefore of obedience. Connecting the Chinese concept of humility with the previous exploration of judgment in that linguistic tradition, we see in 1.11 that in walking humbly one does not leave a footprint, implying that the humble person is invulnerable to judgment. Were Jesus to speak with the author of that vignette he might provide a gloss on the beatitude about the fruits of meekness.[57] Following a conversation with the eighteenth-century Hasidic master known as the Baal Shem Tov about 1.13, he might provide a commentary on humility/obedience, incorporating the Hasidic master's recognition that God has a special affection for those who know that they need God.

Matthew 7:12: "In everything do to others as you would have them do to you; this is the law and the prophets."

Table 2. Friend/Friendship: Gk. *philos* (friend, beloved, dear); Irish *cara* (friend); Sanskrit *sakhi, mitra, suhrd* (having a good heart); Old French *mignon* (darling, little); Lat. *amicus* (closely related to love); Russian *drug* (companion); Chinese 朋 *péng* ("moon" characters side by side to resemble two bird wings, signifying the act of flying as a group; alternatively, it resembles two people standing side by side); Heb. חבר *chaver* (friend/companion, where the root is "connection")

Hinduism	
	1. It is easy enough to be friendly to one's friends. But to befriend the one who regards himself as your enemy is the quintessence of true religion. The other is mere business.
	2. Friendship that insists upon agreement on all things isn't worth the name.
	3. Yes, I am also a Muslim, a Christian, a Buddhist, and a Jew.
	4. Mutual help is the consequence of, not a motive for, friendship.
	5. Since we regard thieves as our kin they must be made to realize the kinship.

(Continued)

Table 2. Friend/Friendship: Gk. *philos* (friend, beloved, dear); Irish *cara* (friend); Sanskrit *sakhi, mitra, suhrd* (having a good heart); Old French *mignon* (darling, little); Lat. *amicus* (closely related to love); Russian *drug* (companion); Chinese 朋 *péng* ("moon" characters side by side to resemble two bird wings, signifying the act of flying as a group; alternatively, it resembles two people standing side by side); Heb. חבר *chaver* (friend/companion, where the root is "connection") (*Continued*)

Buddhism	6. I meet him but know not who he is; I converse with him but do not know his name.
	7. [One who practices *ahimsa* (non-harm) is] ashamed of roughness, and full of mercy, he dwells compassionate and kind to all creatures that have life.
Taoism and Confucianism	8. The supreme good is like water which benefits all creation without trying to compete with it.
	9. The Tao is giving birth and nourishing, making without possessing, expecting nothing in return.
	10. Can you love people and lead them without forcing your will on them?
Judaism	11. The stranger who resides with you shall be to you as one of your citizens; you shall love him as yourself, for you were strangers in the land of Egypt: I the Lord am your God.
Islam	12. None of you [truly] believes until he wishes for his brother what he wishes for himself.
	13. Out beyond ideas of wrongdoing and rightdoing there is a field. I'll meet you there. When the soul lies down in that grass … ideas, language, even the phrase *each other* doesn't make any sense.
Miscellaneous, unknown	14. If it harms none, do what you will.
	15. Do not do unto others what you would not wish done to yourself.
	16. If you want to be kind, be polite.

Table 2 highlights the golden rule. While friendship might not be the first thing that comes to mind in reading this gospel passage, it is an implied outcome. If we treat each other the way we want to be treated, friendship is bound to develop. The Hindu vignette in 2.5 places the responsibility for our treatment of others on our own shoulders and there is no room for grudges or retaliation. The Sanskrit notion of a friend is "one who has a good heart." Using the language of kinship, the vignette has two messages: the guiding principle is that those we perceive as enemies ("thieves") are in fact our kin. It also indicates that it is up to the person who has been robbed, or perhaps to the one who has apprehended a thief, to bear in mind that the person who has done harm remains loveable and should be treated as such. This is the principle behind restorative justice, which focuses on reconciliation between the offender, the victim, and the society rather than punishment and retribution. The philosophy of incarceration modeled at Halden prison in Norway models that society's commitment to treating inmates with respect. Thanks to this piece of Hindu wisdom we might imagine a conversation between Jesus and a frustrated guard, particularly in the U.S. prison system.

Table 2 (2.13) is a quote from Rumi in which the poet implicitly links non-judgment with kinship. The ideological "other" ceases to exist when soul to soul, we find a place where we can truly be in one another's company. Though the culture differs from Rumi's Persian Islamic background, the Chinese character for friendship conveys a similar message. It is formed by the image of two moons. Together they resemble birds flying together as well as two people standing side by side. The Confucian statement in 2.8 about water being useful and generous toward every part of creation evokes for me the image of the thousands of bird species that pollinate flowers all over the world. Like water, they contribute to the growth of life-sustaining crops. In Mt. 23:23 Jesus criticizes the Pharisees for taxing spices, including cumin, which is native to both China and the Middle East. Imagine Jesus meeting a Chinese spice merchant who is traveling along the branch of the Silk Road that passes through Jerusalem. Perhaps he would strike up a conversation with the merchant about the heavy taxation of cumin, which is a favorite seed of birds. What might he make of the merchant's explanation of the Chinese character for the word bird? Perhaps he would suggest to the Pharisees that a seed that is easily accessible to birds and is a staple of the Middle Eastern diet, is a divine gift to humans and that we are meant to stand together. In Matthew 13:31–2 Jesus notes that birds, which also pollinate mustard plants, find rest in the shade of these towering trees that begin as miniscule seeds. Perhaps he would extend his analogy between the reign of God and the mustard seed, noting that the birds accompany one another and rest in those trees together: just as rain faithfully waters all of creation, heaven is open to all who remain faithful in kinship. Historically this imaginary scenario is entirely possible. It is simple, yet it opens the circle of kinship to include a wide array of gentiles who Jesus might have met even though there is no mention of them in the gospels.

Matthew 17:20: "Truly I tell you, if you have faith the size of a mustard seed, you will say to this mountain, 'Move from here to there,' and it will move; and nothing will be impossible for you."

Table 3.   Faith/Prayer. Gk. *Euche* (prayer); Lat. *votis* (a religious promise); Chinese 祈祷 *qídǎo* (asking God or the Buddha for blessings or release from bitterness); Heb. אמונה *emunah* (being certain, trusting); Arabic *salah* (communication)

Hinduism	1. In prayer it is better to have a heart without words than words without a heart.
	2. A sage taught his son to see the One behind the appearance of the many. He said: "Put this salt in water and come back to me in the morning." In the morning he said "Please bring me the salt you put in the water yesterday." "I cannot find it," replied the boy. His father told him to taste it, and the boy acknowledged that it was salty. Then he told him to throw it away. When it had evaporated the boy acknowledged that the salt had reappeared. The sage said: "You cannot perceive God here, but in fact God is here."
	3. To want an answer to one's prayer is to tempt God.
	4. Our difficulty arises through our effort to measure God by our little selves.
	5. God never forgets us; it is we who forget God. And that is our misery.
Buddhism	6. Remember that not getting what you want is sometimes a wonderful stroke of luck.
Taoism and Confucianism	7. Nurture the darkness of your soul until you are whole.
	8. When heaven gives and takes away can you be content with the outcome?
Judaism	9. Israel made a habit of crying aloud while he prayed. Once his grandfather said to him: My son, do you recall the difference between a wick of cotton and a wick of flax? One burns quickly and the other sputters! Believe me, a single true gesture, even if it only be that of the small toe, is enough.
	10. Rabbi Pinhas used to say: "I am always afraid to be more clever than devout, but rather than both devout and clever, I should like to be good."
	11. The rabbi of Koznitz said to God: "Lord of the world, I beg of you to redeem Israel. And if you do not want to do that, then redeem the goyim."
Islam	12. The good-natured sensualist is better than the bad-tempered saint.
	13. There is a force within you that gives you life.
	14. Give up to grace. The ocean takes care of each wave 'til it gets to shore. You need more help than you know.
	15. Give your weakness to one who helps.
	16. Run from what's comfortable. Forget safety. Live where you fear to live. Destroy your reputation. Be notorious. I have tried prudent planning long enough. From now on I'll be mad.
	17. I didn't come here of my own accord, and I can't leave that way. Whoever brought me here will have to take me home.
Miscellaneous, unknown	18. A devout man fell on hard times and prayed regularly: "Lord for years I have served you and asked nothing in return. Now that I am old and bankrupt I am asking you for a favor and you I am sure you will not say no. Allow me to win the lottery." After months had passed, the frustrated man said: God, "Please give me a break." God replied: "Give me a break yourself! Why don't you buy a lottery ticket?"

Table 3 includes the etymologies for the concept of faith/prayer in Greek, Latin, Chinese, and Hebrew. In the gospel passage provided, Jesus indicates that even a small step toward faith has unlimited benefits. Table 3 (3.18) offers an illustrative vignette of unknown origin. The subtext seems to indicate that we should think twice about praying for frivolous things and that if we really want something, we should cooperate with God by trying to help ourselves. In Mt. 12:53–56 Jesus notes that weather forecasters focus on the future but pay no attention to the present. If Jesus lived in an era that included the lottery, he might listen to the storyteller in 3.18 and pass along that piece of wisdom to someone who is complaining that God is not being attentive to her or his prayers. The Confucian vignette in 3.7 suggests that the path to wholeness is to be attentive to what today we would call our shadow side. The Arabic word for prayer, *salah*, is derived from the word for "communication." The vignette in 3.13 acknowledges that the source of life is within us. Just as a newborn must communicate with his or her mother for survival, we must communicate with the One who sustains us. It is as vital as breathing and eating, which is made possible because of our mother's love. From this Islamic vignette Jesus might have used maternal imagery in teaching his disciples to pray.

Matthew: 7:1–5 "Do not judge, so that you may not be judged. For with the judgment you make you will be judged, and the measure you give will be the measure you get. Why do you see the speck in your neighbor's eye, but do not notice the log in your own eye? Or how can you say to your neighbor, 'Let me take the speck out of your eye,' while the log is in your own eye? You hypocrite, first take the log out of your own eye, and then you will see clearly to take the speck out of your neighbor's eye."

Table 4. Non-judgment. Gk. Judgment: *krisis* (decide, judge); Irish *breth* (doom); Gothic *dōms* (fame, glory); German *reht* (law); Middle English *verdit* (decision of a judge or jury); Chinese 審判 *shěn pàn* (the upper portion of the first character signifies a house and the lower portion, an animal: a house where an animal has left their footprint leaving clues for evaluation in search of evidence. The second character represents half of a living creature and a knife, therefore "to make a decision in a court case"); Heb. שופט *shaphat* (to judge or govern)

| Hinduism | 1. A Guru asked his disciples how they could tell when the night had ended and the day begun. One said, "When you see an animal in the distance and can tell whether it is a cow or a horse." "No," said the Guru. "When you look at a tree in the distance and can tell if it is a neem tree or a mango tree." "Wrong again," said the Guru. "Well, then, what is it?" asked his disciples. "When you look into the face of any man and recognize your brother or in him; when you look into the face of any woman and recognize in her your sister. If you cannot do this, no matter what time it is by the sun it is still night." |
| | 2. If you don't meet God in the next person you meet, it is a waste of time looking for God further. |

(Continued)

Table 4. Non-judgment. Gk. Judgment: *krisis* (decide, judge); **Irish** *breth* (doom); **Gothic** *dōms* (fame, glory); **German** *reht* (law); **Middle English** *verdit* (decision of a judge or jury); **Chinese** 審判 *shěn pàn* (the upper portion of the first character signifies a house and the lower portion, an animal: a house where an animal has left their footprint leaving clues for evaluation in search of evidence. The second character represents half of a living creature and a knife, therefore "to make a decision in a court case"); **Heb.** שׁוֹפֵט *shaphat* (to judge or govern) *(Continued)*

Buddhism	3. Though gold dust is precious in the eyes it obscures the vision.
	4. The perfect way knows no difficulties except that it refuses to make preferences; Only when freed from hate and love does it reveal itself fully and without disguise . . . to set up what you like against what you dislike, that is the disease of the mind.
Taoism and Confucianism	5. The soft and the pliable overcome the hard and inflexible.
Judaism	6. Rabbi Rafael asked his teacher: "Why is no face like any other?" Rabbi Pinhas replied: "Because humanity is created in the image of God. Every human being sucks the living strength of God from another place, and all together they make up humanity. That is why their faces all differ from one another."
Islam	7. A Sufi saint set out on pilgrimage to Mecca. At the outskirts of the city he lay down by the road, exhausted from his journey. He had barely fallen asleep when he was brusquely awakened by an irate pilgrim. "This is the time when all believers bow their heads toward Mecca and you have your feet pointed toward the holy shrine. What sort of Muslim are you?" The Sufi did not move; he merely opened his eyes and said, "Brother, would you do me the favor of placing my feet where they won't be pointing to the Lord?"
	8. Christian, Jew, Muslim, shaman, Zoroastrian, stone, ground, mountain, river, each has a secret way of being with the mystery, unique and not to be judged.
	9. I have chased out duality, lived the two worlds as one.
Unknown, miscellaneous	10. An old woman in the village was said to be receiving divine apparitions. The local priest demanded proof of their authenticity. "When God next appears to you," he said, "ask God to tell you my sins, which are known to God alone. That should be evidence enough." The woman returned a month later and the priest asked if God had appeared to her again. She said yes. "Did you put the question to God?" "I did." "And what did God say?" "Tell your priest I have forgotten his sins."

The Jewish tradition offers a conversation between a rabbi and his teacher. In table 4 (4.6) the younger rabbi asks the elder why each face is unique. In his response the sage notes that each person "sucks the living strength of God from another place." Implied is the idea that since our own features come from God's very being, we ought not interpret differences as defects. If Jesus lived among these fellow rabbis, he might further the conversation by challenging them to consider the relationship between charity and kindness toward those who are differently abled, rather than to label them as unclean. He might encourage them to teach their congregations about God showing up in the most unlikely places. He would not have to reference his divine identity in order to teach about charity. This might have facilitated his fellow rabbis' ability to hear his message. Within the Buddhist tradition, the vignette in 2.4 can be considered from a spiritual rather than religious perspective. That is, in seeking wealth, one is distracted from the Buddhist's desire to experience a clear mind and an awareness of the present moment. While Jesus would be more likely to see this as an admonition about praying for frivolous things, he might learn something from the Buddhist sage about the way that glitter obscures our ability to focus on God.

John 14:2: "In my Father's house there are many dwelling places"; Jn 8:32: "And you will know the truth and the truth will make you free."

Table 5.   Wisdom/Truth. Heb. *Hokhmah* (Wisdom, beginning point Truth); Heb. *emet* (faithfulness, firmness, truth); Lat. *Veritas* (truth, truthfulness, reality in the abstract sense. Legal: as opposed to a lie; likeness of life in works of art; the truth of nature; rectitude; integrity); Gk. Truth *Aletheia* (reality as opposed to appearance or something fake). *Alethes* (truthfulness; sincerity, frankness, candor). *Alethinos* (agreeable to truth; trusty); Sanskrit *Satya* truth; Chinese 智 *zhi* (Wisdom, a term that is comprised of three characters: 1.矢: arrow 2.口: mouth 3.日: sun, signifying the wholeness created by the yin and yang as the sun moves between day and night. Wisdom is like an arrow coming from the mouth, bringing great knowledge.

Hinduism	1. It is unwise to be too sure of one's own wisdom. It is healthy to be reminded that the strongest might weaken and the wisest might err.
	2. Happiness is when what you think, what you say, what you do are in harmony.
	3. Truth is one, paths are many.
	4. An error does not become truth by reason of multiplied propagation, nor does the truth become error because nobody will see it.
	5. A "No" uttered from the deepest conviction is better than "Yes" merely uttered to please, or worse, to avoid trouble.
	6. An idle person stands on the shoulders of two.
	7. As one can ascend to the top of a house by means of a ladder or a bamboo or a staircase or a rope, so diverse are the ways and means to approach God, and every religion in the world shows one of these ways.
Buddhism	8. The fifth Zen Patriarch, Hung-jun, chose Hui-neng from among five hundred monks to be his successor. When asked why, he replied, "The other four hundred and ninety-nine showed a perfect grasp of Buddhism. Hui-neng alone has no understanding of it whatsoever. He's the type of person that ordinary standards will not measure. So the mantle of authentic transmission has fallen on him."

(Continued)

Table 5.   Wisdom/Truth. Heb. *Hokhmah* (Wisdom, beginning point Truth); Heb. *emet* (faithfulness, firmness, truth); Lat. *Veritas* (truth, truthfulness, reality in the abstract sense. Legal: as opposed to a lie; likeness of life in works of art; the truth of nature; rectitude; integrity); Gk. Truth *Aletheia* (reality as opposed to appearance or something fake). *Alethes* (truthfulness; sincerity, frankness, candor). *Alethinos* (agreeable to truth; trusty); Sanskrit *Satya* truth; Chinese 智 *zhi* (Wisdom, a term that is comprised of three characters: 1.矢: arrow 2.口: mouth 3.日: sun, signifying the wholeness created by the yin and yang as the sun moves between day and night. Wisdom is like an arrow coming from the mouth, bringing great knowledge. (*Continued*)

	9. He who knows the law fears it.
	10. There's no cool spot in a pot of boiling water.
	11. Calmness is the substance of wisdom and wisdom is the function of calmness. Whenever wisdom is at work, calmness is within it.
	12. Buddha seemed quite unruffled by the insults hurled at him by a visitor. When his disciples later asked him what the secret of his serenity was, he said: "Imagine what would happen if someone placed an offering before you and you did not pick it up. Or someone sent you a letter that you refused to open; you would be unaffected by its contents, would you not? Do this each time you are abused and you will not lose your serenity."
Taoism and Confucianism	13. Vacuity, tranquility, mellowness, quietness, and taking no action characterize the things of the universe at peace and represent the ultimate of Tao and virtue.
	14. The highest good is not to seek to do good but to allow yourself to become it.
Judaism	15. Every word and every action contains all the ten *Sefirot*, the ten powers emanating from God, for they fill the entire world. . . . There are no words which, in themselves, are useless. There are no actions which, in themselves, are useless. But one can make useless both actions and words by saying or doing them uselessly.
	16. The words of the mouth are deep waters; the fountain of wisdom is a gushing stream.
	17. They say that, in his youth, Rabbi Israel studied eight hundred books of the Kabbalah. But the first time he saw the maggid [itinerant preacher] of Mezritch face to face, he instantly knew that he knew nothing at all.
	18. Rabbi Pinhas told his disciples: "I have found nothing more difficult than to overcome lying. It took me fourteen years. I broke every bone I had, and at last I found a way out." He also said: "For the sake of truth, I served twenty-one years. Seven years to find out what truth is, seven to drive out falsehood, and seven to absorb truth."
	19. The Baal Shem said: "What does it mean, when people say that Truth goes over all the world? It means that Truth is driven out of one place after another, and must wander on and on."

(*Continued*)

Table 5. Wisdom/Truth. Heb. *Hokhmah* (Wisdom, beginning point Truth); Heb. *emet* (faithfulness, firmness, truth); Lat. *Veritas* (truth, truthfulness, reality in the abstract sense. Legal: as opposed to a lie; likeness of life in works of art; the truth of nature; rectitude; integrity); Gk. Truth *Aletheia* (reality as opposed to appearance or something fake). *Alethes* (truthfulness; sincerity, frankness, candor). *Alethinos* (agreeable to truth; trusty); Sanskrit *Satya* truth; Chinese 智 *zhi* (Wisdom, a term that is comprised of three characters: 1.矢: arrow 2.口: mouth 3.日: sun, signifying the wholeness created by the yin and yang as the sun moves between day and night. Wisdom is like an arrow coming from the mouth, bringing great knowledge. *(Continued)*

Islam	20. The art of knowing is knowing what to ignore.
	21. "I long to learn spirituality," said a neighbor to Mullah Nasruddin. "Would you come over to my house and talk to me about it?" Nasruddin did not commit himself. He saw that the man did indeed have a spark of intelligence above the average, but he also realized that he was under the delusion that mysticism can be transmitted to another by word of mouth. Some days later the neighbor called from his roof, "Mullah, I need your help to blow my fire. The embers are going out." "Why, of course," said Nasruddin. "My breath is at your disposal. Come over to my house and you can have as much of it as you can take away."
	22. Be melting snow. Wash yourself of yourself.
	23. Do what you should do when you should do it. Refuse to do what you should not do. And, when it is not clear, wait until you are sure.
Unknown, miscellaneous	24. Those who know do not say, those who say do not know. Therefore the wise are silent. The clever speak. The stupid argue.

In John's Gospel Jesus tells the disciples that the truth will make them free. How might Jesus engage with people who are looking at truth/wisdom through a neighboring window? In table 5 (5.4) the Hindu tradition asserts that a falsehood does not become true by spinning it this or that way and no matter how firmly one refuses to accept the truth, it does not become falsehood. Jesus might have used this insight with his disciples in the face of impending persecution. If we know that we are being faithful to the truth, any mistreatment we suffer is temporary in light of the truth of *Kairos*. Given Jesus' Jewish context, his understanding of divine wisdom (*Hokhmah*) as the beginning point of Truth would have made it difficult to waver. What might Jesus say to politicians in the frenzy of accusations about fake news in which truth is dismissed? I imagine that he would have a pointed remark about the energy wasted in manipulating both the basic facts and the logic we learned as children.

With our Chinese neighbors Jesus might find the character for Wisdom (*zhi*), illustrated in table 5 to be a refreshingly direct, deeply symbolic representation. Like a straight arrow, abundant wisdom streams from the mouth of a sage in the light of day, under the sun that is also continually connected to the night. In 5.12 the Buddha used a brief example of the relationship between stillness and wisdom. This mirrors Jesus' calm demeanor when those who were intent on his death sought to spin his words. He simply did not take the bait. In 5.7 a Hindu master notes that there are many ways to climb to the roof of a house, such as a ladder, a rope, or a staircase. Given his special love of the poor and those in need of healing, Jesus might add to this that we can also carry one another to greater heights.

NOTES

1. Khalil Gibran, *Jesus The Son of Man: His Words and His Deeds as Told and Recorded by Those Who Knew Him.* "Peter-On the Neighbor." (New York: Penguin Books, 1997), 161.

2. Leviticus 18:22 and 20:13 are believed by most biblical historians to be in response to pagan sexual rituals. The often-cited story of Sodom and Gomorrah is believed to be about hospitality and an admonition against gang rape.

3. In Mt. 15:19–20 and Mk 7:20–23 Jesus is concerned about *porneia*, a general term for sexual impropriety, such as adultery, but he does not single out homosexual practices.

4. This core teaching about the mind of Jesus is found in seed form in Lk. 2:52 where the author states that Jesus grew in wisdom and in years. The idea is seldom explored at the popular level. However, it is one of the seminal achievements of the Catholic intellectual tradition. I see its fruition in the thirteenth century, particularly in question 7 of St. Bonaventure (1221–1274). Bonaventure notes that because Jesus is both fully divine and fully human, he apprehends by *ecstasis* everything that is appropriate for a creature to know. As a result, he knows perfectly *that* God is wisdom, but because through the incarnation the Logos voluntarily relinquished some of God's knowledge, he does not comprehend *precisely* the fullness of God. Just as Bonaventure believed that God illuminates human beings (including Jesus) only in ways that God deems appropriate, it is helpful for contemporary believers to recognize that God continues to refract divine light/wisdom differently according to time, social location and other aspects of people's lived experiences. *Disputed Questions on the Knowledge of Christ*, trans. Zachary Hayes (Saint Bonaventure, NY: The Franciscan Institute, 1992).

5. Gianluigi Pasquale and Hamad Mahamed, "San Francesco e il Sultano. Un modello per il dialogo," 63–74 in *Città di Vita*, 73 (January–February 2018), 69.

6. Ibid., 67.

7. Until 1936 Najrān was in Yemen. Today that territory that is now claimed by Saudi Arabia.

8. Martin Lings, *Muhammad: His Life Based on the Earliest Sources*, 2nd ed. (Vermont: Inner Traditions, 2006), 324–325.

9. Bonaventure, "Legenda Maior," in *Francis of Assisi: Early Documents*. Vol. 2 (New York: New City Press, 2000), ch 9, 603.

10. Teilhard de Chardin, *Toward the Future*, trans. René Hague (San Diego: Harcourt Inc., 1975) "The Evolution of Chastity," 86–87.

11. Teilhard de Chardin, *The Divine Milieu: An Essay on the Interior Life* (New York: Harper and Row, 1957), 142.

12. David Tracy, *The Analogical Imagination: Christian Theology and the Culture of Pluralism* (New York: Crossroad, 1981), 406–407. With Tracy's insight about the symbol systems of "theologians," I would include nonspecialists who are seeking ways to make meaning of their spiritual commitments and experiences.

13. Robert Schreiter, *Constructing Local Theologies* (Maryknoll, NY: Orbis Books, 1985), 146–158.

14. S. Wesley Ariarajah, *Moving Beyond the Impasse: Reorienting Ecumenical and Interfaith Relations* (Minneapolis: Fortress Press, 2018). Ariarajah defines intercultural hermeneutics as "the theory and method of interpretation and understanding across cultural boundaries," 117. This has been at work in the church since its inception.

15. Rory McEntee and Adam Bucko, *The New Monasticism An Interspiritual Manifesto for Contemplative Living* (Maryknoll: Orbis Books, 2015), 28.

16. Jorge Ferrer, "The Future of World Religion: Four Scenarios, One Dream," *Tikkun* (Winter, 2012), 16.

17. I agree with Ferrer's characterization of Teilhard de Chardin's insight that "religious cross-pollination will lead to spiritual creative unions in which diversity is not erased but rather intensified" but not with his suggestion that "a historical precursor of [reciprocal illumination] can be found in religious syncretism," 15.

18. Brother Emile, "Inexhautible Joy" retreat at Mercy Center. May 19, 2018.

19. The *Guidelines* describe this process as one "that encourages us to share and emphasizes consensus building." This makes sense for a community that must make decisions that impact the daily experience of members who live together. While the spirit of the *Guidelines* is very helpful, outside of religious communities, in the context of inter- or intraspirual dialogue, I do not believe that consensus is necessary goal.

20. An example of an unnecessary escalation was the U.S. president's comment at a press conference on November 7, 2018, that he would take a "warlike posture" against Democratic leaders if they pursued an investigation of possible corruption by him or his administration. https://www.washingtonpost.com/politics/trump-attempts-to-take-victory-lap-despite-republicans-losing-house/2018/11/07/8cec8226-e2a7-11e8-b759-3d88a5ce9e19_story.html?noredirect=on&utm_term=.e4115b0265d3 (accessed March 31, 2019).

21. Tracy, *The Analogical Imagination*, 409.

22. Ibid., 410.

23. Interview with Fr. Thomas Matus, OSB Cam, February 27, 2018.

24. Panikkar, The Trinity and the Religious Experience of Man (New York: Orbis Books, 1973), viii.

25. Teilhard de Chardin, *The Divine Milieu an Essay on the Interior Life* (New York: Harper and Row, 1968), 142.

26. McEntee and Bucko, *The New Monasticism*, 28.

27. Michael Amaladoss, *Interreligious Encounters: Opportunities and Challenges*, ed. Jonathan Tan (Maryknoll, N.Y., 2017), 14.

28. Doug Lubbers, Director of Spiritual Care and Interpretive Services at St. Francis Memorial Hospital (San Francisco).

29. Accessed March 31, 2019. http://www.neighborhoodarchive.com/mrn/episodes/.

30. Raimon Panikkar, *The Intrareligious Dialogue* (New York: Paulist Press, 1978), 50.

31. "Welcome to the Neighborhood Mr. Rogers Soft Sell Still Smooths the Way," http://articles.baltimoresun.com/1993-05-14/features/1993134131_1_fred-rogers-ro gers-neighborhood-top-of-photos (accessed March 31, 2019).

32. Episode 1,197 aired on February 22, 1972.

33. Matthew 18:3.

34. Shortly after completing this chapter, in an article about the 2018 film *Mr. Rogers' Neighborhood*, *New York Times* columnist David Brooks shared other pertinent insights about the legacy of Mr. Rogers. For example, "During the civil rights era, when black kids were being thrown out of swimming pools, Rogers and a black character bathed their feet together in a tub." He also writes: "And here is the radicalism that infused that show: that the child is closer to God than the adult; that the sick are closer than the healthy; that the poor are closer than the rich and the marginalized closer than the celebrated." "Fred Rogers and the Loveliness of the Little Good," https://www.nytimes.com/2018/07/05/opinion/mister-fred-rogers-wont-you -be-my-neighbor.html (accessed March 31, 2019).

35. The prosperity gospel includes the belief that material wealth is a sign of God's favor and a reward for correct faith. Placing an emphasis on the importance of financial contributions to the church and the organizations it supports, prosperity theology encourages the exploitation of those who are economically underprivileged and favors those who can give from their surplus. In terms of Catholic Social Teaching, it is the doctrinal opposite of the Preferential Option for the Poor.

36. Daily Jolt, April 8, 2016. https://bustedhalo.com/jolt/you-pray-for-the-hungr y-then-you-feed-them-this-is-how-prayer-works-pope-francis (accessed March 31, 2019).

37. Dorothy Day, *All the Way to Heaven: The Selected Letters of Dorothy Day*, ed. Robert Ellsberg (New York: Image Books, 2010), 457.

38. https://www.telegraph.co.uk/women/sex/self-help/9536381/Brene-Brown-on -the-power-of-vulnerability.html (accessed December 23, 2018).

39. David Richo, *How to Be An Adult in Faith and Spirituality* (Mahwah, NJ: Paulist Press, 2011), 71.

40. Bishop Ken Untener, *Preaching Better: Practical Suggestions for Homilists* (Mahwah, NJ: Paulist Press, 1999), 67–68.

41. Matthew 12:1–8: At that time Jesus went through the grainfields on the sabbath; his disciples were hungry, and they began to pluck heads of grain and to eat. [2] When the Pharisees saw it, they said to him, "Look, your disciples are doing what is not lawful to do on the sabbath." [3] He said to them, "Have you not read what David did when he and his companions were hungry? [4] He entered the house of God and ate the bread of the Presence, which it was not lawful for him or his companions to eat, but only for the priests. [5] Or have you not read in the law that on the sabbath the priests in the temple break the sabbath and yet are guiltless? [6] I tell you, something greater

than the temple is here." [7] But if you had known what this means, "I desire mercy and not sacrifice," you would not have condemned the guiltless. [8] For the Son of Man is lord of the sabbath.

42. Company: *cum + pane* ("with bread").

43. Henri Nouwen, *The Wounded Healer: Ministry in Contemporary Society* (New York: Doubleday, 1979), 89.

44. Dante describes this body language masterfully in the *Divine Comedy*. The image of those in hell as being *incurvatus in se* "curved in on themselves" is present in seed form in several of Augustine's writings, including *City of God*, Book 14 chapter 28.

45. Some Burners who can afford it have chosen to create posh "turnkey," "plug and play," "concierge camps" complete with a staff to set up and maintain supplies. "Turnkey Camping," https://burningman.org/event/camps/turnkey-camping/ (accessed March 31, 2019).

46. Cf. Gal. 3:26–28

47. Panikkar, Raimón, *Christianity: Opera Omnia, Vol. III.2, A Christophany*, ed. Milena Carrara Pavan (Maryknoll, NY: Orbis Books, 2016), 127.

48. This is the best description I have heard regarding what we mean in asserting that Jesus is both fully divine and fully human. It was offered by Brian Daley, SJ, in a Christology course at Weston Jesuit Theological Seminary in 1995.

49. https://earlychurchtexts.com/public/augustine_sermon_272_eucharist.htm (accessed March 24, 2019).

50. https://demellospirituality.com/297-2/ (accessed March 24, 2019).

51. Hugh of St. Victor, *Libello de quattuor voluntatibus in Christo,* ed. J. P. Migne (Paris: Garnier), 1844–155 (PL 176, 841).

52. https://onbeing.org/programs/lawrence-kushner-kabbalah-and-the-inner-life-of-god. The episode aired on March 10, 2016.

53. https://www.youtube.com/watch?v=vbfO_Ml1auo (accessed March 24, 2019).

54. Bill Bishop with Robert G. Cushing, *The Big Sort: Why the Clustering of Like-Minded America Is Tearing Us Apart* (Boston: First Mariner Books, 2009), 309.

55. Dante Alighieri, *The Divine Comedy: Inferno*, trans. Allen Mandelbaum (New York: Bantam Dell, 1980), 28, 22–30.

56. Bonaventure, *Disputed Questions on the Knowledge of Christ.* See the "Conclusion" to Question 7, 186–188. Bonaventure argues that inasmuch as it is appropriate for humans to know something, Jesus does to the fullest extent possible. He draws an important distinction between knowing *that* something is true and knowing *precisely why*, from every angle. Comprehensive knowledge is limited to God. In order to become human, in Jesus God relinquished some of the comprehensive knowledge of the preincarnate Logos.

57. In the context of Mt. 5:5 (blessed are the meek), the word meek (*praeis*) is related to the biblical Greek word for humility (*praus*).

Chapter 3

Church outside the Walls

Health, Healing, Wholeness, Holiness

WHY BURNING MAN?

Roman Catholics will recall that four months into his pontificate Pope Francis responded to a question from a reporter about what she referred to as a "gay lobby" in the Vatican. Taking aim at lobbies in general, Pope Francis made a distinction between any lobby that functions through secrets whispered in the dark and a gay individual who "is searching for the Lord and has good will."[1] His response came in the form of a question: "Who am I to judge?" As I was writing this chapter, I wondered about what conclusions Pope Francis would draw should he spend time at the new ecumenical camp at Burning Man. Would he appreciate the ministers' focus on radical hospitality and their profound commitment to non-judgment? Would he find the attitudes, rituals, and sacramental vision too far out of bounds? Would he be inspired to sit with his questions and suspend judgment? I hope that he would recognize that the camp is hosted by Christian ministers, both lay and ordained, who are trying to help the church get out of its own way. His recognition of the church's responsibility in the egregious abuse of minors and other vulnerable people seems to indicate an awareness that the church is indeed in its own way. Perhaps Pope Francis would suggest that the success or failure of these ministries should be assessed by those who serve and are served. Along with a critique, I believe that Pope Francis would take seriously the faith-filled intentions and commitment to pastoral outreach that inspire this growing community. Given that Burning Man is an event that raises the eyebrows even of some "Left Coasters," perhaps a willingness to learn would be enough to ask of a pope who is creative and curious.

Chapter 2 mentions two street ministries that exemplify bold hospitality. In this chapter and the next I will explore more fully how these two radical

California-based Christian ministries can help the church get out of its own way and bring the gospel to those who are often underserved or simply rejected. Both ministries emerged out of a spirit of generosity and are supported by mainline churches: Episcopal and Roman Catholic. My goal is to create a three-dimensional picture of the success that is possible among ministries that occupy the margin. I will make the case, adding additional layers in subsequent chapters, for why the institutional church should be more open to learning from radical and other marginal ministries. By "radical" I mean those that give primacy of place to non-judgment in the practice of hospitality; ministries that might be considered fire-starters because of the ways in which they harness the power of light to provide safe passage, life-giving warmth, and clarity. For various reasons, radical ministries have been planted in soil that borders the garden of the institutional church. Recognizing the unconventional settings and pastoral concerns at the heart of these ministries, the chapter begins by connecting pre-Christian wisdom that influenced the church's sacramental theology and ecclesiology, and these contemporary life-giving endeavors. In this chapter I will explore the gifts offered by a ministry that, in 2018, was in the nascent phase of establishing a Christian ecclesial presence at Burning Man, the annual event that began on a beach in San Francisco in 1986. I will also explain why the camp received a very fitting, very edgy name.

Today Burning Man draws 70,000 people to the Nevada desert. The event provides creative opportunities to explore some essential aspects of the human condition. According to the organization's vision statement the "Burning Man Project will bring experiences to people in grand, awe-inspiring and joyful ways that lift the human spirit, address social problems and inspire a sense of culture, community and personal engagement."[2] During the Burn I attended in 2018, I became aware of some of the desires, gifts, needs, habits, fears, and values that people carried with them into the desert. My objective was to be present to what emerged without judging or making assumptions.

A poem by Emily Dickinson illustrates why it is sometimes necessary to take an oblique approach to the development of provocative ideas and practices.

"Tell all the truth but tell It slant"[3]

Tell all the Truth
but tell it slant
 Success in Circuit lies
Too bold for our infirm Delight
The truth's superb surprise
As Lightning to
the Children eased

With explanation kind
The Truth must
dazzle moderately
Or every [man] be
blind—

Dickinson understood that intense energy, such as a lightning bolt, can scorch everything in its path. It helps to be judicious when sharing a "dazzling" insight. *Il modo soave*, the gentle way of missioners, discussed in chapter 1 is one example. By contrast, some European Christians used the *tabula rasa* approach in sharing the gospel. Intentionally or unintentionally, their method expunged from the historical record many of the true and beautiful cultural expressions that preceded them.

Throughout this book I suggest that in an era in which the relevance of the church is increasingly difficult even for Christians to discern, the church at every level—administrative, pastoral, catechetical, mystical, and liturgical—would benefit from re-evangelization. Ministries that flower at the tips of the branches can scatter seeds that create new life, sometimes against all odds. This is not new. The Christian tradition did not develop with the hierarchy as the hub of a wheel and the laity along the rim. For most of Christian history communication was too spotty to operate through a tidy network. In moving away from a clergy-centric ecclesial model, I am not suggesting that the careful theological reflection that resulted in essential doctrinal formulations or liturgical norms should be jettisoned. I believe that a structured church can provide the consistency and support that many people need in a chaotic world. Rather, I am taking a both/and approach, one that collates values and practices that convey the integral process by which ministries at the margins can fortify the structure and clarify the mission of the church. As Fr. Steve Bevans, SVD, noted several times in conversation: "The church does not have a mission: the mission has a church."

I am inviting church leaders to revisit and expand their vision of how the mission and ministry of Jesus can be lived more effectively in the third millennium. Because this chapter explores a radical ministry curated in part by an individual who has a specific role in presiding at Eucharist as a priest,[4] the topics that will help develop a composite picture of this new camp as a prophetic church include (1) layered connections between health, healing, wholeness and holiness; (2) the healing and leadership roles of priests in the pre-Christian Mediterranean and their influence on Christian sacramental ministry; (3) the function of the ancient Temple of Asclepius, the god of medicine and sleep, as well as resonances with contemporary sacred spaces; (4) the physics of healing: Eucharist as a focused, unconstrained transfer of energy; (5) the "Conventional" church: Eucharist at science fiction conventions; and (6) the dusty church at Burning Man.

Health, Healing, Wholeness, and Holiness

Though the church did not create this confluence, it can be both inspired and challenged by the fact that in many languages associated with Christian history, such as Latin, German, Italian, and French, there is a link between health, healing, wholeness, holiness, and salvation. Western, allopathic medicine triggered an unintended rift between the mind and the body that resourceful health-care providers are now trying to mend through Ayurvedic and other forms of traditional medicine. Those who take a holistic approach to the practice of medicine respectfully recognize that allopathic medicine has a very short history compared with the arc of indigenous medicine: approximately 200 years compared with several thousand. What the modern world gained in terms of medical breakthroughs, it gradually lost in spiritual insight. In its most sterile form, allopathic medicine separates the mind and body, ignoring or negating the emotional and spiritual root causes of physical illness. In therapeutic terms, these two facets of human beings (and some other animals) are indissoluble until death. For example, experienced allergists know that an unsettled soul or mind can create a somatic reaction, such as a rash. Psychiatrists recognize that a chemical imbalance can lead to schizophrenia or psychosis. The shortening of telomeres, the endcaps of chromosomes, leads to cell death, resulting in illness.

The worldview through which peoples of the ancient Mediterranean made meaning helps explain why, for example, in Italian, health (*sanità*) and holiness (*santità*) as well as salvation (*salvatio*) and a blessing for good health (*salute*) are etymologically related. Throughout the ancient Mediterranean, including Jesus' own culture and community, people attributed ailments like seizures, skin diseases, and fits of rage to demonic or other possessions. Since they had no knowledge of the scientific causes of conditions such as epilepsy, leprosy, and ergot poisoning, they developed what they saw as reasonable explanations and treatments for crises that affected the health of their communities. What ancient people knew by intuition, today many remain skeptical about: that what is good for the mind is good for the body and vice versa. I became especially aware of this connection while working as a hospital chaplain. We often received calls from the inpatient psychiatric unit for patients who had requested Communion. Those who identified as Catholic, regardless of whether they practiced their faith regularly, believed that their healing would be aided by receiving the essence of Christ in the form of consecrated bread. I personally witnessed changes that accompanied patients' reception of the sacrament. Whatever the causality of healing, faith in the power of a religious ritual to impact one's physical well-being reflects the wisdom of the unitive approach taken not only by patients but also by holistic healers.

PRIESTHOOD IN THE ANCIENT MEDITERRANEAN: PRE-CHRISTIAN AND CHRISTIAN

For the earliest Romans, a *templum* was a place set aside for a spiritual purpose, especially for reading the auspices (signs) in the sky. The Latin word *templum* is a cognate for the Greek *temenos*, which originates with *temno* "to cut off." According to Servius, the *templum* "was any place that was circumscribed and separated by the augurs from the rest of the land by a certain solemn formula."[5] It was the role of augurs to interpret the flight of birds. Italians still consider it good luck when bird droppings land on someone's head. The word "*augur*" is also etymologically related to the Italian "*auguri.*" For example, to wish someone a speedy recovery the phrase is: "*Augurare una pronta guarigione.*" One can also use "*auguri*" to curse a person or object (*augurare il male*). In English the term "inaugurate" also comes from the concept of an *augur*. As we know, an inauguration does not guarantee a good beginning, but it signifies a desire for a good beginning. The word is connected to a ritual, such as the role of a judge in the inauguration of an elected official. Wherever well-wishing, cursing, or expressions of disappointment occur, the notion of an augur is implied both linguistically and conceptually.

The broadest interpretation of an augur would involve a priest or a chaplain: one who serves as midwife for the hopes, curses, and disappointments that people carry and express. The priest or chaplain prepares the space and ensures its safety and sanctity. Augurs can both lead and accompany the sojourner who temporarily resides in a shelter, camp, or other residence as well as the wandering pilgrim who goes to a foreign place for a particular purpose, and the seeker who is scanning both the horizon and the landscape in search of nourishment. The shared Latin/Indo-European root of "to seek," *sagire*, means "to perceive by scent." Therefore, whether one is well prepared or scarcely equipped, the spiritual journey is an intuitive one.[6]

Since rituals are connected to places, it is helpful to note that the Greek term "*naos*," dwelling place, is often used interchangeably with "*hieron*," a holy place or shrine. The Latin cognate, *templum* is "the space in the heavens marked out by the augur." In other words, the notion of a temple is both fixed and flexible, according to the needs of those who use it. Depending on the language, culture, and beliefs of those who use the space, it can be a place where God or a god dwells, a shrine to be visited and/or a place designated by heaven as holy.[7]

Though there is no etymological connection between the word "temple" as it pertains to the brain and the spiritual temple, they are connected by function. The physician-philosopher Galen (129–200/216 CE) wrote a treatise on the interpretation of dreams for medical treatment.[8] Though he had no way of knowing it scientifically, the temporal lobes (where the temples are located) are responsible for hearing, and distinguishing between different frequencies, visual memories, and language recognition. A serendipitous coincidence, an important goal of contemplation is to develop a habit of hearing differently, or to hear different things through silence, such as our own voices, divine breath, or consolation. As one might expect, contemplation while walking was a significant feature of processing the dreams received under Galen's care.

THE ASCLEPION AND THE ORIGIN
OF CHRISTIAN PRIESTHOOD

The ancient city of Pergamum, now Bergama, Turkey, once housed the Temple of Asclepius, the god of sleep. A deeply embodied form of prayer, the ancient Greco-Roman religious practice of incubation, or sleeping at a holy site, witnesses to the connection between spirit and flesh, dreams and healing. Galen studied medicine at the *Asclepion*, where people went in the hope of receiving healing dreams and a cure for various illnesses, whether physical or what today we would consider psychological. A native of Pergamum, Galen served as imperial physician to several Roman emperors, beginning with Marcus Aurelius.[9] Believing that the Temple of Asclepius (the *Asclepion*) in Pergamum was a place of healing and blessing, the emperor's regard for the site, the god, and the physician elevated the status of all three.[10]

In a dream in which Asclepius appeared to Galen's father, he learned that the deity wanted his son to study medicine.[11] After completing his medical studies in Alexandria, in 157 Galen returned to Pergamum, where the chief priest of the temple appointed him physician for the gladiatorial school. The position provided an opportunity to study anatomy closely.[12] Around the year 160 Galen moved to Rome, where the *Pax Romana* enabled him to obtain pharmaceutical supplies from all over the world.[13] Believing that the mind and body were fully integrated, Galen was highly regarded for his philosophical training as well as his knowledge of medicine.[14] In a study of medicine in the ancient Mediterranean, Julius Rocca notes that "in this intensely competitive world, a 'thorough philosophical training . . . was . . . above all a mechanism for acquiring social respectability in a society in which rhetors, sophists and rhetorically educated elite-members increasingly dominated urban politics.'"[15]

On one occasion Galen provided medical care to a man who had fallen and lost his voice. Both his "organs" and his voice (divine spirit/breath) were healed. He was also believed to have cured the Roman philosopher Eudemus of malaria. It is interesting that he emphasized Galen's healing work more as a philosopher than as a physician.[16] Galen's experience as a philosopher-physician helped gather varied ancient wisdom sources into a single store-room. Believing that "the soul lies in the body of the brain, where thought takes place and memory is stored"[17] Galen practiced in an era in which it was unthinkable to separate physical ailments from emotional distress. His work is a fortuitous example of an integrated approach to the healing arts. Whether anchored in intuition or what today we consider a holistic approach to wellness, Galen's *pneuma*-based physiological model produced results.

As a pilgrimage destination for patients who worshipped the god of medicine, they spent a night of incubation in a purposefully designated sleeping hall, the *abaton*. "It was believed that whilst there Asclepius would send his worshippers dreams with medical prescriptions, if he deemed them worthy of cure."[18] A treatment offered by another local physician, Theodotos, for a patient named Aelius Aristides included singing by a chorus of boys. Aristides reported that he felt comfort from their singing, which is a principle underlying the modern field of music therapy.[19] The miraculous powers attributed to Asclepius are supported by the testimony in Aristides' *Hieroi Logoi* in which the author reports that Theodotos and other physicians were sometimes baffled by Asclepius' prescriptions, but followed his instructions nonetheless. The text makes it clear that the healers followed the god's lead regardless of whether they had faith in particular remedies.[20] For the way in which the patient faithfully insists on following the god's instructions even against the will of physicians, the *Hieroi Logoi* reveals that the patient is the catalyst for his or her own healing. At the Asclepion, physicians, priests, and the patient himself collaborated in the healing of Aristides.[21] In fact, Aristides refers to one of his caregivers, Asclepiacos, interchangeably as a temple warden and a physician.[22] Fully immersed in his holistic medical practice, Galen was both a physician and a devotee of Asclepius.[23] He and other physicians at the Asclepion provided the medicine prescribed by the deity. These vignettes demonstrate often hard-won trust and collaboration between the source, the practitioner, and the beneficiary of healing that was witnessed throughout the Mediterranean world.[24]

The practice of incubation in ancient Judaism has been described as "an activity in which an individual goes to a shrine or a sacred site and engages in some ritual activity . . . in order to obtain a revelation from the deity."[25] Within the Jewish tradition there are several references to "unintentional" or "incidental" "incubations" which are dreams at holy places.[26] "Most commonly . . . incubation is a process one enters deliberately, intentionally, on one's own behalf, with an eye to hatching dreams of power."[27] In Gen. 28:10–22 Yahweh speaks to Jacob, which is how he discovers that the place is sacred. He does not lie down there already believing that it is sacred. "Tablet 4 of the *Epic of Gilgamesh* shows Gilgamesh performing a ritual and asking the Mountain for a dream, and sleeping in a specially built hut near a mountain"[28] Job 33:15 states that God speaks "in dreams and in night-visions/when slumber has settled on humanity/and people are asleep in bed." Job does not refer to a ritual, preparation for a ritual or a sanctuary setting.[29] In antiquity Jews who lived outside of Jerusalem, or within Palestine but far from Jerusalem, prayed regularly in synagogues rather than in the one and only Jewish temple, where the Holy of Holies was understood to be the unique dwelling place for God.[30] Therefore it is not surprising that this practice was less common among Jews than it might otherwise have been.

Given the healing stories associated with the ministry of Jesus, especially those done on behalf of people who were experiencing liminal states such as physical and mental illness, one might wonder whether he saw himself within the tradition of what we might call Mediterranean "naturopaths." In Mark 2 Jesus links sin and illness, especially in the healing of the paralytic. Before the man takes up his mat and walks, Jesus tells him that his sins are forgiven. It is impossible to say how or even whether there is something fundamentally different about the type of healing Jesus performed compared with the type of healing attributed to Asclepius by his followers. However, evidence from the biblical and apostolic eras indicates that those who were healed by Jesus experienced his touch as life-changing. His refusal to judge those whose suffering was considered by others to be the result of sin caused those who were captivated or bewildered by his pastoral presence to flock to him. He was in such high demand that in the story of the hemorrhaging woman, there were so many people in the crowd that when "he felt the power go out of him" he did not know who had touched him.[31] Continuing Jesus' healing work, Christian priests and other ministers attribute their healing work to God, but not without the full participation of the believer. The hemorrhaging woman sought Jesus out, not in the temple, where she could not go because of purity laws, but in the street. Formally stated by Augustine in the fourth century, the church still maintains the necessity of cooperation on the part of the one seeking healing: "God who created you without you will not redeem you without yourself."[32] The section that follows will explore a contemporary application of this principle through the healing work of those who offer a ministry of presence and accompaniment, not in a traditional church, but in a new iteration of street ministry, in a temporary city in the Nevada desert.

As far as I know there is no evidence one way or another about the physical or spiritual focus of those who expressed faith in Asclepius' healing powers, and no information about the long-term spiritual impact of the cure. What we do know is that the Asclepion was a popular pilgrimage destination. Even considering the unique features of the Christological formulas of the Patristic era, it seems fair to view Jesus as the Great Physician within the wider context of Mediterranean healing traditions. In suggesting this I am not relativizing the uniqueness of Jesus' healing power as the incarnate Logos but, rather, situating his work among the therapeutic traditions of his neighbors. I give full credence to the Chalcedonian Christological formula that proclaims Jesus as the incarnate Logos who heals through the power (*dynamis*) of God. Whether Jews, Jewish followers of Jesus or devotees of Asclepius, those in the ancient Mediterranean who believed in the healing power of heaven, along with the full participation of pastoral caregivers and those who sought healing did so in a way, and in diverse settings, that can model for the church what it might look like to open up new contexts in which to receive God's unbounded healing grace. The attribution of that grace is a matter of creed.

The Physics and Metaphysics of Healing: The Unbounded Real Presence of Christ in the Eucharist

On September 14, 2015, 100 years after Einstein posited the existence of gravitational waves, scientists at LIGO detected their existence. They measured the impact on the earth of "two massive waves spiraling into each other," which caused it to expand and contract to a miniscule, but quantifiable degree. In doing so they proved that hugely significant, very real things are not solid or even what we generally think of as enduring. They consist of barely measurable fleeting particles of energy that moves in waves.[33] The fact that this has finally been proven can help reframe the symbolic terms that people who prefer the language of spirituality have long been exploring. Ironically, physicists have only begun to express the "particular" facts (comprised of and caused by particles) pertaining to their own field. It seems to me that the language that physicists are currently using in describing their proven thesis correlates with the Roman Catholic belief (as well as Episcopal and Lutheran) in the movement of "substances" between body and blood, bread and wine. Physicists and theologians both offer models that attempt to explain a single reality: that the most real things are not solid or visible, but consist of energy which, by definition, moves. In 1927 the physicist Sir Arthur Eddington presented his Gifford lectures on quantum physics. In the section called "Reality" he said: "Something unknown is doing we don't know what."[34] Nearly a century later, despite substantial advancements in quantum physics, the "something unknown" remains. From a theological perspective, assuming that something, rather than nothing, occurs in the consecration of the Eucharist, the movement of substances (the Really Real aspect of an object) between body and blood, and bread and wine, is an invisible but real manifestation of divine energy. Though the thirteenth-century theologians who formulated the doctrine of Transubstantiation did not have the benefit of Einstein's understanding of the connection between matter and energy, I would suggest that his model of "particular" energy (which moves in waves), as well as more recent discoveries in quantum physics, can help the contemporary church, and possibly physicists, understand what the medieval theologians were attempting to explain through faithful intuition. As it pertains to this book it can also help us understand the healing power of the Eucharist that is freely communicated through grace (divine energy), whether celebrated within or beyond the walls of a traditional church.

Appealing to the Greek metaphysics that was rediscovered by Latin theologians in the thirteenth century, at the Fourth Lateran Council (1215), the doctrine of Transubstantiation was presented as the church's official explanation for how the faithful receive the Real Presence of Christ in the Eucharist. Though on a popular level it has been more misunderstood than understood, medieval theologians proclaimed that the Really Real, the true presence of Christ in the Eucharist, is not received in the substances of the bread and wine on the altar, but because the (Really Real) substance of Christ in heaven replaces (or joins, as the Lutherans later nuanced the doctrine) the substances of the bread and wine in the prayers of consecration. As the formal explanation for how Christ is received in the Eucharist, Transubstantiation was the best, though still inadequate, model provided by the Latin Church.[35]

A familiar yet ethereal scientific model might also help explain the divine energy at work in Transubstantiation. The specific wavelength of electromagnetic radiation has been proven to destroy cancer cells by disrupting molecular bonds. The spiritual and scientific concepts of energy are two channels by which theologians and scientists can tunnel through to a shared reality from their respective ends. The phenomena that scientists explore through the mathematical principles that govern physics, theologians investigate through the principles of metaphysics. What they learn in winding their way through their respective mineshafts provides data about how energy works according to the models and metaphors of their own fields. The theologian Thomas Hosinski notes that perception is a fluid reality: "An observer in a moving frame of reference will see events occurring at different places and times than an observer in a stationary frame of reference observing the same events."[36] Theological and scientific inquiries offer complementary findings about healing energy and together provide a more vivid image of reality. It can be jarring for some Christians to reevaluate the standard thirteenth-century metaphysical model of how Christ is present in the Eucharist. I am hopeful that because scientific inquiry follows a method that differs significantly from the processes used by theologians, it will be easier for Christians to welcome insights about divine energy through a scientific lens than it is through theological exploration. Whether one's vision becomes sharper because she or he moves closer to the object or because she or he dons a new pair of glasses makes no difference regarding the outcome.

If, as the church believes, the risen Christ is truly alive, he has energy. As physicists have now demonstrated, energy moves in definite, but enigmatic ways. Atomic particles known as quarks can appear, disappear, and reappear in ways that remain mysterious.[37] Heisenberg's Uncertainty Principle asserts that the more we know about the velocity of an electron, the less we know about its position, and vice versa: "Indeterminacy characterizes the entire quantum world."[38] Perhaps it would be fruitful for physicists to design an experiment that allows them to measure the movement of energy that occurs during the consecration of the Eucharist. It seems that the most disappointing potential outcome would be that energy is perceived (because it is everywhere) yet the conclusions about how it behaves with regard to the consecration of the bread and wine are no more demonstrable than what physicists can prove about the relationship between the Uncertainty Principle and the strong wave nature of atomic and subatomic particles. In other words, the movement of energy in the consecration of the Eucharist is unlikely to contradict what physicists know about the indeterminacy of energy in quantum physics. It is likely that theologians as well as Christians who are nonspecialists would still maintain that the energy perceived is likely related to the transfer of substances. It is unlikely that secular physicists will be drawn to a model that asserts that the energy is generated or directed by the Real Presence of the risen Christ. Nevertheless, I believe that these recent discoveries in quantum physics can help the church engage a new model for explaining how the Real Presence of Christ manifests in the Eucharist, and why it is both legitimate and pastorally relevant to celebrate it beyond the traditional boundary of church walls. That is, if divine energy is everywhere, why wouldn't we allow ourselves to follow it?

The Eastern Orthodox perspective on the Real Presence of Christ in the Eucharist also provides valuable insight into why it is helpful to revise our thinking about what we see as appropriate contexts for the celebration. Unlike the Latin Church, the Eastern Orthodox tradition developed a cosmotheandric model, a way of envisioning "the undivided consciousness of the totality," without getting bogged down in the language of metaphysics.[39] In that tradition, the Real Presence received in the Eucharist is a mystery.[40] One might say that this claim is similar to the way in which scientists treated as true for a hundred years Einstein's theory involving gravitational waves, though it had not been proven. Eastern Orthodox Christians profess their belief in the Eucharistic Real Presence of Christ through prayer that is done in *anamnesis*, a type of "unforgetting," in which our consciousness gravitates toward the divine presence of which we are typically unaware. This model does not accentuate a divine breakthrough, but an occasion in which well-meaning, often spiritually inert human beings awaken to divine omnipresence.

With the descent of the Holy Spirit upon the gifts, the Christian tradition developed an understanding of the change by which mystery unfolds through the Eucharistic celebration. Whether it is through the metaphysically rich explanation of Transubstantiation or the Orthodox view that, for our benefit,

God sanctifies the gifts of bread and wine during the Greek *anaphora* (Eucharistic prayer), this familiar sacrament can serve as a model for the church's belief that, as the energizing principle of the universe, God and human beings interact through tangible matter, bringing about discernable changes in behavior and emotions. A parallel example for a physicist might be the light that radiates from a light bulb, a fire or the sun. The energy is both visible and invisible. Theologian Anthony de Mello included in a book of thought-provoking vignettes a humble remark attributed to Guglielmo Marconi, credited as the inventor of the radio. Despite Marconi's success in creating a useful device, he is said to have admitted to a friend that there was something that still puzzled him about radio telegraphy: *why* it works.[41] This seems to me a healthy approach to self-efficacious mystery.

Eucharist beyond the Church Walls: Mass at Science-Fiction Conventions

The Celtic Christian Church (CCC) traces its apostolic succession through the Old Catholic Church, and through Bishop Duarte Costa (1888–1961), a Roman Catholic bishop who founded the Brazilian Catholic Apostolic Church. He had been excommunicated by Pope Pius XII for his strong criticism of Vatican foreign policy following World War II. Katherine Kurtz was the presiding bishop of the CCC from January 19, 2016, until October 31, 2018. She is also an esoteric science-fiction writer who made an impact in that field through a series of well-known books published in the 1970s–1990s. Several of her books feature a fictitious group of Deryni, a community of monastic Christians who possess psychic powers and use magic as a spiritual practice.

Bishop Cait Finnegan of the CCC explained that as a young priest, perhaps in the 1980s, Kurtz began celebrating the Eucharist at science-fiction conventions.[42] Not only did Christians tend to find one another at those gatherings, the celebrations were open to everyone who was drawn to the Eucharist. Though the leadership for those celebrations has since been handed on to other priests, the practice was established and continues to be supported by Bishop Katherine. The decision to encourage the celebration of the Eucharist with open Communion in the context of esoteric conventions is striking in that a bishop who sets the pace and the parameters for her Christian community's prayer life is doing so in a setting that is appreciative both of magic and radical inclusivity. This reminds me of the ministry of Rev. Nadia Bolz-Weber, founding pastor of the Lutheran ecclesial community *House for All Sinners and Saints* in Denver, CO, and author of *Accidental Saints: Finding God in All the Wrong People*. On her website Bolz-Weber describes her encounters with God in "the least likely of people—a church-loving agnostic, a drag queen, a felonious Bishop and a gun-toting member of the NRA."[43]

She notes that "I just don't think belief should be the basis of belonging to a community like this."[44]

Millennial Worldviews and Spiritual Inclinations

Any discussion of practical theology, including the role of the sacraments, must have in mind real people, each with distinct spiritual needs. Several recent demographic studies illustrate some key features of U.S. Catholic parishes in the first two decades of the twenty-first century. The primary focus of those studies is to understand and address the felt needs of Millennials who are nominally Catholic or disaffiliated. Though they do not intentionally focus on these issues within Protestant and Eastern Orthodox churches, theologians from those traditions might find some of these studies' findings relevant. For example, while 23 percent of U.S. Americans are between the age of eighteen and thirty-four, they represent only 12 percent of Orthodox parishioners.[45] As of 2016 only 15 percent of Orthodox parishes saw young adult ministry as a high priority and only 9 percent had developed strategic plans for creating young adult ministries.[46] Since my exploration focuses both on Roman Catholic renewal movements and that tradition's Episcopal sibling, members of which often refer to it Catholic, data from the Pew Research Center is particularly helpful for comparing affiliation among Protestants, Catholics, and a general group that they call Other Christians as well as disaffiliation among U.S. Americans. While I draw on those demographic studies, my purpose in this chapter is to take their findings a step further by imagining what is needed for the cardiovascular health of the future church. These churches' efforts to be more hospitable involves a risk: integrating into their core commitments the gospel values modeled by daring ministries such as Episcopalians at Burning Man and The Gubbio Project, which are discussed in this chapter and the next.

Millennials are typically divided into two groups: Older (b. 1981–1989) and Younger (b. 1990–1996). According to the Pew Research Center's report "America's Changing Religious Landscape (2015), 34 percent of Older Millennials are religiously unaffiliated."[47] Data gathered over the course of two decades by Beloit College presents many of the issues that impacted Older Millennials during their formative years. By the time they reached school-age, HIV and AIDS were a global health crisis, and sex education (as it was then called) emphasized the dangers of sex. While they were still in elementary school they were introduced to e-books. Spelling Bees included the gender-inclusive language found in dictionaries beginning in 1991. By middle school, the European Union helped shape their understanding of the world. Kids in this group might have been taught by an openly gay rabbi, and/or a Jewish or Christian minister who used gender-inclusive language for

God. Preschool and elementary school children of this generation recognized Mr. Rogers as the most trusted man in America. While they were raised with multicultural curricula in schools, including the celebration of Martin Luther King Jr. Day as a national holiday, their earliest memories of radio included partisan stations. They saw wars unfold in real time as well as police activity. They were the first generation since the Cold War to grow up without the fear of nuclear war, and they did not experience a recession until they were in their late teens or twenties. By the age of ten, Older Millennials were the first generation in the United States since the Industrial Revolution not to inherit the idea of personal privacy as a right. By the time they developed a sense of world events, there was no clear delineation between serious news and entertainment news, which blurred the line between fact and fantasy. In his 2017 convocation speech at Harvard Divinity School, Cornel West referred to this now fully developed phenomenon as "the normalizing of mendacity."[48] Though Gen Xers and even Baby Boomers were not raised with the view that facts are flexible or even untrustworthy, it is becoming more common for them to capitalize on this trend, blurring the line between fact and opinion. This undermines the historical and potential role of elders as fonts of wisdom and truthfulness for young adults.

The 2015 Pew study *America's Changing Religious Landscape* notes that 36 percent of Younger Millennials are religiously unaffiliated, a 2 percent increase over Older Millennials.[49] People in this group were raised with email as a standard means of communication. Their parents might have contacted them by cell phone or text beginning in elementary school, which cultivated a preference for texting, often between people seated in the same room and, in some, a fear of speaking on the phone. Due to the availability of GPS devices they might never have used a paper map, leaving them without a sense of direction. Their experience of television has always included programs featuring people who are famous for being famous. Catholics and Lutherans have been engaged in formal dialogue and the cloning of some mammals has been possible since the oldest members of this group were in first grade. They also have had television available on demand since elementary school. Those born in 1996 were in kindergarten on 9/11, introducing to them the idea of the world as a dangerous place. It was also a small place for those who, since first grade, had access to Google and might have seen their parents using Skype since they were toddlers. If they received Christian catechesis as children, they might have belonged to the first group to receive a vision of hell as nothingness rather than the assortment of torments cemented in the Christian imagination by Dante 800 years ago. The youngest among them, slated to graduate from college in 2021, have always known laptops to be more common than desktops. Younger Millennials have never known the peril of tripping over a phone cord or the pleasure of flipping through a new set of encyclopedias. Exposed bra straps are for many of them a standard wardrobe choice. They do not recall seeing billboards advertising cigarettes but were raised with television ads for hard liquor. These competing realities in the sacred and secular spheres created for Millennials a spiritual landscape that can be difficult to navigate.

The 2016 *American Values Atlas* published by the Public Religion Research Institute indicates that 46 percent of LGBTQ Americans are religiously unaffiliated. Fifty-six percent of LGBTQ Americans ages eighteen to twenty-nine are unaffiliated, compared with 25 percent of all Americans aged sixty-five and over. Only 34 percent of LGBTQ Americans identify as Christian. In a 2009 Pew study, 56 percent of former Catholics disagreed with the church's teachings on abortion and homosexuality. The number remained steady in 2016.[50] This group believes that homosexuality does not have a negative impact on the heterosexual population, indicating an appreciation for where "I" end and another begins. For example, Gen Xers and Baby Boomers might not understand the appeal of the hip-hop music that is marketed to Millennials. Those who do not share their culture but spend a great deal of time with them, perhaps in the classroom or in the context of faith formation, have a responsibility to try to understand why it appeals to them. For me, lyrics that consist of little more than a chain of four-letter words seem vacuous. However, Generation X is not the culture that contemporary hip-hop is meant to appeal to, so it would be strange not only if I related to it but made it my issue. The fact that it does not suit my taste is a reflection of my preferences rather than a judgment of the music that I do not enjoy. Even older adults who do not spend much time with Millennials are indirectly involved with them through public policies and social services, giving them a shared responsibility to try to understand younger adults. In the case of the latest generation of hip-hop, the only opinion that means anything, the only one from which we stand to learn anything, is that of Millennials. Blaming them for a cultural expression that older adults do not understand would weaponize our opinions given that we tend to be in positions of authority. Music producer Quincy Jones recognized that in the 1970s he did not understand the emerging art form that became hip-hop but that it reminded him of be-bop.[51] He supported hip-hop artists because he loved their energy and saw the way that their music inspired young people. Quincy Jones and like-minded visionaries recognize that each generation has a unique window onto the world. We have a responsibility to try genuinely to understand our young adult neighbors' experiences, knowing that we will fail. Twenty-first-century educators must give young adults opportunities to articulate their values more fully and more critically than when they began their formal education as children, teaching them how to think rather than what to think. A group that has been particularly alienated is young adult LGBTQ Christians. Their issue is not with Jesus. However, they have walked away from the church because they are judged by heterosexual Christians. The LGBTQ young adults I know have made it clear that they would be more likely to remain in the church if heterosexual adults listened more and spoke less.

Burning Faith

Each year I teach a growing number of undergraduates who report that they find church boring and irrelevant. Christianity's symbolic language is foreign to most of them and though courses such as Theology of Sacraments and Introduction to Catholicism can lead them to understand the church's prayer patterns and rituals, the liturgies often leave students with the sense that they should find more nourishment from the church services than they do. The emerging ministry I explore in the second half of this chapter is served by a group of lay and ordained ministers. They recognize that if the church is going to reach Millennials and Nones who are seeking to make meaning in their lives, it must transform its listening. It must become more courageous in its willingness to go where the need is, and flexible enough to surrender some of its "givens" so that the church will remain faithful to the gospel in a changing world. Just as Jesus grew frustrated with the religious establishment in his own context, reminding its leaders that the sabbath was made for human beings rather than the other way around, as a conduit of Jesus' mission, the church must be willing to root out its own forms of idolatry. In his 2013 address to pilgrims at the Shrine of Our Lady of Guadalupe, Pope Francis recognized the church's obligation to identify and venture into the mission fields beyond its comfort zone: "We need to go forth from our own communities and be bold enough to go to the existential outskirts that need to feel the closeness of God."[52] The case study that follows is one model of radical evangelization as a response to a growing spiritual crisis.

Playing and Praying on the Playa

In 2018 I attended the thirty-second Burning Man event in Nevada's Black Rock Desert. For nearly two decades the annual gathering has occurred on a dry, heavily alkaline silt and clay lakebed. Each summer Black Rock City is rebuilt and populated for one week by festival enthusiasts, spiritual seekers, fatigued executives, escapists, artists, academics, grandparents, billionaire tech moguls, and a small percentage of resourceful individuals who are food insecure and struggling to find or maintain housing. Long before I had attended, many of the people interviewed said some version of: "Whatever your freak is, you can get it on at Burning Man." During that week, interactive art, fantasy art cars, naked bodies, circus apparatuses, fire-breathing dragons, hallucinogenic substances, vaudevillian costumes, and electronic dance music are as normal as birdseed at a wedding.

In 2010, Lee Gilmore, a theologically trained sociologist, wrote a book called *Theater in a Crowded Fire: Ritual and Spirituality at Burning Man.*[53] She examines topics such as Burners' perceptions and experiences regarding the differences between religion and spirituality, the value placed on ritual, their widespread rejection of dogma and their experiences of the event as a pilgrimage. Though her research predates mine by eight years, which is roughly one generation, she reports many of the same findings described by the Millennial Burners I interviewed, especially regarding the restoration of their faith in humanity, as well as the "opportunities for participants to peel away layers of default cultural messages and constructions of identity," leading to a deeper sense of self.[54] She notes that she is seeking "to demonstrate that Burning Man not only is a space in which to ritualize alternative and individualized constructions of spirituality but also calls into question both academic and popular culture assumptions about what constitutes religion, ritual, and spirituality in the first place."[55] Through interviews she explores why most participants, 69 percent in 2010, rejected institutional religion but found Burning Man life-giving.[56] She includes an insightful section on the design and uses of the temple, first erected in 2000. It is a shrine packed with memorial dedications and mementos which, together with the structure itself, is burned on Sunday, the last evening of the gathering.

In addition to reporting on some individual participants' experiences of how they experience the Really Real, I will focus on their responses to the presence of an Episcopal priest who is cultivating a full-time ministry at Burning Man after having spent decades as a priest in a parish setting. His vision of ministry is to reach those who view the church as unwelcoming by introducing mainline Christianity beyond the brick-and-mortar for those who call the Playa home. A pilgrimage destination in a barren desert, the emerging church at Burning Man provides spiritual care in an unconventional setting, where it clearly impacts those who seek a blessing, community, solace, or healing.

This section explores how people who do not attend church at all or only rarely have been touched either for the first time, or in a new way, by Christian rituals that are celebrated in an open-air setting within a community that takes seriously the principles of universal welcome and full participation. The Ten Principles of Burning Man prepare people to leave behind the disheartening daily realities of the default world, especially the tendency to take ourselves too seriously, as well as inclinations toward materialism, social isolation, exclusionism, unhealthy self-imposed limitations, and co-dependencies.[57] The array of small-scale, interactive, and monumental art installations, mutant vehicles, workshops, and costumes, as well as an emphasis on creativity and play are unmatched in the default world. The emerging church at Burning Man can help the wider Church to rethink its approach to mission in the third millennium.

The temple is located beyond the purposefully outlandish monumental art installations, set designs, dance parties, and theme camps, where people from every socioeconomic background explore their bodies and souls, both their own and one another's, often under the influence of drugs and alcohol. Burning Man makes a Bacchanalian feast look like a kindergarten birthday party. However, I will make a case for the sanctity of the temple and the new camp founded by Episcopalians at Burning Man, drawing on the relationship between Galen's healing work and the ministry of presence offered through the camp and its ministers, both lay and clerical. I will also explore some features of the Episcopal Mass (as the resident priest calls it) and other Christian celebrations at Burning Man, which enable the church to reach people who otherwise, for various reasons, either would not go for Mass, or who would not have a meaningful experience during a traditional service. I will refer to the connection between waves of energy as understood by physicists and the free movement of divine energy in the Eucharist as described above. Whether according to the Orthodox or Roman Catholic explanations, or those of Protestant churches that profess faith in the Real Presence of Christ, at the heart of the church's teaching on the Eucharist there has always been a faithful intuition that God connects the divine nature with matter (bread and wine) and humankind (body and soul). Having listened closely for many hours to both nominal and fully committed Christians as they described their experiences of the Really Real at Burning Man, I will try to convey the holiness of the temple and the camp, especially the sacramental efficacy of the Eucharist led by several Episcopal priests and facilitated by a group of lay ministers.

Indulging a long-held secret desire to attend Burning Man, and because he wanted to spend time with his daughter, Rev. Baker accepted her invitation to attend the event in 2015. He did not anticipate experiencing it as a retreat, yet that is how things unfolded. His goal was simply to bless people and to provide opportunities for spiritual growth. A committed priest, Rev. Baker wants people to change their view of the church. In getting to know him it became clear that he has long been looking for ways to bring the life-giving elements of the Christian tradition to people who have rejected the church and/or have been rejected by it, or who are seeking a relationship with God for the first time. He is intentional and pragmatic in his effort to make both the church and the society more hospitable and humane. He has helped yoga instructors understand Christianity in order to meet the needs of Christian students. Today he incorporates the Episcopal Church's *Safe Church* guidelines into his workshops in the hope that instructors will "use their power effectively" and "in order to establish norms and accountability."[58] He thinks deeply and broadly about his pastoral role and his approach to living the gospel. Hardly an anarchist, Rev. Baker works to reaffirm the value of tradition and church structure. This is so evident that during our initial phone conversation I pictured him as rather "vanilla." I had a hard time imagining him doing ministry at the outer edges of human experience. As is often the case, my judgment was way off (probably because it was a judgment). What I learned by participating in the camp is that he and other ministers who know *who* they are can discern *where* they are and adjust their pastoral presence for a new context. Rev. Baker knows that if the essential elements of the Christian tradition are treated as museum pieces, he will eventually be preaching to an empty room. Fortunately, his love of God and the church preclude complacency.

One of the first things Rev. Baker described of his participation at Burning Man is that it was six days of practicing non-judgment and generosity. He was open to whatever that would look like and recalled a moment in his conversion experience halfway through his first Burn. Delighted by the hospitality and fellowship he found at the Kentucky Fried Camp from Lexington, which serves bourbon and fried bologna sandwiches for breakfast, he recognized how the gospel is alive and well through various kinds of communities. In the TED Talk he recorded at Burning Man in 2016, he noted how different this is from the default world, where "we judge ourselves and one another based on the worst we have done rather than the best we could be." In that brief reflection on the value of compassion he notes that the only thing God told Adam and Eve not to eat was fruit from the tree of knowledge of good and evil. His TED Talk leaves the viewer with a deep appreciation of the fact that judgment is the single most important thing that God instructed humanity not to do.[59]

Whether or not we are conscious of them, symbols communicate with an immediacy that words cannot. We evaluate, assess, and judge words, but symbols have an inherent power to convey what they represent in a way that is unique to the viewer. Rev. Baker's chosen symbol was a self-efficacious blessing. He described an encounter with a young man who was wearing a mouse costume complete with a black bra fashioned into ears. Sitting together on a park bench, the young man received the blessing as he sobbed. Perhaps it was Rev. Baker's gold lamé cope, made from a coat turned inside-out or the flowery hat and magenta cassock ensemble that signaled both non-judgment and a form of authority that does not take itself too seriously. Whatever the reasons that brought people to seek a blessing, a conversation, or a hug, Rev. Baker was surprised at how open they were to what he was offering in his clerical role. One young woman said that, having been raised in the church, she believed that non-judgment was possible but has only ever witnessed it at Burning Man. She said that her faith has been renewed and that she has a new appreciation for the real possibility of transforming the world through Christianity.

Some might see the name of the new camp as offensive, so it is important to provide the context. Rev. Baker was having a conversation with a young man who was sharing details about his personal life. Because costumes are ubiquitous at Burning Man, the young man was shocked to learn that Rev. Baker did not just happen to be wearing a gold cope and white lights in the form of a cross on his back. He said, "Wait, you're actually a priest?" "Yeah" Rev. Baker said. "I'm a priest." The young man started back-peddling, as if he had foolishly entrusted an imposter with his deepest secrets. He said: "I'm not religious as all." Wanting to reassure the young man that he was not being judged, he responded in the other's "language." He said: "Well I'm religious as fuck."[60] Not only did his response help the man relax, it became the camp's calling card: based on that encounter Rev. Baker decided to name the camp *Religious as Fuck*. I spent several days with the fledgling group at the newly formed a camp in 2018. To readers who might recoil at the name, I will offer a gentle reminder that St. Paul, an ingenious preacher and faithful realist, distinguished between blasphemy and explicit language used for emphasis or edification. In fact, in reflecting on apostolic ministry, in 1 Cor. 4:13 Paul says that ministers should think of themselves as *perikatharma* and *peripsema*, both of which are vulgar terms for "scum." Of the things he left behind from his earlier life, in Phil. 3:8 Paul uses the word "*skubalon*" (excrement). What unfolded seems to be an apt contemporary example of the need not to take ourselves too seriously: though I'm not sure how it began, no one seemed surprised or offended when frequent visitors playfully nicknamed the campers "The Religious Fuckers." I should also note that during a planning session in Sacramento, we discussed boundaries around nudity among the camp members. Two people said that they preferred to be at least partially nude if possible. While I had no desire to undress, I was willing to consider what other people preferred for themselves. Rev. Baker suggested that since some of the members of the camp also work together professionally outside of Burning Man, it would be best if the ministers kept their clothes on. His reasoning made sense so that's what we did. In other words, though it was in some ways a very edgy endeavor, the camp organizers carefully discerned our mission and boundaries around our ministry of presence.

Rev. Baker's care of the soul had a lasting impression on an astute Older Millennial named Leif, whose peripatetic journey began in the Church of Christ in what he described as a cowboy town in Southern California.[61] In his early teens he began smoking pot and getting into trouble. He describes himself as having been a "restless redneck" who needed to turn over stones. In his search for insight, as a young adult he experienced a psychedelic mushroom trip in which he talked to God and battled demons. Leif was the first person to welcome Rev. Baker to camp Perky Parts Playground in 2015. Then-rector of a church in Sacramento, Rev. Baker traveled by motorcycle and arrived at a camp that was designed as a circus tent with a lounge, couches, and a stage that shot fire fifty feet into the air. Someone had posted on Facebook that a priest was going to be staying at the camp. When he arrived, there was a line of people waiting to talk with him. Leif observed how people reacted to the welcome and blessing they received. He described him as offering "a clearing where you can talk about whatever you want. He doesn't make you wrong." He consistently observed a physical change in people who received a blessing: "The pressure rolled off of them and they left in a space of grati- tude, taking deep breaths." Flipping the calendar back 700 years to the time of St. Anthony of the Desert, Rev. Baker would have been at home with the monastics who welcomed pilgrims and offered counsel. Reconciliation in the desert is an ancient treasure that merits celebration in evolving contexts. Using holy oil to anoint those who accepted his offer of a blessing Rev. Baker recited these words:

> May your eyes be so blessed you see God in everyone
> Your ears, so you hear the cry of the poor
> Your hands, so everything you give,
> and everything you receive is a sacrament
> And your feet, so you run to those who need you.
> And may your heart be so opened
> So set on fire
> That your love
> *Your* love
> Changes everything.[62]

It is important to keep in mind that the priest who offered this poignant blessing is the same person who, according to a Millennial named Joy, was enthusiastically yelling profanity in the street and inviting people to have drinks at a Prince Purple Rain party. One of my most powerful lessons about radical hospitality came from a visit from a woman whose Playa name I will substitute for Marvelous.[63] People would ride by our camp on their bikes playfully yelling: "How religious are you?" As you can now imagine, the group replied: "As fuck!" In that context it would have been considered rude not to respond in kind. I was intrigued by Marvelous who rode into our camp dressed as if she had just auditioned for the Rocky Horror Picture Show. She seemed to be sizing us up. Though I would not describe her as hostile, I sensed that she was not entirely comfortable as she approached our living room. One of our camp members sprung to her feet and asked our visitor if she could bless her. According to my slow clock, the offer seemed a bit hasty. I hoped that my campmate's embrace of Burning Man's principle of "Imme- diacy" would be well received. Perhaps she sensed that our guest would have declined if we had invited her to hang out in the living room. Whatever she was feeling about the offer, Marvelous accepted the offer of a blessing. I would not be surprised if she was thinking: "Well, I wandered into this camp, so I might as well." And then I was even more amazed. As if she were settling into a massage chair, I saw Marvelous' face softening as she focused on the words and gestures of the lay minister. Anointing the woman's eyes, hands, and feet she began with: "The world is too dangerous and too beautiful now for anything but love." Our visitor seemed to be fully present throughout the prayer. As soon as it was over, she snapped back into her initial posture. Smiling and ready to be on her way, she proudly proclaimed: "Well, I'm going to go tell my boss that I found religion and she's going to flip and then we're going to jump into a shower together." "There it is," I thought: "Poetry in motion. 'NON-JUDGMENT' etched into the desert floor." It was everywhere. The singular focus of that transient wilderness church is to welcome people like Marvelous and other oddly dressed (or undressed) Burners in the name of God. An enduring memory of grace, here in the default world I'm sure I would recognize Marvelous without her silver glitter body paint and punk summer haircut. And I imagine that, before I settle into a more helpful mode, my first reaction will be laughter the next time someone says something like "I found religion."

When I returned from Burning Man my first class was in a Christology course. We were working through Paul's letter to the Ephesians. When we probed 2:14–22 two things stood out in neon letters: the harmony between people of radically different backgrounds and the practical implications of Paul's "ethical imperatives." Here he focuses on Jesus as the one who unites Jews and gentiles:

> For he is our peace; in his flesh he has made both groups into one and has broken down the dividing wall, that is, the hostility between us. He has abolished the law with its commandments and ordinances, that he might create in himself one new humanity in place of the two, thus making peace, and might reconcile both groups to God in one body through the cross, thus putting to death that hostility through it. So he came and proclaimed peace to you who were far off and peace to those who were near; for through him both of us have access in one Spirit to the Father. So then you are no longer strangers and aliens, but you are citizens with the saints and also members of the household of God, built upon the foundation of the apostles and prophets, with Christ Jesus himself as the cornerstone. In him the whole structure is joined together and grows into a holy temple in the Lord; in whom you also are built together spiritually into a dwelling place for God.

There were no strangers in our living room. Marvelous, the woman who in the span of half an hour, received a blessing and showered with her boss, might have assumed that we considered her to be living on the other side of Paul's "diving wall of hostility." In having been treated as "a fellow citizen of God's people," I hope she realized that some Christians celebrate the fact that a prism reveals all colors of the rainbow.

Several years into what had become a friendship, Leif and Rev. Baker attended a memorial service for a Burner who was a mutual friend. Leif described it as excruciating due to the "thirty-minute Bible thump" delivered by a woman who did not know her audience. Knowing how badly the minister had missed the mark, Rev. Baker gathered everyone at a park and invited the group of about 100 people to sit in a circle. He started with a mini-sermon about how their friend embodied love, and invited people to shout out memories and words, which the group experienced as a collective catharsis. His ability to perceive and address the emotional needs of those he meets makes Rev. Baker an effective conduit for healing grace.

Though the gift of healing through a sacramental action is not unique to priests like Rev. Baker, it was new to the Nones and unaffiliated Christian seekers who said that at Burning Man they finally witnessed effective ministry in the work of someone who is ordained.[64] What Rev. Baker does: welcome, listen, bless, and help heal, is the work of a priest. The setting is new and the costume witnesses to his openness to being impacted by the local culture. The transformative experiences of those who meet with Rev. Baker and other ministers, both lay and clerical, in that unique setting offer an opportunity for church leaders to reflect on their preparedness to adapt to the changing contexts of ministry. If they reject this radical form of ministry, they must also be mindful of the long-term impact of clinging to what they see as necessary norms and customs. Essentially, they must ask themselves whether they prefer to be religiously right or pastorally effective.

Unlike some of the Millennials I interviewed, Leif believes that the community established at Burning Man, and the culture of gifting can, in fact, be continued in the default world because of the way in which it unlocks something in people. In the *Burning Man Journal*, an author who uses the moniker Caveat Magister, reflected on the biblical story of the Widow's Mite. She or he notes:

> Giving what you don't have is a profound experience, one that has the capacity to change how we relate to the world and who we are. It is one that I think happens a great deal on the playa, [which] in many ways is baked into Burning Man culture, where principles like Immediacy, Communal Effort, and Radical Inclusion push us in directions that we otherwise tend to use money to avoid going in. Sometimes, that is, we use financial gifts—giving out of our surplus—not in a spirit of generosity but to avoid engaging. To protect ourselves from having to spend time or pay attention or reach out.[65]

After walking away from a lucrative job in a company whose culture he described as toxic, Leif tested his theory about the enduring generosity of Burning Man during a six-week trip across nine European countries. His Burning Man friends living throughout Europe offered him the same hospitality as they did in Black Rock City. In fact, during his six-week trek he paid for only two hotel rooms. He had managed to make friends with people who valued the culture of gifting as something desperately needed in society. Those who view the practice of gifting at Burning Man as an opportunity to receive swag will return to the default world unchanged by the virtue of generosity. However, as Leif demonstrated, those who are reflective can be transformed by the paradigm-shifting experience of Burning Man. Through his interactions with Rev. Baker and others, Leif recognized that it is possible to see the world through the eyes of love, and that Jesus offers a model for how to do that authentically. After a long hiatus, Leif, who is a talented project manager, legendary bartender, and tattoo model, attends a Christian church that has what he describes as "a large production value: it's in an auditorium, has great music and engaging speakers." His choice of church is consistent with how I would describe Burning Man: a protracted experience of improvisational musical theater with interludes for discussion.

Recontextualizing Ritual

The Burning Man temple is designed and constructed by various artists and is burned on the final night of the gathering. By the time it is burned it includes a vast array of objects, such as wedding dresses, ashes, pictures, and notes. The list of emotionally charged items echoes the litany of petitions spoken at Mass. Over the years among the ones that Rev. Baker found the most moving were a picture of an older man in a tuxedo with the inscription "Daddy" and the words "I miss you more than words could ever say. You will always be in my heart. I love you. (You would be proud of me)." Another was "Fuck you man who raped me, police who didn't believe me, judge who laughed at me. Fuck you." There were also pleas for forgiveness, expressions of loss, and longing, as well as cathartic declarations such as "My anger for my father ends now" and "Hug them now." In the temple, people automatically respond to one another with compassion.

In 2016 Rev. Baker presided at the first Eucharist in the temple. Because one of the Ten Principles of Burning Man is radical acceptance, anyone who had a frame of reference for the consecrated bread and wine knew they were welcome. Since that first Eucharist, people began to request it daily. He noted that people were amazed by "the two pieces of themselves coming together." This new camp is seeking to create a sustained community by reenvisioning the traditional design of a church. Aware that we are "mourning the loss of the front porch," Rev. Baker noted that he wants to address the void that was once filled with neighbors who cared for one another. For our "Good Friday" service on August 31, 2018, we provided strips of fabric and Sharpies so that people could write the names of deceased loved ones and tie the strips to the structure. The idea was that the names would ascend to heaven with the smoke when the temple was burned. I wrote "Bob Powell," to whose memory I dedicate this book, and another for my mom.[66] Although I was not able to stay for the Temple Burn, Rev. Baker and others have noted that other than the sound of sobbing, the crowd is quiet while the structure burns for about an hour.

The form and function of the camp serves as a place where people who want to live in a temporary faith-based community can experience church beyond the walls. It is intended to be a place where people can have open discussions about faith and spirituality. Returning for a moment to the function of an ancient temple, "When the augur had defined the *templum* within which he intended to make his observations, he fixed his tent in it . . . and this tent was likewise called a *templum*, or more accurately, *templum minus* (small temple) . . . and in the city it was the *arx* (refuge)."[67] Campmates offer a ministry of presence in two hour shifts in the temple and in the camp's living room. As with the ancient Asclepion, *Religious as Fuck* provides a place of welcome, safety and an opportunity for spiritually healing encounters. Like the Asclepion, it is not a place where pilgrims reside permanently, but a temporary dwelling place established as a refuge. This is especially significant given that those who attend Burning Man leave behind their office cubes and other stale work environments, where nightmares often get played out. Kimberley Patton, professor of the Comparative and Historical Study of Religion at Harvard Divinity School, noted that "European and American sanctuaries are decorous places of the daytime, locked up like vaults at night against theft, and are by no means used for collective sleeping."[68] Entirely lacking in doors and walls, *Religious as Fuck* has the potential to jostle and ultimately relax the rigid components of mainline Christianity. The camp functions similarly to Orthodox churches throughout the Mediterranean that are visited for the purpose of incubation. Patton notes, "In modern biological incubation, a period of heat hatches new living creatures."[69] Drawing on that old archetype, the communal ordeal of living in the desert heat combined with the experience of sleeping on land that Burners recognize as sacred, the space has the potential to function as a healing "temple" through the divine energy of Jesus. As the campers grow in their appreciation of the communal space as sacred ground, it might become a place that is conducive to healing dreams. As of spring, 2019, twenty people had expressed an interest in camping with the group, more than double the number who attended the first year.

While Jesus modeled love and offered the assurance of God's infinite compassion, he did these things through his awareness that life is painful and real relationships are difficult. In his TED Talk Rev. Baker reflected on the human condition as depicted through the story of the Fall of Adam and Eve. His point was not that Adam and Eve earned divine disappointment through disobedience, but rather, that the author chose to focus on our knowledge of good and evil. At the core of human sinfulness is the tendency to judge someone as evil because she or he holds different views or behaves differently than we do. Differences are not inherently problematic. In the story of creation, Adam and Eve were different, but all was well in the beginning. Our subsequent response to difference is where human beings do harm. Rev. Baker believes that because of the spiritual damage we do to one another, the church should focus on the grief and anger we experience, noting that if we don't get hold of our demons, they will get hold of us.

Rev. Baker and the camp's co-ministers have an ambitious view of the future of *Religious as Fuck*. He has retired from his position as Dean of Trinity Cathedral in Sacramento and moved to Los Angeles to focus full-time on evangelization for this emerging ecclesial community. Currently there are around seventy-six people on the Episcopalians at Burning Man list, four of whom are priests. Eventually the camp will have designated hours for things like Reconciliation, foot-washing, and counseling. In 2017 Rev. Baker kept ashes from the burning of "The Man." Modeled after the practice of keeping the palms from Palm Sunday to mark the beginning of Lent the following year, he and several lay ministers led a late summer Ash Wednesday service in 2018. They gathered ashes in 2018, as well. Drawing on the beauty of the Christian liturgical celebrations, at the service he used the traditional words: "Remember you are dust and to dust you shall return." Going forward the community also plans to use the ashes for burial services. Though only a few of the campers are Roman Catholic, the model of priesthood they practice is an example of the vision that emerged in a study conducted by a group at Boston College. The members of that seminar determined that "a concentration on functions unique to priests also runs the risk of isolating priests from the community of faith or even of defining priests in terms of power over the community. If priesthood becomes a path to power, priests can understand themselves as gatekeepers of 'discipline, rules and organization,' rather than as disciples among disciples."[70] The Burning Man ministers' commitment to the priesthood of the people involves a wide vector compared with the efficacious but narrow pre-Christian priesthood practiced in the ancient Mediterranean.

At Burning Man, priests and other ministers who are willing to meet people in their spiritual location/desolation, whether in a setting that is akin to the Asclepion or more explicitly ecclesial, have at their disposal the person's faith in the potential for healing to occur, and the healing power of Jesus for those who seek it. When St. Paul was walking through Athens, he noticed many temples that he believed to be dedicated to false idols. However, he told the Athenians who expressed an interest in learning about Jesus that he recognized their genuine faith. Rather than rail against what he saw as "false idols," he focused on the altar dedicated to "an unknown God."[71] He used that as a starting point for contextualizing salvation history. Scripture tells us that some, but not all, were unreceptive. The temple at Burning Man is hardly a Godless place. Those who minister there go where most religious leaders have yet to venture, offering healing that both draws on the authority of the apostles and reaches beyond the boundaries of hierarchical jurisdiction. Drawing on courage, the church can learn from the fluid boundaries between medicine and prayer. People have always gone where they believe they will be healed. Faith in the power of Asclepius, the god of healing dreams, along with medical treatment, proved to be effective treatment. It is as well for those who minister in the name of Jesus at Burning Man.

The ancient world was more comfortable than contemporary Westerners are with the fluid boundaries between worship and medicine, but that does not have to be the case. When medicine and religion were not treated as exact sciences, devout people placed their faith in the mystery of healing. Formally, the church gives assent to the mystery of God but in terms of behavior, it functions as if formulary prayer and invariable patterns of worship are essential for cultivating an authentic relationship with God. This message leaves the church at a disadvantage in reaching people who cannot digest the nourishment offered by the Eucharist in traditional liturgical environments. I am not advocating for the priests at Burning Man to offer a drug made of vipers, as was prescribed to one of Asclepius' devotees. I believe that the Eucharist and the other sacraments of the church are excellent medicine. Equipped with these appropriate salves for nominal, fatigued Christians or other seekers, the priests, and other ministers at Burning Man are doing groundbreaking work in reaching people who otherwise would not participate in the sacramental life of the church. Their vestments, name, method, and setting are unconventional, yet as ministers they are effective in rekindling the faith of those who enter the liturgical space on the Playa. I agree with Rev. Baker that if Jesus were ministering today, he would be at Burning Man, not to admonish those who prefer the Bacchanalian feasts, but to welcome them into God's house should they need a safe place to rest when the music stops pumping. As the Psalmist says: "I will both lie down and sleep in peace; for you alone, O Lord, make me lie down in safety" (Ps. 4:8).

NOTES

1. http://w2.vatican.va/content/francesco/en/speeches/2013/july/documents/papa-francesco_20130728_gmg-conferenza-stampa.html.

2. https://burningman.org/network/about-us/

3. Emily Dickinson, Amherst Manuscript #372. Amherst College Archives and Special Collections. I have used unpublished word variants under the guidance of the collection's archivist.

4. Though Rev. Baker has support from Episcopal Diocese of Los Angeles for the umbrella organization: *Episcopalians at Burning Man*, as of March 2019, there were seventy-six members, both laypeople and clergy.

5. Maurus Servius Honoratus, *Commentary on the Aeneid of Virgil*. I.446 http://www.perseus.tufts.edu/hopper/text?doc=Perseus%3Atext%3A1999.02.0053% 3Abook%3D1%3Acommline%3D446, accessed March 25, 2019 and William Smith, ed., *A Dictionary of Greek and Roman Antiquities* (London: John Murray, 1873), 1104. http://penelope.uchicago.edu/Thayer/E/Roman/Texts/secondary/SMIGRA*/Te mplum.html (accessed March 25, 2019).

6. The Latin *intueor* means "to contemplate."

7. Carl Darling Buck, *A Dictionary of Selected Synonyms in the Principal Indo-European Languages: A Contribution to the History of Ideas* (Chicago: University of Chicago Press, 1988) "Temple" 22.13, 1465–1466.

8. Galen. *De dignotione ex insomnis libellis*. https://www.ucl.ac.uk/~ucgajpd/ medicina%20antiqua/tr_GalDreams.html.

9. Julius Rocca, *Galen on the Brain: Anatomical Knowledge and Physiological Speculation in the Second Century AD. Studies in Ancient Medicine*, Vol. 26, ed. John Scarborough (Leiden: Brill, 2003), 1.

10. C.R. Haines, trans. and ed. *The Correspondence of Marcus Cornelius Fronto*. Loeb Classics. Vol. 1. (London: William Heinemann, 1919) "Letter to Fronto," 51.

11. Israelowich, Ido. "The Authority of Physicians as Dream Interpreters in the Pergamene Asclepion," in *Medicine and Healing in the Ancient Mediterranean*, ed. Demitrios Michaelides (Oxford: Oxbow Books, 2014), 294.

12. Rocca, *Galen on the Brain*, 4.

13. Ibid., 5–6.

14. Ibid., 5.

15. Ibid., 6., quoting HW Pleket "The Social Stauts of Physicians in the Graeco-Roman World," *Clio Medica* 27 (Jan 1, 1995), 27–34, 33.

16. Ibid., 7 n.40. Eudemus might have been Galen's philosophy teacher.

17. Ibid., 197.

18. Israelowich, "The Authority of Physicians as Dream Interpreters," 291.

19. Ibid., 292.

20. Alexia Petsalis-Diomidis, *Truly Beyond Wonders: Aelius Aristides and the Cult of Asklepios* (New York: Oxford University Press, 2010), 145–146.

21. Petsalis-Diomidis, *Truly Beyond Wonders*.

22. Ibid.

23. Ibid.

24. Ibid., 293.

25. R. Gnuse, "The Temple Experience of Jaddus in the Antiquities of Josephus: A report of Jewish Dream Incubation," *The Jewish Quarterly Review* 83 (3/4) (Jan–April 1993), 365.

26. Gnuse, "The Temple Experience of Jaddus in the Antiquities of Josephus," 365.

27. Kimberly Patton, "'A Great and Strange Correction': Intentionality, Locality, and Epiphany in the Category of Dream Incubation," *History of Religions* 43 (3) (2004), 203.

28. Juliette Harrison, "The Development of the Practice of Incubation in the Ancient World," in *Medicine and Healing in the Ancient Mediterranean World* (Oxbow Books, 2014), 284–290, 288 citing Butler, S. *Mesopotamian Conceptions of Dreams and Dream Rituals* (Münster: Ugarit-Verlag,1998), 224–227.

29. Harrison, "The Development of the Practice of Incubation in the Ancient World," 285.

30. Even if, as some scholars believe, Job lived during the First Temple period, there is no evidence that he ever visited it. He seems to have lived where southwest Jordan, southern Israel and eastern Egypt intersect.

31. Mark 2: 25–32.

32. St Augustine, *Sermon* 169, 13 (PL 38,923).

33. LIGO is the acronym for Laser Interferometer Gravitational-Wave Observatory housed in Hanford, Washington, and Livingston, Louisiana. See "Gravitational Waves, Einstein's Ripples in Spacetime, Spotted for First Time," *Science* (February 11, 2016), http://www.sciencemag.org/news/2016/02/gravitational-waves-einstein-s-ripples-spacetime-spotted-first-time.

34. Arthur Eddington, *The Nature of the Physical World* (Cambridge: Cambridge University Press, 1928), 291.

35. For a detailed explanation of the metaphysical problems with the doctrine of Transubstantiation, see Gary Macy's *The Banquet's Wisdom: A Short History of the Theologies of the Lord's Supper* (Akron: OSL Books, 2005).

36. Thomas Hosinski, *The Image of the Unseen God: Catholicity, Science and Our Evolving Understanding of God* (Maryknoll, NY: Orbis Books, 2017), 64.

37. See Adrian Cho's article "The Social Life of Quarks" in *Science Magazine* (January 14, 2016), 217–219.

38. Hosinski, *The Image of the Unseen God*, 70.

39. Panikkar, *The Trinity and the Religious Experience of Man*, 75.

40. Ware, Timothy, *The Orthodox Church* (London: Penguin Books, 1964), 290 ff.

41. Anthony de Mello, *Heart of the Enlightened: A Book of Story Meditations* (New York: Image Books, 1991), 71–72. Though de Mello attributes this remark to Marconi, the staff at Marconi Archive in the Bodleian Library were unable to identify the specific publication in which the remark occurs. Regardless of the historicity of the comment, the statement reflects the humility that is called for in the presence of mystery.

42. Phone interview with Bishop Cait Finnegan July 6, 2018. The Old Catholic Church broke from Rome in the 1850s through 1889 and was not in union with Rome until the 1950s.

43. http://www.nadiabolzweber.com/book/accidental-saints (accessed February 15, 2019).

44. https://www.npr.org/2015/09/17/441139500/lutheran-minister-preaches-a-gospel-of-love-to-junkies-drag-queens-and-outsiders (accessed December 20, 2018).

45. The study I read includes the following Orthodox Churches: American Carpatho-Russian Orthodox Diocese, Antiochian Orthodox Christian Archdiocese, Greek Orthodox Church of America, Orthodox Church in America, and Serbian Orthodox Church. http://www.assemblyofbishops.org/assets/files/studies/2017-U SOrthodoxParishesYoungAdultsFinalReport.pdf.

46. Ibid.

47. McCarty and Vitek, *Going, Going, Gone: The Dynamics of Disaffiliation in Young Catholics*, 4.

48. Cornel West, "Spiritual Blackout, Imperial Meltdown, Prophetic Fightback," YouTube Video, August 29, 2017. https://youtu.be/7wCIWF1rYak

49. McCarty and Vitek, *Going, Going, Gone*, 4.

50. http://www.pewforum.org/2009/04/27/faith-in-flux/. See also the 2016 the Pew Study http://www.pewresearch.org/fact-tank/2016/05/12/support-steady-fo r-same-sex-marriage-and-acceptance-of-homosexuality/.

51. "Quincy," Netflix documentary (2016). Directed by Alan Hicks and Rashida Jones.

52. http://w2.vatican.va/content/francesco/en/messages/pont-messages/2013/ documents/papa-francesco_20131116_videomessaggio-guadalupe.html.

53. Lee Gilmore, *Theater in a Crowded Fire: Ritual and Spirituality at Burning Man* (Berkeley, University of California Press), 2010.

54. Ibid., 13.

55. Ibid., 14.

56. Ibid., p. 51. By contrast, in 2006, 63 percent of U.S. Americans said that they were members of a church or synagogue

57. The "default world" is the expression Burners use to describe society beyond the Burning Man event. The Ten Principles are Radical Inclusion, Gifting, Decom-modification, Radical Self-Reliance, Radical Self-Expression, Communal Effort, Civic Responsibility, Leaving No Trace, Participation, and Immediacy. https://bu rningman.org/culture/philosophical-center/10-principles/ (accessed March 27, 2019).

58. "Model Policies for the Prevention of Sexual Exploitation of Adults" https:// www.cpg.org/linkservid/3F324A36-DBAE-DF27-E38DBB7F33C4670F/showMeta /0/?label=Model%20Policies%3A%20Preventing%20Sexual%20Exploitation.

59. "Seeing Through the Eyes of Love," https://www.youtube.com/watch?v=ku0 dXTzNQ0I (accessed March 28, 2019).

60. In this context the term "as fuck" is an expression used in social media as a hyperbole, sometimes written as AF. A rough equivalent might be the phrase used by Baby Boomers: "As all get out."

61. Other than the directors of religious organizations, in this book I have changed the names of the people I interviewed.

62. This prayer was written by Rev. Brian Baker.

63. A "Playa name" is one that people only use at Burning Man or in a social circle affiliated with the event.

64. By the term "sacramental" I am including the practices and objects that are not necessarily found among the seven sacraments recognized by churches that identify

as Roman Catholic, but which serve as resources in healing rituals for those who identify with a Christian worldview. See chapter 4 n.23.

65. Caveat Magister, "The Parable of the Gift," https://journal.burningman.org /2017/12/philosophical-center/spirituality/the-parable-of-the-gift/ (accessed March 27, 2019).

66. Bob was married to Micky Powell for forty-six years. It was in their dance studio that I wrote the majority of this book.

67. William Smith, ed., *A Dictionary of Greek and Roman Antiquities* (London: John Murray, 1873), 1104. http://penelope.uchicago.edu/Thayer/E/Roman/Texts/ secondary/SMIGRA*/Templum.html, (accessed March 25, 2019).

68. Patton, "A Great and Strange Correction," 196.

69. Ibid., 196.

70. Boston College Seminar on Priesthood and Ministry for the Contemporary Church. "To Serve the People of God: Renewing the Conversation on Priesthood and Ministry," *Origins* 48 (31) (December 27, 2018), 484–493, 485. The reference to "discipline, rules and organization" is from Pope Francis' address to pilgrims at the Shrine of Our Lady of Guadalupe, cited in n.52.

71. "Then Paul stood in front of the Areopagus and said, 'Athenians, I see how extremely religious you are in every way. For as I went through the city and looked carefully at the objects of your worship, I found among them an altar with the inscription, 'To an unknown god.' What therefore you worship as unknown, this I proclaim to you.'" Acts 17:22–24.

Chapter 4

Sanctuary and City

A Radical Ministry of Presence

THE CITY

In Book 1 Part 2 of *Politics*, Aristotle asserts that "[man] is by nature a political animal." Most cities develop organically because the residents of a geographical area have the same basic needs and similar interests. To this simple reality Aristotle adds a poignant observation: that the purpose of a city is for people to live well. The term he uses, *polis* (city), evolved into words like politics, polite, and polity. Within Aristotle's paradigm, the function of government, of the systems and policies it implements, is to create an environment that enables its residents to thrive.[1] This can be difficult to actualize in an era in which the middle class seems to be an endangered species and those who are living paycheck to paycheck are preoccupied with survival. Beginning the week of February 24, 2017, *The Washington Post* incorporated the slogan "Democracy dies in darkness" beneath its online masthead. That day it included an article in the Style section explaining that the reference is about government secrecy.[2] In addition to the ethical violation of governing through secrets whispered in the dark, governments that claim to be inspired by Judeo-Christian values, but fail to help as many people as possible to "live well," undermine themselves. Myopic capitalism weakens all societies that profess a belief in good will and the dignity of all of creation. The church is well positioned to challenge government policies that neglect the basic needs of the struggling majority, especially where poverty and violence are widespread.

From 1972 to 1977 there was a popular television show called *The Streets of San Francisco* starring Karl Malden and Michael Douglas. It was a police drama that portrayed urban crime from the perspective of heroic detectives.

Episodes highlighted daily events such as muggings, homicides, violence against women and children, greed, revenge, drug deals, immigration raids, and class warfare. While the storylines echo the issues that have significantly impacted San Francisco residents since the 1970s, the events were depicted through the eyes of crime fighters. The brunt of urban misery, however, cannot be accurately represented through one-sided narratives. People who live and work in the Tenderloin and other depressed areas of the city understand the experiences of residents who are caught at the intersection of vexing problems such as mental illness, violence, drug addiction, social isolation, and poverty. This chapter illustrates the experiences of those who most San Franciscans would prefer not to see, and the ministry of those who serve them.

Above all others, the theme that has dominated Bay Area news throughout the first two decades of the twenty-first century is the glaring reality of income inequality, which continues to rise. Fifty years after canned images of the Summer of Love (1967) and high-speed chases became hallmarks of the city and county of San Francisco, it is a growing plutocracy. In February 2018 the annual income needed in order to buy median-priced home in the city ($1.5 million) was $303,000. Only 12 percent of potential buyers were able to afford an average home, which was up 4 percent since 2007.[3] The reason that the percentage increased along with the continually increasing cost of homes is that there are now more people who are very wealthy, even by San Francisco statistics. In 2016, the national median income for the "1 percent" was $305,553.[4] In San Francisco in 2015 the number was $558,046.[5] In January 2018 the median monthly rent for a one-bedroom apartment in San Francisco was about $3,400.[6] Twenty-three percent of households earned more than $200,000, while 8 percent earned between $10,000 and 20,000.[7] People aged 25–44, approximately 50,000 residents, were the largest group with an annual median income of more than $200,000, compared with approximately 25,000 people aged 45–64 in the same income bracket.[8] In 2016 there were 20,133 individuals (5.6% of the population) in a city with a population of 870,887 who earned less than $10,000. Approximately 25 percent of these, or 5,033 individuals, were homeless. Twenty-two percent of residents earn between $11,000 and 50,000, not nearly enough for a one-bedroom apartment in a city in which around 58 percent of adults are single.[9] It is within this context that those affiliated with the Franciscan ministry known as The Gubbio Project labor daily to serve both the working poor and the people who are living in desperate poverty.

The Gubbio Project was named after an Italian town that has been a role model for collaborative relationships since the thirteenth century.[10] Franciscan communities continue to celebrate the story of "The Wolf of Gubbio." Perhaps more than any other, this vignette captures the spirit and charism of St. Francis (1180/1–1226), the founder of the Franciscan Order. About thirty miles from Assisi, a wolf was attacking both the livestock and the residents of Gubbio. Wanting to be safe from what they saw as a savage animal, the villagers' instinct was to hunt down the wolf. The legend memorializes the saint's remarkable intervention between the wolf and the villagers. Instead of persuading the wolf to leave town in search of another food source, Francis upended the model of civic power, convincing the villagers to feed and shelter the wolf.[11] They did not kill, cage, or relegate Brother Wolf, as Francis called him, to a remote part of the woods, but welcomed him into the community.[12]

The peace accord that Francis established between the wolf and the citizens of Gubbio included an agreement by the community to feed the wolf if it agreed to stop attacking them. Francis' embrace of this perceived threat grew out of a spirit of generosity, which gently unfolded in the form of *courtesia*, a medieval virtue that governed morality and social conduct. As the model peacemaker in the Middle Ages, the literary tradition that developed around the life and work of St. Francis includes a narrative about the possibility of creating a genuine, lasting peace: one in which no one loses. Francis seemed to believe that when there is a winner and a loser, the power struggle might come to an end, but harmony does not arise merely from the absence of chaos. From a Christian perspective, the apparent winner loses by having won the battle through aggression. Gubbio built the church of San Francesco della Pace over the cave in which the wolf lived for about two years after the encounter with Francis. Renovations undertaken in 1873 revealed a sarcophagus embossed with a large cross, containing the remains of a large wolf. Seven centuries after the death of St. Francis, the parish honored the wolf yet again, this time by burying the remains under the altar.[13]

The Gubbio Project is a Franciscan ministry that evolved out of the Tenderloin Reflection and Education Center in San Francisco while Fr. Louie Vitale, OFM, was pastor of St. Boniface Catholic Church in the 1990s. A social activist who was arrested dozens of times during his years in active ministry, he was responding to the need for housing for people living on the streets during a particularly cold, wet winter. The Gubbio Project was designed as a program that would provide what some see as radical hospitality to people in the blighted Tenderloin district who need a safe place to sleep. Confronting the common mistreatment of people who lived on the streets and were considered threatening and lacking in dignity, The Gubbio Project established this center for hospitality in the sanctuary at St. Boniface. People who struggled to find rest and to maintain basic hygiene practices would be treated as beloved guests. The word "hospital" originated from the Latin *hospes* (guest). The basic objective of hospitality is to take care of those who are suffering, as the sultan did for St. Francis after a long journey into a foreign land.[14] Today hospitality monitors, staff, and volunteer chaplains at The Gubbio Project develop genuine relationships with the guests. So authentic is the employees' compassion and solidarity that it is sometimes difficult to distinguish guests from staff.

Now housed both at St. Boniface in the Tenderloin and at St. John's Episcopal Church in the Mission district, The Gubbio Project provides places for people who are unhoused to sleep safely during the daytime hours when the shelters are closed. This ministry is a radical expression of the Preferential Option for the Poor, as well as a creative, highly effective model of spiritual care. It is also a direct response to Jesus' mandate in Matthew 25 to care for "the least of these," which is an ever-changing challenge for the church. If a society should be judged according to how it treats its weakest members,[15] The Gubbio Project is a pastoral *exemplar* from which San Francisco's urban plutocracy can learn how to be a more just city.

San Francisco was a pioneer in the early years of the sustainable living movement, and in many ways is still at the forefront of innovations that enhance people's quality of life. However, because of the ways in which capitalist democracies can become twisted, many of the startups that focus on sustainable living have been so successful that, with the growing income disparity, their companies have unintentionally fueled San Francisco's housing crisis. The Gubbio Project seeks to address the impact of this irony from a distinctly Franciscan perspective. As stated on their website, the organization's eight principles are as follows:

1. All people, especially those who are living on the streets or have mental health or substance abuse issues, are worthy of respect, dignity, and loving kindness.
2. The church has historically been an open space of sanctuary and shelter for those seeking shelter.
3. While The Gubbio Project's specific activities might change over time, our mission to provide a sacred space and care services for those in need of a safe, compassionate respite that places dignity and respect in the highest regard will not change.
4. The Gubbio Project is on the front lines of homelessness, and addresses basic needs of all people: a sense of safety, belonging, and calm.
5. Compassion is a covenant between equals; not a relationship between healer and wounded.
6. The Gubbio Project is unconditional giving. Everyone is welcome.
7. The Gubbio Project works to nurture a sense of understanding and shared responsibility in the broader church, school, and neighborhood communities.
8. The Gubbio Project's homeless guests are served best by staff and volunteers who have a firsthand understanding of their struggles.

Franciscan Peacemaking

Laura Slattery, executive director of The Gubbio Project from 2010 to 2018, described the program's success in this way: "It calls out the community's normal response to those who are homeless, including people who struggle with drug-addiction and mental health issues, and invites a different one." Another important element is that Gubbio has continued to cultivate its original elasticity. For example, when I became involved with this ministry in 2009, the policy for those sleeping in the pews at St. Boniface was that they were welcome but had to sit up during Mass. This is no longer the case. In fact, the organization's harm reduction model means that, though it is in no way encouraged, a guest who is intoxicated can be in the church if she or he does not interfere with anyone's ability to rest, sleep, or worship. The shift seems to be related to the organization's message, or perhaps my way of reading it, about what makes sleep sacred. A decade ago what impressed me was the fact that a church, a place that is typically seen as holy ground, where one steps lightly, invited people to sleep in the pews. The church build- ing and the friars who generously offered the space facilitated The Gubbio Project's desire to provide sacred sleep. Today the focus is not on the church building or even on the love of the community that offers the space, which is a given, but on the divinely ordained dignity of those who sleep in the church. A basic need and a human right, what makes the guests' sleep sacred is the fact that they are loved by God. The transition from The Gubbio Project as an ecclesiological model to an expression of the community's theological anthropology has both fortified and clarified the radical mission of the parish and the Franciscan community that provides support. As this ministry devel- oped, the orientation between the power brokers and those they served shifted from vertical to horizontal: from hierarchical to egalitarian. The guests' use of the space was the catalyst for this shift, while those with decision-making authority had the wisdom and generosity of spirit to follow the lead of those they served.

St. Francis of Assisi is rightly seen as a model for solidarity with the poor. However, this is due neither to his humility nor to his appreciation for the natural world. The Christian tradition is full of saints who have been typecast as exemplars of peace and humility. In order to understand Francis' impact on the church we must remove him from the birdbath. Far from the hippie stereotype, Francis began his life as the privileged son of a textile merchant during a time in which fine silk and pure wool were highly valued. If the teenage Francis were alive today, he would be a viable candidate for a reality TV show about Millennials with too much money and equally poor judg- ment. In medieval Italy he would have had a very comfortable life if not for his restless spirit. His wanderlust led him to join his friends in a war against the neighboring city-state of Perugia, where he seems to have contracted what today we know as PTSD. That traumatic event marked the beginning of his conversion and is a good reminder that "the occasional brush with the unexpected . . . breaks open the 'everydayness' that ensnares us and brings something awesome and terrifying to our reluctant attention . . . God."[16]

The Legend of the Three Companions emphasizes Francis' innate generosity. However, it is also candid about his early aversion to the lepers in the colony near Assisi. Having been one of four hospital chaplains who were responsible for the morgue, part of our job was to accompany the transport staff and funeral directors who had come to retrieve a body. We also regularly attended to any number of "issues" related to the morgue. I understand Francis' dread at the sight and smell of the lepers' deteriorating bodies. In his youth Francis would ride past the leper colony, tossing coins to the people he saw. However, people change and having become disillusioned and traumatized by war, when Francis was trying to figure out what he wanted to do with his life, he returned to a familiar place: the leper colony. The difference was that with his change of heart and hard-won maturity, he began to care for the lepers in proximity. He became their friend and neighbor (*proximus*).

Sister Mary Litell, OSF, is a Gubbio Project board member. She suggested that the encounter with the leper in which Francis learned that "what before had been bitter . . . was turned into sweetness," might have been initiated by a leper who Francis had previously known from a distance.[17] She imagined that the leper reached out to hug Francis when they encountered one another on the street. The friendliness that Francis had exuded even when he was afraid to interact with the lepers physically could have prompted one of them to come out of the shadows when she or he saw Francis after the war. Seen this way, Francis' change of mind and heart (*metanoia*) was not a matter of the healer reaching out to someone who was wounded. Their sacred exchange occurred on a horizontal plane rather than in a hierarchical encounter. Thereafter Francis was no longer merely an almsgiver, but an integrated member of the community of lepers. In response to my question "What makes The Gubbio Project a successful Franciscan outreach?" Sister Mary returned to the leper's embrace of St. Francis, noting that "wisdom comes down the path to meet you before you've even thought about asking her."

The grace that healed St. Francis stemmed from his desire to serve others, thanks in part to his innate affability. His earlier longing to taste and touch the material world was transformed into a desire to reach out to others and in turn to be touched by the suffering and joy at work in the world. His own vulnerability opened up a willingness to be wounded by the impact of social sin. His courage enabled him to go where people who wanted to protect themselves from the ugly realities of suffering would not venture. An unlikely ally, PTSD seems to have created an opening through which the Holy Spirit was able to slip in and make God's presence known. Francis did his work in choosing to accept God's invitation to change course, reminding us that grace and freedom of the will are inseparable.

Sacred Sleep and Compassionate Care

Gubbio is staffed by a handful of paid employees and a host of volunteers. It is a ministry that attracts pragmatists with a self-possessed grittiness and a keen awareness of human dignity. Some of the people who serve at St. Boniface and St. John have experienced homelessness and/or are in various stages of recovery from addiction, often stemming from the forms of trauma that also impact the lives of guests who sleep in the churches. Quick-witted and earnest, Carmen is one such employee. She pays careful attention to everyone who walks through the door and has taken the time to get to know them. She is so attentive, in fact, that one day she anticipated a seizure in a guest, based solely on his unusual aloofness. Her realization occurred mere moments before his head would have hit the floor. She caught him just in time to slowly lower him to the ground. Carmen greets those who enter the church with the gratified smile of someone who has just returned from a dental cleaning. In working with her I had the sense that joy might have been a precipitating factor in her conversion, which is a core theme in her spiritual narrative.

Carmen was raised in a home with an alcoholic father who beats her mother. When she was in her teens her father turned his violence against her, so she left home. Her childhood perspective on "normal" family life led to some difficult but valuable lessons. A fierce survival instinct led Carmen to create her own family. However, at such a young age and with no adult role models, her effort to escape violence led her into a life of gangs and drugs. At around the age of fifteen, Carmen lost sight of her childhood faith, letting go of what had been a deeply embedded habit of prayer. For the next fifteen years Carmen routinely cheated fate. Looking back at that extended period she realizes that there were many times that her poor choices could easily have led to death. When her children were ages five and six, her slumlord ignored too many of his responsibilities. Carmen lost her apartment, leaving her and her children homeless for about six months. One night while she was intoxicated, her children were taken by Child Protective Services. The impact of losing her children was a catalyst for Carmen's change of mind and heart, but things got worse before they got better. Having long been indifferent to the faith of her childhood, she shared an experience that literally brought her to her knees. While crossing the street one night, Carmen was struck by the car closest to the crosswalk in a three-car, rear-end collision. While lying on the ground she opened her eyes and saw that her head was next to the wheel. She heard a voice that said: "Get up, get up, get up!" As soon as she did, the

car she had been lying next to was hit again. Having narrowly escaped decap-
itation, the traumatic accident coupled with the loss of her children caught
Carmen's attention. A native San Franciscan, she remembered that the city is
known for its social services. Within two weeks of seeking help she was in
an inpatient facility for drug rehab. Though anxious to keep busy, she waited
patiently until she completed the program that paved the way to employment.
The first position that caught her attention was at The Gubbio Project. Having experienced addiction, loss, and homelessness, Carmen is aware of how
important it is that these churches allow people to sleep in them. A year later
she is still beguiled by the fact that her job literally thrust her back into the
church. She started attending services at St. John's, and is focused on instill-
ing faith and morals in her children who once again are in her care.

What helped me understand how deeply personal Gubbio's ministry is for
Carmen was her story about her alcoholic father's reentry into her life. While
she was still in rehab, Carmen received a call from her aunt saying that her
father had been found unconscious in the Tenderloin and was in the hospital.
He had just had emergency heart surgery and had been fitted with an artificial
valve. Though she had not seen him for ten years, Carmen acquired resources
for her dad, including a social worker, and advocated for him to be placed in a
respite care facility. She was also listed as his emergency contact. Eventually
he was placed in a Single Room Occupancy (SRO).[18] She knew that he had
been sober for about a year until, shortly after beginning her work at The Gubbio Project, she saw her father sleeping in one of the pews. She shared with me
the empathy she felt for him at that moment, noting that she often thinks about
him when it rains. Though she has no legal obligation to do so, she offers her
father the support that he could not provide for her as a child. Transformed by
love, the once-abused child has become the mature, caring parent.

Though Carmen's father has been told that his synthetic valve is fragile
and that he must take care of himself, he does not. Carmen said that she realizes that her dad does not want help yet also does not stay away entirely. In
fact, the day before she shared her story with me, he was asking for her at St.
Boniface. Carmen's practical and theoretical education in addictions counseling, combined with her work among the guests at The Gubbio Project, have
taught Carmen that the will is a tricky thing. A longing for a drug-free life,
without the full participation of the will by the one receiving help, creates a
thorny situation for caregivers, who must attend creatively to the needs of
people whose lives might not change. Carmen practices a pure form of hospitality: paying attention to the guest, without the expectation of receiving
anything in return.[19] The fact that Carmen is able to do this, not just with the
many guests at Gubbio, but with her own father, witnesses to the depth of her
metanoia. With each passing day, her compassion for her father and the other
guests molds her more fully into an exemplary parent for her own children,

disrupting what could have become a dysfunctional cycle. Carmen has integrated her grief with love, empowering her to stand shoulder to shoulder with guests who are also grieving while seeking to love and be loved. Like St. Francis, Carmen chooses not only to see but also to befriend those who others see as wolves or lepers.

Power Equity for a Ministry of Presence

In 2011 I was catapulted from the high-speed life of inner-city chaplaincy into a rural university where I teach theology and pastoral ministry to undergraduates. During my sabbatical in 2018 I was back in the city, where I spent a few hours each week offering a ministry of presence at Gubbio for anyone who might want to talk with a chaplain. In order to illustrate the kind of work that the Gubbio staff and volunteers do in responding to a constant stream of human needs, I will share some of the conversations I had with guests across seven months as a volunteer chaplain. The two Gubbio sites are very different, not only because one is Roman Catholic and the other Episcopal, but because the physical spaces are distinctive. The sanctuary at St. John has chairs rather than pews, so guests sleep on camping mats on the wood floor. At St. Boniface they sleep in pews, which elevates them off the floor. This elevation has the added benefit of providing warmth and dignity that they do not experience when they are sleeping on the street. At St. Boniface two of the confessionals have been repurposed as supply closets for hygiene kits, socks, and blankets, continuing to provide an essential service for those who look to the church for help. As we will see toward the end of the chapter, the confessions continue but usually outside of the confessionals.

At St. John the chaplains and "listeners" sit in front of the altar on the *bema*, which is covered with a musty carpet that is stained with who-knows-what.[20] On average there are about forty people sleeping on the floor, and five or more sitting at a table. Like large medieval monastic dormitories, during the day both churches function as "snoratoriums." Other human noises also emerge. For example, on my first day at St. John, a man who was half asleep rolled over and spat on the floor. He appeared to be so exhausted that it would surprise me to learn that he realized he was sleeping indoors.

On a rainy January afternoon, I entered St. Boniface where a small group of parishioners at the noon Mass were receiving the final blessing. I was both excited and surprised to see the change that had been described by staff members: in the first six pews people were focusing on the liturgy. The sparkling images in the gilded apse looked like the scene Zeffirelli's film *Brother Sun, Sister Moon* in which a dazed Francis in a grubby habit meets Pope Innocent III in the Lateran Basilica. The pontiff's dazzling white vestments accentuate the contrast between high and low church. In the back two-thirds of St.

Boniface people were sleeping, many of them snoring loudly. The makeshift dormitory called to mind the Temple of Asclepius, where people slept in small cells in the hope of receiving healing dreams from the god of sleep. In this Christian setting I thought: "Interesting: these guests are suffering from psychological, spiritual and physical illnesses and are seeking healing dreams from the God of sleep. Of course." For the God of the universe, there is nothing new under the sun. I began to wonder whether the Mediterranean world's shift from polytheism to monotheism was, from the beginning, part of God's cosmotheandric design.

On a chilly spring morning I visited with a frequent guest who I will call Chris. She had a long list of complaints both for and about God. During our first conversation she said that when she was four, God promised to make her whole, only to abandon her as a broken young woman. After many decades she was still waiting for God to return. That day she announced: "God pimped me out." She described the various ways in which men had abused her. We returned to this theme during subsequent conversations. I was unclear about why she blamed God for what had happened, rather than those who abused her. Ad-libbing, one day I asked: "If God pimped you out, what was the pimp's role?" That resulted in a well-deserved blank stare. When she left, I realized that when we spoke again it might be helpful to invite her to reflect on what seemed to be an important distinction: how she sees the difference between God and Satan, who was also part of her narrative. That morning the train derailed as soon as it left the station. She stormed into the church, sat next to me and said: "God is a lazy cockroach and Jesus is a pedophile." I knew that she saw God as the cosmic disappointer, but the rest came as a surprise. She continued: "Easter was a beautiful day" for two reasons: because of the baptism celebrated at St. John's and because "everyone saw Jesus for the fraud he is." Chris would not consider the possibility that the people who abused her are not, in fact, the God who hated what they did. During a subsequent conversation she returned to "God is love so why did God make Jesus suffer?" I invited her to consider a new ending to her story: that crucifixion was humanity's answer to God's love, not a masochistic twist to the paschal mystery. Other than showing up, I failed to reach Chris. She had so deeply internalized the message that God had abandoned her that she could not reflect on the possibility that the abusers were responsible for their own behavior. As I watched Carmen interact joyfully with guests across the room, I was reminded that sometimes the only thing the host can do is open the door and sit with whoever walks through it.

Another guest, James, is a reflective, lonely, sensitive person who was grieving the loss of his wife and mother within the span of six months. In a flash of rage, he vented to me his frustration with his daughter for making demands on him that he could not meet. He was incensed at "how selfish that grown-ass woman is." I was surprised at how quickly his anger dissipated when I asked whether he loved his daughter. In fact, he seemed confused about why that was unclear. Half an hour later our conversation ended with James sobbing in dismay about how women are treated in society. The quiet of the sanctuary provided the stillness James needed in order to express his anger. That opened the door to anger's estranged sibling: sadness. James' great emotional bandwidth reminded me of the importance of suspending judgment, which is one of the primary tenets of this book. He helped me see that when strong emotions are involved in conversations, people rarely lead with what they want to say. I find that the most difficult and necessary part of ministry is to step aside and stay put simultaneously.

A young man named Anthony had a shelter space at night. His mind was overwhelmed by conspiracy theories and he was struggling with his identity, noting several times that he could not trust anything he thought he knew about himself. Wondering even about his own goodness he asked me if I thought the devil should have a chance. I asked for clarification: "Do you mean with you or with God?" His answer: "Yes." I peeled a page from Anselm's *Cur Deus Homo?*[21],suggesting that the devil has no rights over us and that if the devil wanted to return to God, it is in God's nature to receive those who have a change of heart. I told him that I could not imagine a God who would reject anyone. Because of his constricted affect I had no idea whether any part of our conversation was helpful, but he said that he would take me up on the offer to meet the following week. As it turned out, the following week was Holy Thursday and I missed him because the church had to close early to prepare for the liturgy. It was several months before we reconnected. Our conversations continued to focus on trust, though I could not detect in him any new awareness or satisfaction. In the end I felt like I was in his way. If I was at all helpful to Anthony, I was not aware of it. As vexing as it was to try to reach him, I do not regret making the effort. I learned from this experience that what we think people need is often wrong. Regardless of the earnestness with which Anthony asked theological questions, theology was not going to provide him with any relief. He was visibly frustrated that his brain injury made it impossible for him to communicate clearly what he needed. I can only hope that Anthony knew that I saw him and was glad to stay put while he drifted off to sleep.

Sierra is one of several guests whose companion is a beautiful, sweet dog. When I met her on a lovely spring day little Brady was having a hard time resting and was keeping Sierra awake. Since they were both restless, I initiated a conversation. Sierra said that she'd had a rough night but was relieved that Brady had been able to sleep. She didn't share the reason for her restless night, and I regret that I did not ask. However, she shared the circumstances that had recently left her without a home. Sierra is an artist who had been living in her RV. When it required repairs that she could not afford, she put her belongings into storage. When we met, she and Brady had been living on the street for five weeks. She told me that she was relieved because she would soon have the use of a studio space during the day so that she could earn some money. It would not provide a place to sleep but she was hopeful because she had a mechanic who was on the lookout for an affordable RV. In the meanwhile, she and Brady were without a home. When I asked about her social support network, she said that many of her family members had died and that she would have asked an ex-lover if she could stay with him but did not because he had recently gotten married. I kept thinking that she reminded me of any number of my well-educated friends and that, if I weren't a chaplain in that setting, we might have become friends. Sierra's circumstances made me aware of the fragility of the social web that protects most people from living on the street. Humility. *Humus*. Dirt. The life we think we have can become a memory. The most I was able to do for Sierra and Brady was to call the storage facility to make sure they were open since it was a holiday. For an afternoon, she would be able to access symbols of stability and the safety that she was longing to provide for herself and Brady. It wasn't enough, but it was more than she'd awoken with in the shelter or doorway where she and Brady had slept the previous night.

Johnny and Ronald are the parents of another timid little mutt named Linus. Until recently the couple had been living in a trailer in Ronald's brother's backyard. An interpersonal conflict had arisen with the brother, and Johnny was no longer welcome. Though it meant leaving the trailer's modicum of security, Ronald also moved out in order to be with Johnny and Linus on the street. When we first met at St. Boniface, Johnny was furious about a conflict that had arisen with another unhoused individual at a local institution that feeds whoever walks through the door. It was clear that because the confrontation had scared Linus, it was very upsetting to Johnny and Ronald. I was worried that Johnny was on the verge of a stroke or heart attack, so I spent an hour with them listening to their story and getting to know them. Above all, I wanted them to know that I was listening. My goal was to calm Johnny down and to give Ronald my full attention. Before they left, I asked if Linus has a favorite treat. Ronald smiled and said: Yes! Milk Bones! I told them that I would bring him some the following week. It was painful to watch Johnny struggle to stuff their belongings into two suitcases. I wondered how they would manage their load while also caring for Linus.

The following week Johnny and Ronald were not at St. Boniface. I was told that they had been going to St. John's, so I gave the Milk Bones to a couple with two dogs who were hanging out at the drug hub known as "The Stock Exchange." I was hoping I would see Johnny and Ronald the following Monday. When I arrived, Ronald was sitting in the lobby with Linus, charging his phone. Johnny was waiting for the restroom. A few minutes later, he returned, frustrated because someone was taking his time smoking crack in the bathroom. I kept him company while he tried to fish out his clean pair of jeans. Exasperated that they were not in his suitcase, he tried to try to find his shorts. We stuffed their sleeping bags back into the suitcases, which were to the point of bursting. I asked if they were familiar with Space Bags, which they were not. I explained that they are designed to squeeze the air out of bulky fabrics. They were receptive to the idea so I told them that I would have some for them the following week, along with some original flavor Milk Bones (Linus is not fond of peanut butter).

A couple of weeks later Johnny, Ronald, and I had set a date to meet at St. John's. I brought the Space Bags and the Milk Bones. This time Linus relaxed when I went to pet him. His dad, Johnny, also dropped his polite façade, and vented about a confrontation he'd had with another guest outside the restroom. For a few minutes I slipped into the role of community member, forgetting that I was there to provide a service. That distinction tends to become blurred over time at Gubbio. While Ronald slept, Johnny and I talked about the history of the upcoming Pride Parade, a veritable Feast Day in San Francisco. Meeting at the intersection of our shared experience as "Left-Coasters," that morning marked the beginning of a deeper relationship. I began to understand that knowing Ronald and Johnny and caring about their quality of life made the difference between empathy and action. I realized that showing up for them in a small way served a practical end in that, for as long as the Space Bags lasted, they would have less difficulty closing their suitcases as they rifled through them for pants, toiletries, food for Linus, and all of their other belongings. They taught me that the proverbial "little things in life" are huge for those who struggle to meet their basic needs.

On my final day at St. John's, I texted the site coordinator to tell him that I was running a few minutes late. His response was: "Ok. See you soon. Lots of need today." When I arrived Ronald and Johnny were walking down the street and were visibly upset. I was parking so I rolled down the window and waved. Johnny yelled, "We need to talk to you!" They were having a lovers' quarrel based on a misunderstanding. It was obvious to everyone who knew them that they loved each other. I tried to help them see the situation from the other's perspective. Because their love is a mile deep it didn't take much before Ronald was sobbing in Johnny's arms, loosening his partner's suit of emotional armor. That day Ronald said several times that he was tired: tired of sleeping on the street, tired because he knew that being dirty all the time bothered Johnny, tired of dealing with drug addicts and the many other stressors of homelessness. Knowing that I could not resolve the housing issue, I introduced them to someone who could potentially find them a place to live. However, when I visited them the following Christmas, they were still living

Figure 4.1.   St. John's Episcopal Church. *Source:* Photo © James Earl Scott.

on the street. As a connection to The Gubbio Project and to Johnny, Ronald, and Linus, I purchased one of Johnny's drawings of the interior of St. John's (see figure 4.1).

In getting to know people who lament being treated as if they are invisible or even despicable, I understood more fully why those of us who are materially comfortable have a responsibility to draw near to those whose physical appearance and living situations might threaten our own sense of security. I imagined that if Jesus were working in the inner city, every day he would make it a priority to provide not only Space Bags but breathing room. Since the *Parousia* has not yet begun, we have work to do for Johnny, Ronald, Sierra, Anthony, James, Chris, and the thousands of people and pets who are unhoused. If Jesus were practicing street ministry today, I imagine that he would prod the consciences of those who have the resources to address the housing crisis for which they are partly responsible. The Gubbio Project is a horizontal (power equity) community not only because its mission is to create an environment in which people can experience sacred sleep, but also because it models a nonhierarchical structure at the heart of the church. Despite the stereotype of the wild-eyed beggar, the deprivation experienced by those who are unhoused does not always lead to depravity. From a biblical perspective, the latter is a real danger for those who are privileged. Sister Mary Litell, OSF, noted that on Maslow's Hierarchy of Needs, Gubbio provides a necessity that is frequently overlooked yet is vital in order for human beings to flourish: safety. Ironically, those who take safety for granted do not always flourish.

When I lived in Italy in 1998, I became involved with a group of musicians and other artists under the leadership of Peter Dulborough. They were in the final production stage of a musical called *The Prince and the Rose*, a play by Ann Davis based on *The Little Prince* by Antoine De Saint-Exupéry. The core message of both stories is the value of mutuality: that we are responsible for those we love. The playful Fox tells the prince that friends "tame" one another. We keep each other in check and are unafraid to speak the truth. When we do so with respect and a light-hearted approach thanks to friends like the coy Fox, we can offer difficult feedback without the other experiencing it as a swipe. Friends do this with the understanding that we are equal in dignity. Those who have more power in caregiving relationships should be attentive to the impact of real differences such as income, housing status, education, and mental health challenges. It is important to be mindful of the fact that mutual enrichment and friendly affection are not the same as mutuality.

The Gubbio Project provides a bridge that spans the social ravine between those who are housed and unhoused. In this organization, though it exists, the boundary between the two is often indiscernible. As previously noted, some of the people who serve have themselves been displaced. Unlike most people who are living on the street, St. Francis chose poverty as a way of life. For someone who had been sheltered and coddled, relinquishing security was a necessary step in learning about and meeting people's needs, especially the need to be loved. In capitalist democratic societies such as the United States, most can try to imagine, but cannot remember, what those who are unhoused need most because they have never experienced it. Unlike St. Francis in the thirteenth century, the majority of those who struggle daily to survive on the streets of San Francisco have not made a free choice to live outdoors. Members of this Franciscan community who work as hospitality monitors, organizers, chaplains, and listeners as well as the volunteers who provide breakfast and other services are deeply aware that any number of circumstances could unfold that would leave most of us materially impoverished.

The Gubbio Project stresses compassion not only through its mission statement but by the ways in which the staff are trained and the guests are treated. I had an opportunity to attend a staff workshop about accompanying people who have experienced or are currently experiencing trauma. The facilitator shared with us what it was like to grow up in low-income housing in San Francisco, where the sound of gunshots and the reality of people being caught in the crossfire were daily occurrences. We reflected on the forms of trauma that the guests experience. In a follow-up conversation Laura Slattery described long-term transformation among the staff, noting that "we are all working on love, and this requires doing." For example, one person said that working at Gubbio has helped her understand transgender people's experiences. Others have learned to recognize the connection between mental health issues and behavior. As Laura noted, these outwardly focused ministries require that we "put judgment on the shelf and take down compassion." Gubbio provides an important witness to the wider church: that love is only transformative in relationship. Rather than being annoyed with the sound of snoring during Mass, one Franciscan novice commented that it makes the sanctuary feel like home. To those who would say that church is church, and home is home, I will offer a frank remark made about St. Boniface by executive director, Christina Alvarez: "This is the bedroom of a hundred and fifty people."

Amy, a Younger Millennial who volunteers at Gubbio, offered valuable insights about what the organization can teach the wider church about social sin. Having moved to San Francisco for graduate school, her other points of reference are in the global south and the East Coast of the United States. She described San Francisco as a playground for the rich. Though the percentage of homelessness in San Francisco is less than it is in Seattle, Los Angeles, Washington, D.C., Las Vegas, and Boston, the income disparity is the highest in San Francisco.[22] The degree of inequality has contributed to what Amy described as social apathy. She told stories about what she has witnessed on public transit: one person asking for money while the ten other people in the train car or the platform completely ignore the individual. If someone "acts up," the bystanders become paralyzed. She noted that their day-to-day behavior does not match the views they present on social media. As a Younger Millennial, Amy believes that the problem is that there are too many young people with too much money, such as the 50,000 San Franciscans ages twenty-five to forty-four with an annual income of more than $200,000. "They want a beautiful city and homelessness is not pretty, so they collectively ignore it." They have no idea how to respond appropriately. Their awkwardness is not limited to their discomfort with poverty. These are the same people who isolate themselves in public with headphones, cell phones, and laptops on public transit. At Gubbio there are unhoused people who do not like each other yet will sleep in the same church. This is a witness to society about relationship building. We do not have to like one another in order to share space, breakfast, eye contact, and small talk. In part because people who live on the streets cannot safely possess smartphones and other expensive devices, and in part because of the cost, the scarcity of technology in that community can teach us how to live without our devices and cultivate our innate need for relationships. That way of life makes personal demands in a way that filling the void through superficial means does not. Through

Gubbio the church can model what Jesus' ministry looks like when people put away their devices and focus on no-tech human needs. For the church in the third millennium this Franciscan outreach ministry lights the path toward St. Paul's "more excellent way."

Perhaps the historical approach I have used elsewhere in this book can lend perspective to what might be an emotionally charged issue: the repurposing of a church from a place primarily designated for worship to a place set aside for sacred sleep. As we saw in chapter 3, a temple is a place that is designated as sacred by those who use it. Fundamentally, it is a dwelling place where a god/God and people are at home. From both the Greco-Roman and the Jewish traditions, there is continuity between ancient Mediterranean religious practices and the early church's appropriation of liturgical clothing, architecture, and governance structure. One example is the Church of Concord in Agrigento, Sicily, which was converted from a Greek temple in the sixth century CE. In antiquity it required only minor modifications to the existing structure in order to be transformed into a church. This pattern is especially striking in the Cathedral in Ortigia, Sicily, where in the Temple of Athena, walls were erected between the Doric columns that are visible both from the nave and from the exterior. In addition, Latin and Byzantine liturgical vestments were adapted from Roman senatorial clothing. Over time the churches of the Latin West followed the Jewish tradition of keeping the "bread of angels" in a special place within the sanctuary (Ps. 78:25). For nearly 1,000 years the tabernacle containing the Real Presence of Christ has been placed near the altar, where a lit candle reminds the faithful that God dwells within.

At St. Boniface Catholic Church, and St. John's Episcopal Church, the physical sanctuaries function as places of sanctuary, as they did for asylum seekers in the Middle Ages. An important difference is that in the medieval church, those who had committed crimes were required to confess them in the church and might eventually be exiled from the realm. At Gubbio there is no such condition attached to the offer of sanctuary. Guests might or might not "confess" to having done some form of harm, but judgment is not part of the social contract. It is a covenantal relationship based on compassion rather than an act of mercy extended by the powerful to the powerless. In the centuries before the legalization of Christianity, churches were small, and it was common for members of the community to confess their sins in the presence of the entire assembly. The administration of what would become the seven sacraments was not yet concentrated in the clergy. In the Eastern Orthodox world, it was very common for people to bring their spiritual burdens to the women and men who were recognized as holy. Occasionally they had the title of deacon or deaconess, but not necessarily. The example of permaculture gardening offered in the Introduction illustrates the messy process by which the church at the margins can help transform the church at its center.

The example that follows points to a species of new growth that seems to be slowly migrating inward.

Plugging Theology into a Grounded Outlet

If it is possible to describe a pastoral approach at Gubbio, I would say that it is "of the moment," in a place where things change by the minute. The following example mirrors a Kenyan proverb: "It takes a guest to point out to the owner where the roof is leaking." At both Gubbio locations lay ministers in whom the guests confide their deepest, sometimes dark experiences are aware of the sacramental nature of their work. Amy, the Younger Millennial Roman Catholic graduate student in theology introduced above, described a difficult conversation with her classmates, some of whom were candidates for ordination. In a course on the theology of sacraments she noted that in her ministry she regularly hears confessions and offers absolution because that is what the guests are seeking at that moment.

Since the friars who do sacramental ministry at St. Boniface cannot be everywhere, Amy's willingness to be present for guests in the "confessional" way she describes is the only reasonable response to a direct, time-sensitive need. She expressed her frustration to her classmates, noting that because the work she is doing sometimes demands this specific type of spiritual care, she would benefit from some of the formation that Roman Catholic ordination candidates receive for hearing confessions and anointing the sick. To the seminarians' credit, they were earnest and respectful in grappling with the fluid categories that flow into and out of sacramental theology. Before we slip into a premature conclusion about theological relativism, let's take a moment to revisit essential components of the historical theology of sacraments from a Roman Catholic perspective in order to recontextualize Amy's "sacramental" ministry.

The twelfth-century theologian Hugh of St. Victor understood a sacrament to be a sign that signified something sacred. Unlike simple signs, such as a stop sign, which is a clear indication of what ought to happen, symbols point toward mystery and communicate grace. All sacraments involve symbols and grace, but not all symbols are sacramental. However, whether a symbol conveys grace depends on the individual participant. The number of sacraments "counted" by the church did not become set at seven until the thirteenth century. Seven was where the Roman church was sitting when the music stopped playing during the Fourth Lateran Council (1215). Previously the number had been a moveable feast and so, therefore, were Christians' perceptions about sacraments and sacramentals (the latter is used here as a noun).[23] Keeping in mind this historical fact, we start to see why if a guest at Gubbio initiates a pastoral care moment that she or he experiences as just as effective as the sacrament of Reconciliation, and the experience has a healing impact, the encounter served a sacramental (adj.) purpose for the guest. In other words, as we saw with the Christian ministry at Burning Man, God's grace can go where God wills and is not subject to the limits of our imaginations or theological categories.

Arguments can be made about the important role of ordained ministers, but they cannot legitimately point to qualitative differences between what has often been called the "special grace" received through the sacraments celebrated by clergy and the grace received through Christian rituals celebrated by the laity. In other words, to claim that grace is more efficacious when it involves ordained ministers is a hierarchically motivated, specious position. It is not my intention to trivialize or relativize the function of ordained ministers who celebrate the sacraments, but to contextualize it. To offer an analogy: just as both solar panels and wind turbines are valuable, environmentally responsible means of harnessing electricity, the church needs both lay and ordained ministers. I am suggesting that, scanning the horizon for opportunities to receive grace, Gubbio guests who abstain or are excluded from the sacraments such as Reconciliation and Eucharist, can experience the consolation and healing of relationships that are the fruits of the sacraments of the church. With or without the symbols and rituals that are integral to the sacrament of Reconciliation, the guests who "confess" their sins regularly to the volunteers at Gubbio do so because they experience the grace of God blowing toward, and through them. If the power of any sacrament is visible in the efficacy of grace through human faith in God's presence, it is up to those who seek to cordon off the grace that is conveyed by the seven sacraments to work out a category for the sacramental nature of the informal sacramental (adj.) ministries offered by laypeople. Splitting hairs about precisely how the volunteers at Gubbio are channels of grace would be as productive as pushing water uphill with a rake. Who would benefit from such a discussion? I can guarantee that it would not be the guests. The creative tension that the volunteer and her seminary classmates experienced in conversation illustrates the staying power and mutual respect needed when the people of God, both lay and clerical, discern a better way to be church.

Roman Catholics might find it interesting to learn that the Episcopal Church has in its Canons a contingency plan for the need Amy is trying to meet: "Canon 9 clergy are typically called by their congregation. . . . It is the normal expectation that persons ordained under this canon will not move from the congregation for which they were ordained." These "local priests and deacons" "serve in a particular location which is small, isolated, remote, or distinct in respect of ethnic composition, language, or culture."[24] Of course, those who were ordained for broader ministry are welcome to serve alongside them should they become available, but Canon 9 clergy offer spiritual

care because there is a need. As previously noted, the handful of friars who
serve at St. Boniface cannot be everywhere. Given the unique needs of those
who are unhoused, a case could be made that The Gubbio Project meets the
criteria for a "distinct" population as described by Canon 9. Some of the high-
functioning guests use the term "community" to describe their relationships
to others who also use the program's services. I would go a step further, and
also describe the unhoused population as sharing a culture.[25] Contrary to the
typically anonymous setting used for sacramental Reconciliation, Amy's
work among the unhoused population demonstrates that she can appropriately
meet the needs of a particular community in which intimacy is required for
effective ministry. If she belonged to the Episcopal tradition, Amy might very
well be ordained as a Canon 9 priest.[26] Since her membership in the Roman
Catholic Church is firm and her ministry effective, Amy's lay ministry is
a call to action directed toward Roman Catholic clergy who have the clout
needed to initiate this conversation among ecclesiastical decision-makers.
Perhaps her seminary classmates who have since been ordained will do so.

The center of an organization is a center of gravity, a place of stability
where policies are made, practices develop, and norms become fixed. If the
administrative center of the church, whether local or global, is insulated from
the margins, it becomes a dangerous place where the life-giving water that
it has been commissioned to sustain becomes stagnant. Jesus did not work
alone when he healed the person who was born blind. The man was treated
by Jesus, but he then had to go to the pool of Siloam to wash his own face.[27]
As Gubbio demonstrates, water goes where it will, and it can become tumul-
tuous. Those who serve the guests most effectively are skilled swimmers and
salvage divers. Churning waters are also cleansing. They create the energy
that enables the center and the perimeter flow into one another. The sharing
of ideas, experiences, and horizontal decision-making ensures that those who
are responsible for the day-to-day operations are impacted by those whose
needs determine the organization's evolving mission. This is not a romantic
idea that would annul the need for bishops, other clergy, or for that matter,
school principals and executives but, rather, an example of what can happen
when decision makers celebrate the vivifying potential of communities that
develop organically. In such settings the healing capacity of each person is
enkindled by other members of the supportive community. At Gubbio, the
executive director scrubs the toilets as needed. Regardless of his views on
same-sex relationships, I have also heard from several parishioners about
a high-ranking Roman Catholic cleric who serves in the soup kitchen at a
church with a predominantly LGBTQ congregation. One day a minister is
tasked with stirring a pot of bubbling soup. Another day she or he must tend
to a troublesome toilet. The motto at Burning Man is "Welcome Home."

When ministers who are also power brokers seek out those they might rather avoid, they send the same powerful message.

San Franciscans cannot overlook the multitudes who shoot up and drop their needles on city sidewalks. In July 2018, San Francisco was slated to become the first U.S. city to open safe injection sites. The move was overwhelmingly supported by residents at both ends of the political spectrum. Since the facilities would have violated both federal and state laws, at first only a mock site was created. It was aimed at educating would-be clients, politicians, and the public.[28] In May 2019, a bill was passed by the California State Assembly that could allow San Francisco to open such facilities, despite the illegality at the federal level. The majority of San Francisco residents are deeply concerned about harm reduction for the city's 22,000 drug addicts. In the spirit of St. Francis who churned the waters, joining the margins with the middle, The Gubbio Project is one of numerous ministries and community organizations throughout the Tenderloin that support this politically charged initiative.

The public ministry of Jesus can be described in this way: rather than avoid people who were ignored or actively scorned by society's power brokers, he moved toward them: widows, lepers, beggars, tax collectors, gentiles, women, prostitutes, and children. He broke through the walls that religious authorities had erected in separating the unsavory characters from the love of God and he did so without lording it over them. He did not ask to be thanked or secretly harbor resentment toward those who dismissed him. He offered truth without abandoning people who had chosen falsehood, always inviting them to reconciliation. He extended mercy as a gift (*gratis*) with no strings attached: *gratia*, grace freely given.

While it might seem an odd pairing, both Burning Man and Gubbio emphasize the creative potential of hospitality, defined by Henri Nouwen as "paying attention to the guest." The sixth principle of Gubbio and the first principle of Burning Man articulate a commitment to inclusivity. People who occupy the margins in some societies (such as members of the LGBTQ community, nonconformists of many varieties, eccentric artists, political activists, religiously unaffiliated "Nones," and victims of trauma, to name just a few representative groups) are welcome both at Burning Man and Gubbio. As Rev. Baker noted, these are the people Jesus would gravitate toward today, so one could expect to see him at Burning Man. One Gubbio Project board member wrote in the Archdiocesan newspaper *San Francisco Catholic*: "Can you imagine the impact our local Catholic Church would have in our city and beyond if the parishes of San Francisco considered the welcoming of homeless people into the sanctuary of the church to be an important part of our Catholic identity? Christ is already sleeping at the doors and on the front steps of many of our churches—what keeps us from inviting him inside?"[29]

NOTES

1. For an interesting study of the ethics of political life, see Eugene Garver's *Aristotle's Politics: Living Well and Living Together* (Chicago: University of Chicago Press, 2011).

2. The newspaper noted that the slogan is a general statement rather than a commentary on the then newly formed administration in its own city.

3. "$303K Is the Annual Income Now Needed to Buy a Median Priced Home in San Francisco," https://www.sfgate.com/realestate/article/income-needed-buy-home-San-Francisco-real-estate-12614111.php (accessed March 31, 2019).

4. "What Percent Are You?" http://graphics.wsj.com/what-percent/ (accessed March 31, 2019).

5. "Here's the Income Required to be Among the Top Earners in San Francisco," http://www.businessinsider.com/the-salary-of-the-top-earners-in-san-francisco-2015-11 (accessed March 31, 2019).

6. "San Francisco Rents Freeze in First Month of 2018," https://sf.curbed.com/2018/2/2/16965618/san-francisco-rents-january-2018 (accessed March 31, 2019).

7. "San Francisco, California (CA) income map, earnings map, and wages data," http://www.city-data.com/income/income-San-Francisco-California.html (accessed March 31, 2019).

8. Ibid.

9. Ibid.

10. Videos and other information about Gubbio can be found at https://www.thegubbioproject.org

11. During a presentation given to the chaplains and listeners at St. John the Evangelist on March 2, 2018, Sister Mary Litell suggested that a possible reason for the wolf's aggression was that she had to attend to hungry cubs.

12. Kathleen Manning, "Upstart from Assisi," *U.S. Catholic* 82 (10) (October 2017), 12–17.

13. Musei Uniti Gubbio, http://www.sanfrancescodellapace.it/chiesa/.

14. The story is found in chapter 2.

15. *Dedication of the Hubert H. Humphrey HEW Building* (Washington, DC, November 1, 1977). Speech Text Files. Hubert H. Humphrey Papers. Minnesota Historical Society. "Under this roof . . . new and better efforts to promote human welfare will be developed and administered. . . . All of us will move closer to our goal of insuring to every child the opportunity to grow and develop to his or her fullest potential, to every adult a life of industry and dignity, and to every aged American, a twilight of serenity and independence."http://www2.mnhs.org/library/findaids/00442/pdfa/00442-04138.pdf.

16. Alan Jones, *Soulmaking: The Desert Way of Spirituality* (San Francisco: HarperCollins, 1989), 84

17. Regis Armstrong et al., eds. "Legend of the Three Companions," in *Francis of Assisi: Early Documents*. Vol. 2. *The Founder* (New York: New City Press, 2000), ch. 4, 74.

18. A single-room occupancy building.

19. The theme of hospitality as the art of paying attention to the guest is found throughout the works of Henri Nouwen.

20. *Gubbio* uses this term for those who provide a ministry of presence and accompaniment but do not have formal training in chaplaincy. Functionally, there is no difference between the work done by chaplains and the work done by listeners. The *bema* is the platform in the sanctuary that elevates the altar, lectern, and pulpit.

21. *Why Did God Become Human?*

22. In 2017 the percentage data was as follows: Seattle 1.65; Los Angeles 1.39; Washington, D.C. 1.31; Los Vegas 1.03; Boston .91; San Francisco .79

23. When used as a noun the term "sacramental" refers to objects or rituals that convey grace for individuals but are not universally recognized by the church. Examples include a rosary, a scapular, a religious habit, making the sign of the cross and religious jewelry.

24. "An Episcopal Dictionary of the Church," https://www.episcopalchurch.org/library/glossary/canon-9-clergy.

25. The cultural anthropologist Richard Geertz described culture as "a system of inherited conceptions expressed in symbolic forms by means of which men communicate, perpetuate, and develop their knowledge about and attitudes toward life." *The Interpretation of Cultures* (New York: Basic Books, 1973), 89.

26. I am grateful to Fr. Vincent Pizzuto for bringing Canon 9 to my attention.

27. John 9:1–11.

28. "A Controversial Fix for Overdose Deaths: Safe Injection Sites," https://www.citylab.com/equity/2018/09/building-a-safe-space-for-san-franciscos-addicts/568942/ (accessed March 28, 2019).

29. "The Sanctuary of St. Boniface as the Tabernacle of the Suffering Christ," https://catholic-sf.org/news/the-sanctuary-of-st-boniface-as-the-tabernacle-of-the-suffering-christ (accessed March 31, 2018).

Chapter 5

Action-Reflection

Radical Hospitality and the Contemplative Life

TIME

As both a way of life and an intellectual tradition, monastic spirituality has had a profound influence on the shape of Christian prayer. Originating with the oral tradition of the followers of Jesus in the first few decades of Christianity, the *Didache* is recognized as the church's first handbook on prayer. Its instructions on the reception of guests and best practices for harmonious communal life parallel those of early monastic communities.[1]

As faithful Jews, the earliest followers of *The Way* infused into an increasingly gentile church the Jewish practice of morning and evening prayer, to which they added a third session, all of which were to include the Lord's Prayer.[2] The Roman Church promoted this in a way that aligned with the ancient practice of ringing bells to mark various times throughout the business day.[3] In the Roman Forum the first bell was rung at 6:00 a.m. (*prime*), the second at the third hour, 9:00 a.m. (*terce*). The bell also signaled the lunch break at noon, which was the sixth hour (*sext*). Laborers returned to work at 3:00 p.m. (*none*) and the workday ended at 6:00 p.m. with the ringing of the *vesper* bell. Both the Latin word *vesper* and the Greek *hesperos* mean "west." As one might expect, in the early church, the workday, the Psalms and the prayer times reflected the movement of the sun.[4] The words and images of the Psalms chosen for *prime*, read at the beginning of the work day, often emphasize hope in God's abiding presence and protection from one's enemies. The texts chosen for *vespers* focus on resting in God's protective arms and the promise of a peaceful night. In some European countries, such as Italy, the Roman work hours governed by daylight are still normative, especially outside of commercial areas. Those engaged in manual labor typically rest in the early afternoon when the sun is overpowering. The form and function of the church's earliest prayer pattern integrates the practice of *ora et labora*, of praying throughout the day, whether one's work involved bricklaying, reading, or rocking the cradle. Because the work and prayer times were standardized, whether individuals were literate or recited their prayers from memory, the basic practice was accessible to anyone who could follow the movement of the sun and moon. The established prayer times and varied readings created an inherently flexible pattern of prayer.[5]

BENEDICTINE MONASTICISM

The founder of monasticism in the West, St. Benedict of Nursia (480–547) introduced for those who lived according to his *Rule for Monasteries* a standard order of prayer based on the Psalms. With the marriage of church and state in the eighth century under the Carolingian dynasty, both monastic and liturgical dimensions of ecclesial life became more uniform than they had been in that region. For example, Charles Martel (714–741) made literacy a requirement for clergy, while the laity remained largely illiterate. He also mandated the use of the Roman liturgy throughout his lands. His grandson Charlemagne called himself king of the Romans and the Franks and was received at the twelfth milestone outside of Rome, as had been the custom for the ancient Roman emperors. Though functionally illiterate, Charlemagne effected church reforms under the guidance of the monk, Benedict of Aniane (c. 747–841). Charlemagne's son Louis the Pious (814–841) mandated the Benedictine form of monasticism for monks within the Holy Roman Empire. Within 300 years of the death of the founder of Western monasticism, every monk and nun, as well as some literate laypersons who had the funds to commission books for personal use, used the Benedictine *Liturgy of the Hours* for daily prayer.

With the development of an increasingly serpentine body of canon law, the laity became heavily dependent on ecclesiastical foundations for their spiritual and material needs. Especially significant were monasteries, cathedrals, orphanages, and hospitals. Underscoring the conceptual and historical link between Roman Rome and Christian Rome, the Benedictine monk and cardinal Peter Damian (c. 1007–1073) went as far as to suggest that cardinals are the "spiritual senators of the church," legislators who were to enforce ecclesiastical laws.[6] Influential scholastic theologians including Peter Lombard (c. 1100–1160), Bonaventure of Bagnoregio (1217–1274) and John Duns Scotus (c. 1265–1308) all asserted that the laity were obligated simply to believe church teachings that they did not understand and that, unlike the clergy, they could not be expected to understand theological issues explicitly.[7] In fact, "In a motif popular with later writers, Peter Lombard used the disparaging image of asses pasturing alongside ploughing oxen (Job 1.14) to illustrate how simple Christians without clear knowledge of the articles of the faith might be saved through the faith and doctrine of their betters in the church."[8] Bishops and theologians generally agreed that the most the laity could be expected to understand were the Creed, the Lord's Prayer, the Ten Commandments, the Hail Mary, and the list of sacraments, though they were not necessarily obligated to receive all of the ones that applied to them. This attitude significantly limited the laity's access to spiritual resources. It is no wonder that from the High Middle Ages through Vatican II, a key feature of lay spirituality was recitation of the rosary. There are ample studies that indicate that the laity was underserved by an overtaxed or out-of-touch clergy. The bishops' inability to travel regularly to rural parishes is the main reason that Latin Christians often went without Confirmation.[9] With the expansion of urbanization and now globalization, the contemporary laity can understand, and is longing for, spiritual practices that transcend rote prayer. However, the church continues to underserve people who are not drawn to traditional practices such as Eucharistic Adoration, recitation of the rosary and the traditional scope of Bible study groups. Just as the medieval model of atonement theory that has infused Christian theology in the West for nearly a thousand years does not make sense to those who live hundreds of years after the collapse of the feudal system, the proliferation of age-old Christian practices ought to be reimagined for people whose daily experiences are noisy, frenetic, and anxiety-producing.

Postmodern Contemplative Practices for Christian Renewal: Three Case Studies

a) Taizé Prayer at Mercy Center in Burlingame, CA

The son of a Swiss Protestant minister, Roger Louis Schutz-Marsauche, crossed into Vichy-controlled France in the middle of World War II.[10] While working on his college thesis: *The Ideal of the Monastic Life Before Saint Benedict and Its Conformity to the Gospels*, he found a house for sale in the small village of Taizé, near the demarcation line. Though at that time Roger had not yet formed a permanent religious community, he and a network of friends decided to meet every other month and to live under a simple monastic Rule. The house provided an opportunity for Roger to offer shelter and safe passage to Switzerland for European refugees, including many Jews. In the early 1940s Roger and a few of his friends developed into a residential community of brothers, which quickly became ecumenical. Together with Roger's sister Geneviève the community took care of local orphans. Committed to the confluence of contemplative life and social justice, at the end of the war the community at Taizé continued their ministry at the margins by serving soup to German prisoners on Sundays, despite the fact that it put them at odds with the villagers who had welcomed Roger to France.[11] Just as we saw with The Gubbio Project and the emerging Christian community at Burning Man, prayer and hospitality have always gone hand-in-hand in the community at Taizé.

In the late 1940s the brothers asked the local bishop for permission to use a nearby abandoned Catholic Church for communal prayer.[12] Their request was granted by the papal nuncio in Paris, Angelo Giuseppe Roncalli, who in 1958 became Pope John XXIII. The relationship between the community at Taizé, Roncalli, and the future Pope John Paul II grew over the years. When Pope John XXIII convened Vatican II, the newly formed secretariat for Christian Unity, Cardinal Bea, invited both Brother Roger and the subprior of the Taizé community, Max Thurian, to attend the council as official observers. They attended every session throughout the three-year council. Believing that Vatican II had not gone far enough to heal the divide between Christians of various denominations, they welcomed the opportunity to continue their ecumenical work by supporting the efforts made by CELAM to foster dialogue between Catholics and Protestant missioners in Latin America.[13] Brother Roger was a personal guest of Pope Paul VI at the conference in Medellín, Colombia (1968), and also attended the 1979 meeting in Puebla, Mexico.[14]

Believing that young people would be catalysts for a united church, Brother Roger organized the first Council of Youth at Taizé in 1974. At the first of what would be followed by many subsequent meetings, 40,000 young people gathered for workshops and discussions. The goal was to establish an experience of community and real understanding. In a resounding endorsement of the peacemaking work of the community at Taizé, Pope Benedict XVI gave communion to the Protestant Brother Roger at the funeral of Pope John Paul II.

Urban Hospitality through the Spiritual and Corporal Works of Mercy

Amid urban blight, Catherine McAuley (1778–1841), founder of the Sisters of Mercy, was instrumental in joining and cultivating what she saw as spliced seeds of the gospel: spirituality and social justice. Responding to an immediate need, her ministry in Ireland began with a house that sheltered destitute women and orphaned girls. She taught them using best practices in education at a time in which formal instruction was primarily reserved for the clergy. During San Francisco's infancy, the sisters, who were themselves immigrants, tended to the substantial healthcare needs of gold prospectors and other pioneers. In 1857 they founded San Francisco's oldest continually operating hospital, now St. Mary's Medical Center. Throughout the remainder of the nineteenth century, the sisters would minister to inmates from San

Quentin State Prison, care for quarantined smallpox patients, provide job training for homeless women, including former prostitutes, and care for soldiers stationed at the Presidio who were suffering from influenza and typhoid. Today one of their most impactful, challenging ministries is Mercy Housing, described by the organization in this way:

> Mercy Housing is one of the nation's largest affordable housing organizations. We participate in the development, preservation, management and/or financing of affordable, program-enriched housing across the country. Mercy Housing serves a variety of populations with housing projects for low-income families, seniors and people with special needs. We acquire and renovate existing housing, as well as develop new affordable rental properties.[15]

Sister Patsy Harney has worked for Mercy Housing since 1990. Working with a significant number of families who struggle socially and financially, the sisters continue to take bold steps to address social justice issues. For example, Sister Patsy explained that they boldly declared the illegality of the practice of separating children from asylum-seeking parents who arrived in significant numbers at the U.S.-Mexico border in the summer of 2018. As a response to the needs of unaffiliated Millennials who have a desire to respond to social and spiritual needs, the Sisters of Mercy participate in the Nones and Nuns movement that was established by Wayne Muller and Adam Horowitz in 2016. The organization is building intergenerational communities that collaborate on social justice and spirituality. Some of their planned initiatives are to create Tiny Home Villages for those who are unhoused, initiate green living projects, create support systems for the arts in an era of budget cuts, and transform underused religious houses into intergeneration communities.[16] The sisters have realized that "Challenged to imagine new, unexpected manifestations of God's presence and grace in the world, they can offer hope to the millennials."[17]

Unwilling simply to sit by and watch their community dwindle in numbers, their enthusiasm for sharing their lives and their homes with Nones is a courageous step and a contemporary expression of the inherent flexibility of religious life. A highly successful six-month pilot program was completed in 2019 at Mercy Center in Burlingame, CA. As soon as the young adults moved into the convent, they wanted to discuss the sisters' experiences of their vows. Sarah Jane Bradley grew to appreciate a view of obedience that surprised her: "It sounds like it's about taking orders, but the sisters helped me see it's about preparing the heart for dialogue and a deep internal listening for truth."[18] The young adults did not begin by asking about Catholic doctrine, but longing for rituals, they asked about the sisters' spiritual practices. Sister Judy Carle noted that "One young woman wanted ritual so much that she started going to Mass every morning."[19] The Nones' commitment to meaning making and their hunger for spiritual sustenance helps clarify their desire to understand and integrate practices from another religious tradition. While the Christian Creed is vital for those who embrace the Paschal Mystery, the Nones' experiences indicate that rituals that grew out of Christian faith can be life-giving for those who do not profess faith in the divinity of Jesus. Because I fully embrace the Christology that emerged from the Council of Chalcedon (451), part of me recoils at the idea of separating Christian rituals from faith and doctrine. At the same time, I am aware that Jews in the early years of Christianity felt this way about their brothers and sisters professing faith in Jesus while continuing to practice Jewish rituals.

For nearly 200 years the Sisters of Mercy have been living out the corporal and spiritual works of mercy as inseparable components of a virtuous life. Among their charisms are fortitude, creativity, a commitment to collaboration, and a sense of humor, all of which have served them in their assorted ministries. The sisters' ability to respond rather than react to difficult situations is one of many fruits of a rich contemplative life. Instead of using their spiritual gifts primarily for the benefit of their own community, they invite those who are seeking to make meaning in their lives to join them through various programs. With the founding of Mercy Center in 1981, the sisters created a hospitable environment in which to rest so that retreatants and harried workers can be reenergized as they return to their busy lives. As with the community at Taizé, the sisters' expression of hospitality and commitment to social justice demonstrate that the church can thrive when firmly planted in the deep soil of the gospel.

A Place of Refuge at the Gateway to Silicon Valley

An image that reflects the approach to action-contemplation of both the Sisters of Mercy and the community at Taizé with which they have been affiliated since the early 1980s, is the pilgrimage church of Notre Dame du Haut in Ronchamp, France. The visionary architect Le Courbusier (1887–1965) believed that the church's mission is to move boldly into the world, so he designed the white, concrete structure of Notre Dame du Haut to resemble a steam liner. He made the unusual decision to include both interior and exterior altars. The concave external apsidal wall invites the pilgrim onto the grounds, embracing her at the journey's end. On the interior, the same apsidal wall is convex. The church is full of unusual curved surfaces and has no right angles. Unlike most Roman Catholic churches, it is not a place where one goes to linger in prayer. Le Corbusier's idea was to create a church that would provide spiritual food for pilgrims and then impel them back out into a world in need of sustenance. The convex wall behind the altar symbolically and metaphysically "bounces" the pilgrim out of the church.[20]

Though architecturally very different from the church at Ronchamp, the chapel at Mercy Center in Burlingame, CA similarly offers retreatants an inviting space for temporary respite. Also painted white, it contains wall-to-wall white carpet that enriches the warm setting. A deeply welcoming space, the floor of the over-sized apse is the preferred seating area for many who attend the monthly Taizé service. Located at a crossroads between Silicon Valley and San Francisco, Mercy Center is a place of refuge surrounded by an economic vortex. Easily accessible from a main thoroughfare, some visitors stay for days, others for an hour. It is a place where community is carefully tended to by sisters who understand that a sustainable, fruitful contemplative life is inseparable from a commitment to social justice. As with the Brothers of Taizé, and in their response the spiritual hunger of the Nones, the sisters' approach to spiritual renewal continues to take seriously the connection between action and reflection. They aptly describe themselves as a community that is engaged in a "mission of mercy guided by prayerful consideration of the needs of our time."[21]

On the first Friday of each month since 1982, Mercy Center has hosted prayer in the style of Taizé. When Sister Suzanne Toolan, RSM, already an accomplished liturgical musician, heard an LP record featuring the music of the Taizé Community in France, she immediately realized that she had found her music.[22] She collaborated with Sister Jean Evans and Sister Judy Carle, who were enthralled by the music and the multinational ecumenical community in France. They collaborated with a local Methodist minister, Rev. Braxton Combs, who happened to have connected with the Brothers at Taizé around the same time. In anticipation of their first visit to Mercy Center and in keeping with their focus on young adults, the brothers had asked their U.S. hosts to gather a group of young adults aged between eighteen and thirty-five. The sisters gathered around 350 college students and young parishioners from the Bay Area. Throughout the 1980s, until the fall of Communism made Eastern Europe accessible, the brothers made an annual visit to Mercy Center, which they nicknamed "Taizé West." The gatherings multiplied and were soon hosted at various Protestant and Catholic churches throughout the Bay Area and beyond.

Sister Suzanne noticed that in places where the music had a performative character, the Taizé service did not take root. In fact, she believes that for this form of prayer it is important for the musicians to "stay out of the way" so that the focus is truly on contemplating God. Beginning in the early 2000s, again reflecting the community's abiding commitment to the spiritual growth of young adults, Sister Patsy Harney began a group called MercyWorks, which invites young adults to gather before and after Taizé for fellowship and conversation. Over the years it has cultivated enduring relationships among students, young professionals, and the young-at-heart who would not likely have connected during the liturgy itself.

In May 2018, Brother John and Brother Emile of the Taizé community traveled to North America to conduct workshops in various cities. A Gen X interloper, I joined the weekend retreat at Mercy Center called "Inexhaustible Joy" for Millennials. It took place on the Friday and Saturday before Pentecost. Including a handful of young-at-heart adults, there were about forty participants. When we gathered on the first night the brothers invited us to say a few words about why we were attending the retreat. One courageous, charismatic Millennial said that he decided to attend because his joy had been exhausted. In his opening remarks Brother Emile addressed the spiritual malaise that many are feeling in the current global political context. Acknowledging that so many have described an experience of trauma due to political developments, he recognized that it is difficult to find signs of new life. Reflecting on this generalized angst in terms of the arc of human history, he suggested that the world might be in a Holy Saturday phase. Throughout the weekend I reflected on the theological significance of the political situation he described. I imagined that on the Saturday following Jesus' crucifixion the apostles were grieving and laying low, slowly processing their experiences with Jesus and the events of the previous day. Not knowing what to do with themselves, I pictured them reflecting on what they knew: that in Jesus God had already done something new. How to make meaning of their journey with Jesus following the crucifixion was unclear. When they witnessed Jesus risen from the dead, they had no explanation for that Really Real event, or at least the gospels do not offer a description of their reaction to the risen Christ. Through faith, however, they knew that the one who had appeared to them multiple times beginning on the third day was the one with whom they had traveled throughout Galilee and Judea. Brother Emile's insight gave me hope that we can welcome a variety of mysteries that are too vast for understanding on this side of life.

Throughout the weekend, both in small group discussions and in larger sessions, we reflected on our own joyful experiences as well as obstacles to joy. Given the many, unprecedented stressors confronting Millennials, the brothers' message was that we should try not to be totally absorbed by the current climate. The weekend helped the young adults experience contemplative prayer as a tool for finding nourishment that enables people of faith to live the gospel as fully as possible. As their history and current work with refugees indicates, the brothers are aware of the importance of linking action with contemplation. Brother Emile noted that "for St. Paul, there is no other way to fulfill what Christ asks for than to carry one another's burdens."[23]

As I discovered through subsequent interviews with my fellow retreatants, the connection between this form of contemplation and social justice is less obvious to U.S. Millennials than to older adults. Across many conversations I began to see how this disconnect contributes to a sense of helplessness. It reminded me of Amy, the Roman Catholic Millennial volunteer from The Gubbio Project, who was bothered by the disconnect between her peers' conversations about social justice and their actions.

The majority of Millennials I interviewed after the retreat reported on features of the Taizé service that appealed to them. Delia (aged thirty-two), Agnes (aged twenty-five), Ferdinand (aged thirty-four), and Sara (aged thirty) belong to different Protestant denominations. They were invited by friends to attend a prayer service in the style of Taizé. Sara first visited the community at Taizé when she was sixteen and later spent several months with them. Having received spiritual formation through their ministry at such a young age, she said that she cannot imagine life without a connection to the community at Taizé and its unique form of prayer. The Protestant Millennials who attended the retreat noted that the most fruitful aspect of Taizé-style prayer is that it compels them to focus their attention on God in a way that their Sunday liturgies do not. They described what they experience as the primary distractions: the sermon, music, announcements, and even their fellow worshippers. Delia noted that, during church, her mind wanders toward her weekly calendar and other mundane obligations. She described an unparalleled experience of calm and union with God in community. Agnes said that the profundity of Taizé-style prayer is one of the few things that helps Millennials forget about their phones. She described traditional liturgies of various denominations as "having complex elements that have more in common with shows or performances than with worship." Her observation reminded me of Sister Suzanne Toolan's comment that Taizé-style prayer did not take root in the U.S. host churches where it had a performative quality. I also thought about Leif, the Burner who is fed by the very thing that bothered these retreatants. There the prism revealed complementary colors that might be judged too quickly as clashing.

Each of the Millennials noted the value of darkness for its calming properties and the freedom it provides to come as you are. They are grateful for the opportunity to sink into a liminal, sacred space. That said, I was surprised to learn from Delia and Agnes that they were unaware of the historical connection between the community founded by Brother Roger and the social justice. Having spent time with the community in France, only Sara was aware of the connection between hospitality, social justice, and prayer in the tradition of Taizé. She works for a mainline Protestant church in the Bay Area, where one of her responsibilities is to plan events for the young adults in her church. When asked about their spiritual inclinations, she noted several obstacles:

an unwillingness or inability to make commitments beyond the immediate future, and a dearth of free time. Both she and her husband, who works in information technology, only have about ten days of vacation per year, similarly to their peers. She believes that the scarcity of vacation time, as well as the demands on their time made by their employers leaves them overwhelmed and spiritually dazed: that they see spirituality as something one attends to as an add-on rather than a way of life.

Born in 1984, Ferdinand noted that he belongs to a "middle generation" that went from no cell phones and few computers to the ubiquity of both, all before the age of eighteen. He described the novelty of Taizé prayer as an opportunity to escape from "the constant pinging of whatever is happening in the world." He believes that the liturgy's freedom from doctrinal messages sets aside "shoulds" and invites people to experience Jesus' message of non-judgment and mercy through song: that it creates a space in which to engage spiritually that is precluded by the busyness of daily life.

A social worker who was raised in a mixed Greek Orthodox/Protestant family, Lynne, belongs to an intentional community that prioritizes spiritual practices. Many of her housemates are former Christians and some currently identify as Protestant. Their Sunday night spiritual practices are varied. In addition to what traditionally would be considered prayer, more often they use guided meditation, or have discussions about poems, articles, and films. As committed as she is to her intentional community, Lynne noted that their spiritual life "is not as full" as she wants it to be. Having been raised as a Christian but not belonging fully to either an Orthodox or Protestant church, she craves the ritual that marks more traditional Christian spirituality, such as the prayers of the faithful and the liturgy of the Eucharist. She noted that the sensory experiences of incense, candles, and quietness enable her to engage kinesthetically in prayer. With regard to prayer around the cross in the tradition of Taizé, she appreciates the fact that she can go straight from the gym, not have to think about which part of the liturgy is coming next, and that she "will not have to listen to a homily that might be lackluster or frustrating." As someone who rides public transportation throughout the day in order to visit clients in their homes, she is profoundly aware of the wealth disparity in San Francisco. Asked about the connection between Taizé-style prayer and social justice, she was unaware that there is one, but was excited by the possibility of introducing it, perhaps at the Gubbio sites, for the way in which it might bring together those who are in need of housing and those who have the resources to help resolve the impact of the city's economic disparity.

My conversations with Millennials about their experiences of Taizé prayer indicate that the liturgy feeds them spiritually and provides a sense of community with those gathered in the chapel but does not naturally extend to engagement with the world beyond the chapel. That disconnect, I believe is a growing edge for U.S. churches that encourage this form of prayer. In conversation with two Baby Boomers: Maria, who was raised in Rome, and Sophia, a formerly Catholic laywoman who is now a Protestant minister, I realized that there is an important generational difference in their experience of Taizé prayer. When Maria was living in Rome, she became interested in the community at Taizé because the idea of Christians of different denominations living together was unheard of in Italy. When the brothers organized a meeting in Rome in 1982, she got involved because she was active in her parish. The beauty of the prayer prompted her to learn about the community that shaped it, so she took a train to Taizé as a young adult. Over the years she attended international meetings of Taizé in Barcelona, London, and Chennai. She describes the hospitality offered as one of complete openness and tolerance, in part because the setting in Taizé is "uncluttered." However, unlike the experience of the Millennials I interviewed, Maria sees Taizé as necessarily linked to social justice. As she became more involved with Taizé gatherings in her parish, she witnessed Italians whom she believed unlikely to do so, opening their homes to people from all over the world, to total strangers who needed lodging.

The generational differences in participants' experiences of this form of contemplative prayer are striking. Since water flows to its lowest point, it makes sense that the hollow place that Taizé fills in for Millennials is the need for silence and safety. For the Baby Boomers and Gen Xers who have lived experiences of sacred silence and are able to carve out pockets of it for themselves, Taizé-style prayer provides an opportunity to reach beyond themselves in a way that creates an experience of community and hospitality. These differences are important pieces of awareness for ministers who are hoping to introduce this form of contemplative prayer to a multigenerational community. What these seekers have in common is their awareness of the need to stop moving so that they might become aware of the Holy Spirit dwelling within them. Taizé-style prayer demonstrates that in a frenetic, noisy world, contemplative practices, countercultural as they are, can have an even greater impact toward creating a prophetic church than they did in the earliest years of Christianity.

b) New Skellig Contemplative Christian Community

Although now an Episcopal priest, Father Vincent Pizzuto was raised as a Roman Catholic. He had long felt the call to priesthood but did not want to live the double life of a Roman Catholic priest in a same-sex relationship. His lifelong connection to sacramental worship led him to seek ordination in the Celtic Christian Church, an ecclesial community that recognizes and respects same-sex relationships and traces its apostolic origins through the Old

Catholic tradition.[24] In 2009 I began attending a small faith community called New Skellig at Father Vincent's home. At that point we gathered as a house church for monthly Eucharistic liturgies that were based largely on the Roman rite. This was a pastoral concession to the large number of Roman Catholics who attended New Skellig. Gradually, however Father Vincent incorporated language and rituals that evoke intimacy between God, humanity, and the members of the ecclesial community, which continue to play an integral role in the Celtic liturgy designed by Father Vincent. He encouraged the members, all of whom were Roman Catholic, some of whom were gay men, to continue to worship at their "anchor" parishes, but to attend the monthly Celtic rite of New Skellig at the small house church in Marin County, CA.

The community's demographic as well as his own ecclesial background resulted in Father Vincent's decision to base the liturgy on the structure of the familiar Roman rite. However, because he had flexibility as a member of the Celtic Christian Church, the celebration included parts that would complement the intimate nature of the house liturgy, such as each-to-each Communion around the dining room table using homemade bread, and the practice of bowing to one another after Communion, a ritualized the link between Christ present in the community and the consecrated bread and wine. In a way that reflected the intimate nature of the meal shared at the Last Supper, the New Skellig house liturgy included a shared meal, followed by the Third Hour: a discussion on some aspect of contemplative spirituality. In 2012 he fully revised the Celtic liturgy, incorporating features of the seventh-century Gallican rite as well as more modern adaptations and influences of Celtic liturgical practices. This was largely a result of the fact that the community had expanded to include members of other Christian denominations from Orthodox, Episcopal, Roman Catholic, and Reformed traditions. Having physically outgrown the intimate environment of Father Vincent's home, the community found a welcoming space at St. John's Episcopal Church in Ross, CA, where the liturgy was held on the first Saturday of the month as a Vigil Mass. There were growing pains and a sense of loss as the community adapted to the new, more institutional setting. For example, we began to gather around the altar rather than the dining room table, and the church seemed dark compared with the sun-soaked living room among the hills in which the house church was nestled. But the move to St. John's was precipitated by a dialogue that Father Vincent had begun with the Episcopal Church to be received as a priest and to have New Skellig received as a congregation. The community of St. John's officially sponsored Father Vincent and New Skellig as a whole. On December 6, 2014, both Father Vincent and the New Skellig community were received into the Episcopal Church under the authority of then Presiding Bishop Katharine Jefferts Schori at Grace Cathedral in San Francisco.

Now fully received into the Episcopal Church, Father Vincent was appointed to another congregation, St. Columba's Episcopal Church and Retreat House in Inverness, CA, on January 1, 2017. Since that time Father Vincent has been working to rebuild what was a dwindling ecclesial congregation and to develop his vision for the creation of a center for contemplative Christianity in West Marin. During a recent sabbatical I was fortunate to be able to spend many weekends, including several special occasions, with the now-thriving community at St. Columba's. I was present for the first jointly celebrated liturgy of the Celtic community of New Skellig and St. Columba's. I also attended Father Vincent's formal installation as Vicar of St. Columba's, and his wedding to his partner of fifteen years. The evolving programs and renewed liturgical life at St. Columba's have cultivated a spiritual renaissance. Many seekers from West Marin have noted that "until recently, in West Marin you could be anything but Christian." The growing attendance at St. Columba's is also indicative of the shifting experience of the mission.[25] When Father Vincent began ministering at St. Columba's there were merely seven registered parishioners. By comparison, the average Sunday attendance at the principal Sunday Eucharist in early 2017 was in the low to mid-twenties. After a year and a half, the church was seeing a significant uptick both in members and in church attendance. As of March 2019, there were fifty-eight registered parishioners, with about forty people attending the main liturgy on Sunday. The average weekly attendance at the inaugural contemplative workshop series also drew a weekly attendance of just over forty people, most of whom had been spiritually underserved. Thirty of the participants had not previously been connected to St. Columba's or New Skellig.

Over the course of four workshops, Father Vincent had conversations with roughly twenty participants. He described them as spiritual seekers who were attracted to contemplative spirituality and especially appreciated learning about it within a Christian context. Many of those who attended came with backgrounds in Hinduism, Buddhism, and other spiritual traditions, but reported that what Father Vincent was presenting about contemplative prayer resonated deeply with them. The translation process that was taking place was one of interspiritual learning. For example, visitors' familiarity with meditation provided the comfort level they needed in order to participate in a meditation "sit," in which the community focuses on a gospel passage, image, or Christian theological concept. They had a reference point for the experience of resting in the Holy Spirit. A significant number of those who attended the inaugural contemplative workshops experienced a new sense of connection to Christianity in discovering its long and rich tradition of reverencing the sacredness of creation and learning of its own history of attentiveness to contemplative silence.

The New Skellig community has always been small, with around twenty participants on a given day over the years. The majority are Gen Xers and Baby Boomers. In reflecting on Millennials' consciousness-altering experiences of silence through practices such as Taizé prayer, Centering Prayer, and walking meditation, I have been wondering about the sparse participation among Millennials at New Skellig. I am aware that one of the reasons is the practical issue of transportation. Some who have attended over the years have been Father Vincent's students from the University of San Francisco, which is a Catholic institution. Others attended while they were students but left the area after graduation. Those who came were able to carpool across the Golden Gate Bridge to the various gathering points, which are between seventeen and forty-one miles from the university. Some students were able to arrange for rides with other members. Part of what makes New Skellig so special is the opportunity to leave the city behind, yet the distance from the university is also a hindrance to student attendance. Keeping this in mind, I asked some New Skelligers, including the three Millennials who attend regularly, to help me understand what is special for them about New Skellig and why they make the effort to be present each month.

Conversations with New Skelligers

Jerry is a middle-aged man who has been a member of New Skellig since 2014. A relative newcomer, he brings a colorful background. With degrees in Divinity and Anthropology, he sees New Skellig as "an opportunity to evangelize the New Agers and to be evangelically contemplative." He believes that, for its embodied repetitiveness and the way in which it transcends intellectual arguments, liturgy can appeal to postmodernists. In fact, what appeals to Jerry most about the New Skellig liturgy is the chanting and singing: "When we're all breathing together, we become one. It trains people's nervous systems together." Jerry has explored Zen Buddhism and appreciates the way in which it emphasizes the importance of changing perspectives. Once he realized that Christianity also embraces the importance of *metanoia*, he recognized that "Christianity is the only religion big enough to hold my spiritual quest." Far from a syncretist, Jerry wants each wisdom tradition to celebrate its radical distinctiveness from the others, noting that "the union of opposites is our work." When asked what he thinks it would take to get Millennials involved with New Skellig, he agreed that transportation might be the major hurdle.

Erica is in her early twenties. She was raised in a household that attended either the Pentecostal or Catholic Church, depending on what was happening in her family. When asked to describe what drew her to New Skellig and led her to return regularly throughout her four years of college, she highlighted what she described as the intimacy of Father Vincent's home. She especially loved the smell of bread in the oven, the gentle light and fresh air filtering through the trees, and the joyful birdsongs. Unlike what she described as "a hyper-emotional Pentecostal or Catholic Charismatic Renewal liturgy," she found New Skellig to be informal yet solemn. She said: "During a house liturgy people can drop things, even the Communion bread, and oh well." Noting that she used to hate hugging strangers, she experienced it as a very human and humanizing community. New Skellig helped her to begin to trust her heart as much as her head and not to be so uptight. "Not a speaking-in-tongues, fainting type of person," Erica enjoyed the opportunity to ask questions and have a conversation during the third part of the celebration. In a region in which it is very expensive to own a car, Erica believes that if it were geographically more accessible, Millennials would enjoy the experience, especially the twenty-minute silent "sit" before the discussion. She noted that "social media enables you to mind someone else's business rather than your own" and that the ability to be silent is both healthy and largely unfamiliar among her peers. Her experience of continual noise and frazzled nerves is consistent with what I learned from each of the Millennials I interviewed from the Taizé prayer retreat.

With the shift to St. John's church in Ross, Erica experienced what she described as a loss. For example, she found the sanctuary to be dark compared with Father Vincent's house, and the size, cavernous compared with his cozy living room. With the move to St. Columba's in Inverness, she named two things that she believes the community still needs to work on: cultural diversity and the balance between Bible study and liturgy. As an undergraduate she experienced New Skellig as having a distinct focus on Scripture and that the move to St. John's and St. Columba's included an emphasis on contemplative worship. She recognizes that there are other things about the liturgy at St. Columba's that could simply be growing pains, or perhaps will become a permanent culture clash. For example, she noted that while an earlier, more formal version of herself would have loved the altar rail at St. Columba's, "The New Skellig way is to rip out the altar rail and pass the [Communion] plate." Having attended many liturgies with Erica in all three settings, it seems to me that she enters as fully as possible into whichever experience presents itself and is open to being shaped by God and community. Erica's willingness to try new liturgical forms and practices is a characteristic strength that Millennials bring to faith communities. In reflecting on her experience of New Skellig, she said that she believes its gift is the way in which it can teach her peers how to sit in silence with God, themselves, and one another.

Rose is an Older Millennial. She is a is a cradle Catholic whose parents now attend an Episcopal Church and is a former leader in the Catholic

Worker movement and the Jesuit Volunteer Corps (JVC). She was unfamiliar with New Skellig until the community moved to St. Columba's. She went not because she had a strong desire to experience New Skellig but because her mother asked her to help with the music. As a newcomer it was clear to her that the two groups were experiencing the growing pains of integration. After about a year in this Episcopal setting, Rose was becoming accustomed to the idea that "you don't have to go to a Catholic Mass for it to count [as church]." She had experienced more participatory Catholic Masses through the Catholic Worker and JVC and was glad to see that lay participation was significant at New Skellig. She finds the greater focus on contemplation, nature, and the environment attractive, yet some of the language pertaining to cosmic Christianity is unfamiliar. She said that she is trying not to think about it in terms of something "out there" but as a new experience. Rose experiences the physical touch involved with the anointing and blessing as a special moment. She believes that with their difficulty getting a handle on their own busyness, framing New Skellig as a half-day retreat rather than a burden would be helpful in attracting Millennials.

Rose also enjoys the silent meditation but finds it challenging to do it between the lunch and the group discussion in the Third Hour. She now spends a full ten minutes trying to get settled, whereas when the meditation was integrated with the liturgy she was already settled. She experiences people's willingness to be open and vulnerable about their frustrations and sorrows as a gift and feels less like an outsider each month. She also noted that it is difficult for her to be vulnerable because her parents are present for both the liturgy and the Third Hour. On a practical level the integration with a new community has been difficult. No one ever left a New Skellig celebration hungry. However, Rose is a vegetarian. Sometimes she does not find what she needs at lunch because the established community at St. Columba's approaches the "coffee hour" in a way that is very different from the shared meal celebrated by New Skellig. She sees this issue as a growing pain as the two communities become integrated. Looking down the road five years, Rose hopes that the group will include others who are looking for this type of faith community but also noted that she would not want it to grow too much. Recognizing that the New Skellig community includes people with a wide array of views and a willingness to explore other ways of praying and thinking, she hopes to see more integration and that the St. Columba community will grow to love New Skellig for what it is: In Father Vincent's words: "It is contemplative leaven for the wider church."

Rachel is a twenty-something cradle Catholic who learned about New Skellig during her senior year while taking a course with Father Vincent called Christian Contemplative Practice. Her first experience of the house church was in a member's living room in San Francisco. She shared Rose's initial concern that attending New Skellig on Sunday would not meet her Catholic Sunday obligation. However, from the first liturgy her fear was assuaged by what she described as an intimate, meaningful experience of Christ in community. She describes a New Skellig Eucharist as an experience of *Kairos*, especially each-to-each Communion: holding the bread for more than two seconds, remembering who passed it to you and what it felt like in your hand. During that period of her life she had a part-time job as a sacristan. The contrast between a traditional Roman Catholic liturgy and the New Skellig house liturgy made her begin to feel like she was being paid to attend Mass. She was frustrated by her growing awareness that good theology is largely inaccessible to the people in the pews, and that she had to participate in the academic environment of the Third Hour discussions in order to learn about the Catholic tradition.

Since most of the liturgies are held in Marin, before she had a car Rachel would receive a ride from various members. She soon felt that church was not just about the community gathered for prayer but began with the carpool itself. This is one way to address the concern she shared with Rose about transportation being an obstacle to Millennials. Not only did she courageously acknowledge her need for help in this way, the community graciously and regularly reached out to her. The diverse spiritual practices and backgrounds of people who gave her a ride helped her understand ecumenism in a real way. In getting to know people who might otherwise have remained anonymous faces in the pews, she learned that a diverse faith community requires a willingness to hold many perspectives on God in creative tension. This was a shift from her previous approach to the Eucharist, which she saw herself "patrolling" in her adolescence. Sustained relationships in the New Skellig community taught her that "the Eucharist is out there for the taking, not an object to be policed."

When New Skellig was preparing to be received into the Episcopal Church, the governing body of the General Convention asked not only Father Vincent to speak as vicar, but a member, as well. Rachel described New Skellig through an analogy involving the five senses. These are excerpts from her speech to the General Convention:

> I often tell family and friends that New Skellig gives me a taste and a glimpse of the kingdom of God. The first glimpse is when we are celebrating our liturgy together. . . . I can't help but look around the room and see that our community is made up of different ages, backgrounds, and people with various life experiences who come together to be contemplatives in a world of action, centered in Christ. I think to myself: "This must be what the kingdom of God looks like." After the liturgy, a shared meal is prepared by fellow community members. We gather around the table sharing food and the fellowship of one another. The food always tastes amazing and I can't help but think that it's because we share the

fruits of our labor and follow Jesus' example by breaking bread together. Again, I say to myself, "This must be what the kingdom of God tastes like." In the final part of our gathering, we have theological discussion and faith sharing. This is where we educate our hearts and minds and get a better understanding of our Christian faith. I have learned how to be a contemplative listener during these discussions. I have heard myself and others grapple at times with our faith and pose difficult questions. But I am always comfortable doing so because I feel that I have much to learn from my fellow New Skellig members. "This must be what the kingdom of God sounds like."

Rachel's testimony to those who would welcome New Skellig into the Episcopal fold emphasizes the egalitarian nature of the liturgies. While Father Vincent is the presider, he leads without lording his authority over the members. Between the lines of Rachel's speech are other important facets of the celebration: the presider also bakes the bread that feeds the community. He greets each person by name and makes eye contact as communicants receive the Eucharist. Each member exchanges the sign of peace with everyone present, no matter how long it takes. Protracted silence during the Third Hour is cherished rather than avoided. Everyone's thoughts, emotions, and gestures are received rather than judged. New Skellig is a contemporary example of *Kairos*: time as it is meant to be spent; time blessed by the Holy Spirit and recognized as such by the community.

Both Rose and Rachel recognize that the St. Columba's and New Skellig communities are working to adjust to one another. Rachel noted that it is painful to see New Skelligers struggle with a new space and liturgical format, and that it must be difficult for St. Columba's regular parishioners to have to accommodate monthly visitors whose liturgy is unfamiliar to them. During New Skellig's inaugural liturgy at St. Columba's we watched as seven people walked out rather than receive a blessing during the *Kyrie*. Rachel reported that since then, some who are uncomfortable with the New Skellig Celtic rite have stopped just short of calling the liturgy witchcraft for the use of *Bishop Tírechán's Creed*, along with the simple clay chalice and paten that were made for New Skellig liturgies. The inevitable changes that New Skelligers have experienced with the move to St. Columba's have brought back for Rachel some of the denominational divides that she thought she left behind when she made a home in the New Skellig house church. However, aware of the developmental nature of the Catholic tradition, Rachel knows that over time a third incarnation of New Skellig will emerge that fits within the blueprint of the Episcopal Church that has become its new home. New Skellig is an ever-evolving Christian community. Its future, as well as that of St. Columba's, depends on the full embrace of a both/and ecclesiology.

Ecclesial Hospitality

Through my own participation in New Skellig, along with Rose, Erica, and Rachel, I understand the desire to maintain one's denominational affiliation while also needing a liturgical celebration that provides greater spiritual nourishment, and a more collaborative ecclesial model. Some Roman Catholic communities are bold and creative in liturgical planning, yet still color within the lines drawn by canon law. For example, there are parishes, monasteries, and religious communities that incorporate liturgical dance, readings in multiple languages, gender-inclusive language wherever it is reasonable, petitions spoken by the community, homemade bread for Communion, and Eucharist administered each-to-each. These variances provide enough warmth to sustain some Roman Catholic communities. However, for some individuals who are seeking a substantively egalitarian ecclesial model, New Skellig provides a spiritual home. Its solemn liturgy safeguards against a theological mash-up yet also manifests a contemporary Episcopal ecclesiology by practicing intercommunion. New Skellig makes it possible for Roman Catholics to maintain their ecclesial identity while also participating in a Catholic community that has both a divergent history and a nearly identical sacramental theology. Here I will explore several of the unique, engaging characteristics of the New Skellig liturgy.

The first words spoken by both the presider and the community are *Beannaim Chriost ionat!* (I greet Christ in you!).[26] By using language and gestures that engage the senses, the New Skellig rite cultivates intimacy between individual believers, Christ, and the cosmos. The opening chant conveys this expansive vision. I see the faces and stories of the guests at Gubbio as the community prays for awareness of "Christ in quiet, Christ in danger . . . Christ in mouth of friend and stranger." When I met with guests the day after the monthly New Skellig celebration, I was more aware of who was sleeping, who was anxious, sad, angry, or afraid. The imprint of the chant established continuity between the sacred and the "profane," helping me find an entry point with those who had recently lost their housing and were feeling alone. Sitting at the *bema*, mingling in the courtyard, keeping vigil as the guests slept, Christ was "behind, before, beside and beneath me."[27]

Recited immediately following the Nicene Creed, Bishop Tírechán's Creed (c. 670) proclaims that "Our God is the God of all, the God of heaven and earth, the God of the sea and rivers, the God of the sun and moon, the God of all the heavenly bodies, the God of the lofty mountains, the God of the lowly valleys." Every feature of every planet, each body of water, every animal, plant and the light that nourishes them: no one and nothing is excluded from God's embrace. In reciting those words, it is impossible for a Roman Catholic to miss the contrast between this radically inclusive vision and the limiting revision made to the Roman missal by the U.S. bishops in 2012. The Latin phrase "*pro multos*" from the Eucharistic prayer, which had previously been translated as "the many" was changed to "many," implying that Christ died only for some. "The many" signified an open-ended multitude, an assembly beyond the limits of our imagination, being welcomed home by God. The revised version of the prayer evokes not an image of divine generosity but of the "puny, vindictive God" called out by Father Greg Boyle.[28] The faith professed by Bishop Tírechán is all-encompassing. Incorporating prayers for the bishop of Rome, the archbishop of Canterbury, the ecumenical patriarch of Constantinople, and the presiding bishop of the Episcopal Church, as well as the local Episcopal bishop, the New Skellig liturgy is ecumenically oriented.

As we learned from the travelogue of Rabban Sauma in chapter 1, where there is respect and the inclusion of the other in the Eucharist, Christ is tangibly present in the resulting communion between people. St. Augustine, who laid the theological foundation for much of both the Roman and the Anglican traditions, believed that the elements on the altar cannot be separated from the community that is gathered and, I would add, remembered in prayer. For reasons having to do with the Roman Catholic interpretation of the claim that the bishop of Rome is *primus inter pares*, "first among equals," today the churches of the Anglican communion are not formally in communion with the bishop of Rome. However, by the inclusion of the pope in the Memorial Acclamation as well as the sacramental theology of New Skellig, those who participate in this Celtic liturgy are, through their inclusivity and their Eucharistic theology, in communion with Rome. How Roman Catholic bishops would see their relationships to New Skellig is another matter. Forgiveness between friends is not always mutual. Though for historical reasons it is not ritually Roman, the Episcopal Church makes the case that it is fully Catholic. As members of the denomination that is much more reticent to practice intercommunion, Roman Catholics must ask ourselves whether the now-ancient, interpersonal breach between Henry VIII and Pope Paul III should continue to dampen our mutual good will despite our shared sacramental theology. It seems that we have reached a saturation point in our conversation about these issues. Just as water is lost when it streams out of a soaked sponge, the longer we behave as if we are divided, the longer we continue to waste precious human resources, especially our capacity for trust and creativity. Ideally both churches would recognize that outsized egos led to the schism between Rome, the Tudor king and their successors. Whether in a family or between unrelated individuals, after a suitable period of discernment, people who are spiritually mature choose to stop brooding so that they can be reconciled. Having engaged in the theological discernment necessary to understand the possibility of reconciliation, we actively choose with each passing day to continue remain alienated from our fellow Christians. What makes New Skellig such a special community is the way in which relationships and prayer experiences are negotiated in full recognition of differences. It would be inauthentic to minimize the messiness of the relationships. A Roman Catholic deacon who was an early member of New Skellig once said in a homily: "It's better to be compassionate and welcoming than religiously right." The members of New Skellig have a fundamental disposition toward hospitality and deep listening.

Interspirituality as a Verb

As one who identifies as fully, but not only, Roman Catholic, and has participated unreservedly in the sacramental life of New Skellig over the course of a decade, I envision an ecumenical, interspiritual practice as the building material for the bridge that will eventually be built between religious institutions. As Barbara Brown Taylor noted, it is more important to believe in the bridge than the gorge.[29] The way in which the mission of New Skellig has unfolded reminds me of the story of the Semmering Railway in the Austrian Alps. The tracks were built before there was a locomotive that could manage the structure's gradient and turning radius. The engineers undertook the challenge of building tracks that would incorporate dozens of tunnels, bridges, and viaducts. Not only did they take technical risks in building the railway, they ensured that their tracks would complement the natural environment. The engineers faced challenges and even risked failure in proposing a design that would result in the high-tech locomotive. Working toward a goal was at that point beyond their experience, they summoned courage and creativity.

Like the engineers and builders in the Austrian Alps, church leaders are known to puzzle over perceived obstacles to Christian unity: some are "technical" challenges such as flexibility around the use of liturgical rites and the lectionary cycle, and some are generated by fear of what they see as monumental shifts, such as the ordination of women, clerical marriage, and marriage equality. One thing is certain: sixty years after the initial rapprochement between Roman Catholics and groups of Protestants who hold similar sacramental theologies to our own, it is no longer enough to "talk about talking about" Christian unity. We have the historical perspective and theological expertise necessary to enter with courage into a spiritual collaboration, by living and praying together as the one Body of Christ. As we have seen, the tables in chapter 2 provide tools for Christians to learn about the gospel from people of other faiths. If we can benefit from insights about Christianity from people of other faiths, how much more straightforward should this process be among Christians of various denominations?

Unlike the challenges of keeping a high-velocity train from falling into a gorge, our engineers and builders do not have to participate in this project with consensus about every detail. Practices such as intercommunion and other expressions of Christian unity are human processes. They are not mechanical engineering experiments, and a significant margin of error is reasonable. As I have seen and experienced through the ecumenical community of New Skellig, a spiritual rapprochement between courageous Christians will foster unity between the Episcopal and the Roman Catholic churches in real and unforeseeable ways.

Contemplative Inscape: Reframing Monasticism

While there are times when it is possible to retreat to a monastic setting, as a lifestyle, traditional monasticism has never been an option for most people. New Monasticism focuses on spiritual transformation in everyday life, a fitting interpretation of monastic values for the Third Millennium. Even the reluctant surrender of certainty and ego needs can transform ordinary experiences into mystical ones. A contemporary interpretation of a life of simplicity and prayer, New Monasticism translates for the twenty-first century the instruction from chapter fifty-three of the *Rule of Saint Benedict* to receive guests as one would receive Christ, beginning with communal prayer. Because twenty-first-century life is anything but simple, New Monasticism is a risky countercultural commitment. It has heightened my awareness that "the moral dimension of the spiritual journey has nothing to do with external rules and regulations, but with a fundamental, radical reorientation of the person's inner commitment to be established permanently and concretely in love and compassion."[30] In the next section I take a risk in illustrating the transformation of one of my most mundane realities into a bizarre, life-altering, and, at times, vexing journey with the little lioness in my living room. I have chosen to do so because I believe it highlights an important feature of the map drawn by new monastics: the intersection of the sacred and the profane. There are others who are working to unite those domains, as well. In 2009 Glennon Doyle, Christian blogger, author, philanthropist, and activist, began what I would describe as a public ministry in the spirit of New Monasticism. Her organization is called *Momastery*. While today her work focuses more on activism on behalf of women and children, she began as a blogger who wrote about her awareness of the importance of vulnerability through her history of addiction. In *Love Warrior: A Memoir*, Doyle describes her frustration with motherhood: "From dawn to dusk and then through the night, I am reacting, responding, juggling and dripping with children."[31] She goes on to share the internal dialogue she had when her marriage had reached the boiling point. Her husband would come home from a busy day at the office and ask how her day was. She writes:

How was my day? It was the best of times and the worst of times. I was both lonely and never alone. I was simultaneously bored out of my skull and completely overwhelmed. I was saturated with touch—desperate to get the baby off of me and the second I put her down I yearned to smell her sweet skin again. This day required more than I am physically and emotionally capable of, while requiring nothing from my brain. I had thoughts today, ideas, real things to say and no one to hear them.[32]

My CPE supervisor's mantra: "How can we help people get out of their own way?" permeates young adults' capacity to cultivate mature spiritual lives. They are not deficient adolescents in need of educational supplements, but curious people who can develop a *habitus* of spiritual and intellectual exploration. When they ask whether they are "doing it right" I assure them that everyone who has a prayer/meditation practice of some kind knows how difficult it is to measure spiritual growth: that one never knows that she or he has arrived at the destination because it does not exist. Rather than attempt to define spiritual maturity, I offer my students the image of a timeline with shifting intervals, distinguishing between two conceptual frameworks: *Kairos* and *chronos*. Alexander Schmemann describes *Kairos* as time as it is meant to be experienced. *Chronos*, on the other hand, is the familiar clock consisting of hours, minutes, and seconds, often experienced as a taskmaster. I suggest that when the intervals between experiences of *Kairos* are shorter, and *chronos* holds less of our attention, we are more consistently aware of God's presence. During those interludes, distractions from the Really Real are less frequent: we are calmer, more present, happier, more conscious and more available to give and receive abundantly in relationships. I try to help students reflect on how we might train ourselves to scan the horizon for the glow of God's presence, sifting through the mundane, elongating our experience of *Kairos* and developing an awareness of spiritual opportunities presented by *chronos*. On this side of life there can be no *Kairos* without *chronos*. Every sacred moment occurs within the framework of clock time. When seen through a prism, the refracted light of grace reveals that what we generally recognize as profane also contains what is sacred.

In a pretechnological age, our ancestors in faith were accustomed to focusing on signs of God in creation. At the first sign of an earthquake followed by raging wind, driving rain, a smoky mountain, and a wild fire, on Mt. Sinai Elijah expected to receive a theophany in the form of a mandate. However, God did not emerge in the raging storm as expected, but rather, in a still, small voice (1 Kgs 19:12). Yet even then God did not have Elijah's attention. He was distracted, running for his life in the desert, listening only for what he thought God *ought* to be saying. Yet beyond the noise, danger, and fear, the divine revelation Elijah received on Mt. Horeb manifested as an inaudible voice, reminding us that the God of surprises goes wherever we go, whether we go there willingly or not. She or he speaks in a voice that we might miss if we are not listening with the "ear of the heart."[33] What I describe in the next few pages is the way in which the still, small voice presented itself in one of God's most vulnerable creatures. I am placing this spiritual narrative under the umbrella of the New Monasticism because of the way in which God got my attention. A countercultural decision that cultivated community, compassion, humility, humiliation, and good humor, this commitment required a nearly three-year cycle of action, reflection, and discipline. In a way that is akin to my use of the vignettes in chapter 2 to decontextualize the gospel, here I am decontextualizing Christian monasticism. Whether you find the following section quite new or very familiar, I encourage you to approach it as another tool for reflecting on the scope of your spiritual field of vision. I am aware that this subtle shade of the rainbow is missing from the standard color wheel employed by the church.

LILY B. QUANTZ

In June 2014 my otherwise healthy, highly sociable sixteen-year-old cat, Lily, suddenly stopped eating. It was as if she had suddenly forgotten *how* to eat. I knew her behaviors and tastes intimately so I tried to coax her back into her habit of enjoying certain foods. Even as a kitten, equipped with milk teeth and joie de vivre, that tiny creature relished both her "crackers" (kibble) and soft food from the tuna family. Friends called her "the talking cat" for her habit of echoing the vocal tone of anyone who spoke to her. Lily plugged herself into any and all conversations for sixteen years. But one day, she woke up, looked at her bowl, smelled the contents, and walked away with a blank stare. I understood that cats are often mysterious, but the blank stare worried me. Test after test, and one educated guess after another, the specialists at the university veterinary hospital determined that the cause must be either a brain tumor deep in the primitive part of her brain, or an idiopathic neurological disorder. We tried everything we could think of, including an antidepressant that doubles as an appetite stimulant. The side effect was traumatic for both of us: it failed to trip her hunger awareness and caused her cry and shake like a drug-addicted newborn.

Throughout the testing phase I had been handfeeding Lily with a syringe which, at first, she oddly seemed to enjoy. Without that stopgap she would have starved to death. I knew that Lily was a fighter, and, as I had every reason to expect, she continued to be her sociable, bossy self throughout the summer. I could not see the sense in ending her life just because of a strange behavior and was determined to find a solution. Some people thought I was crazy for resorting to what seemed like a radical remedy, but I knew that I had to ignore the skeptics and critics. I had no idea that the only viable solution would hem me into thirty-three months of a quasi-monastic life. For the rest of the summer and into September I fed Lily with a 10 ml syringe. To minimize the impact on her body and overall comfort, at each feeding I put two newborn bibs around her neck, removing the top bib when it became saturated. Adding to the ridiculousness of the situation, the bibs that were the right size and material were decorated with Disney characters. Once I worked out the mechanics of manipulating two bibs while she reclined in my lap, the major challenge was that the syringes were intended for liquid, not paté. She needed about six ounces of food per day, which meant that I had to repeat the routine every one to two hours from morning till night throughout the rest of the summer. I was losing patience and beginning to resent Lily, but she tolerated the feedings for a full ten weeks. In the eleventh week she began to use her front leg as a baseball bat, knocking the syringe out of my hand. I figured that a cat who had the zest to do that was not only telling me that we needed a new tactic, but that she was still full of life. It was a crazy-making process that often left both of us, and sometimes the walls, floors, and furniture covered in a smelly paté. By September I was at my wit's end.

A friend who lives on a farm with a menagerie of rescue animals had mentioned months earlier that she'd had a feeding tube inserted in her cat's stomach for a brief period during recovery from an illness. I had dismissed that option as an extreme measure, yet with the beginning of the semester came long hours on campus and out of desperation I considered the possibility. I took her to a specialist who explained the PEG (stomach) tube option as well as the technique by which a G-tube is placed directly into the esophagus. The later was described as the safer and more economical model, so that's what we did. After some trial and error, we settled into a routine of feeding two or three times daily, which enabled me to administer the necessary calories, medicine, and geriatric kitty supplements, with minimal interference with my work commitments. Two years later, when I began work on this book, Lily was eighteen and still stable, happy, alert, and opinionated. By then the vet had ruled out a brain tumor because her condition had not changed significantly in two years. However, after thirty-three months of a stable feeding routine, Lily's body began to shut down. To everyone who was trying to be supportive for almost three years, I had explained many times that Lily would have to tell me when she was ready to go and that, until then, the problem was mine alone. On April 3, 2017, Lily told me that she was struggling. The following day we made our final trip to the vet. It was an agonizing decision because, as with many beloved pets and people whose health is failing, Lily was still alert and emotionally present. I could not explain to her what was happening with her body or hear her describe how she felt. I could only respond based on

what I saw: a vulnerable creature whose body was weakening. What follows
is what I learned about myself, Lily, God, and friendship during that intimate,
gratifying, mysterious, and often frustrating chapter of our lives.

Because it forced me to slow down and though I did not seek it out, the
routine that developed revealed my strengths, fears, and other emotions. After
a while I noticed that our three-daily feeding sessions mirrored the monastic
prayer periods that are interlaced with established times for work. Those
regular intervals generated for me a new understanding of time. Because
feeding Lily was a two-handed process that required full, active participation, during those thirty or so minutes I could not surf the web or talk on the
phone. Regardless of what I had to do next or where I had to be shortly, I had
to feed her slowly enough that she was able to keep the food down. Since I
had become accustomed to taking students to a monastery, I was aware that
each feeding lasted approximately the same duration as Lauds, Compline, or
Vespers. I remembered that in a monastery the Psalms correspond to the time
of day. Our mealtime ritual was similarly predictable, with slight variations
depending on the supplements and medicines she received at different times
of day. Like prayer, sometimes the experience was mundane and other times
intimate and gratifying. Whether the experience was rewarding, boring, or
crazy-making, every feeding session was relational. Lily conveyed how she
was feeling and, whether I was conscious of it or not, I'm sure I did, as well.
I often expressed frustration to God and at other times, gratitude, especially
when I was able to settle down and enjoy Lily's sweet personality. With
the help of some intrepid members of my community, every part of me was
engaged in the act of feeding Lily.[34]

Even monastics who have been in religious life for fifty or more years have
reported that one never becomes fully comfortable waking up in the middle of
the night to pray. Lily experienced time in her own way, so it was no surprise
that she awoke me at all hours of the night throughout those years. For all
she knew, sleep and a nap were the same. The sound of her purring loudly
in my ear vibrated like a boat motor and her new habit of drooling evoked
the same annoyance and jarring anxiety I experienced as a hospital chaplain
when the pager would go off in the middle of the night. In place of the chapel
bells to signal the beginning of a prayer period, my signal for Lily to settle in
was *"metteti a sedere"* (have a seat), which prompted her to hop into my lap.
When we had finished, her signal to resume whatever she had been doing was
a kiss on her head and the phrase "all done." As with monastics who must
request permission to spend the night away from the monastery, throughout
those many months, I could not be away from Lily for more than eight hours.
Just as there is no point in arguing with an abbess, I took my direction from
Lily. Though a few people were able to step in to feed her occasionally,
understandably my family and close friends were afraid of something going

wrong with the tube. Being away overnight required significant preparation and, if I had to be gone more than forty-eight hours, for everyone's sake, I had to take her with me.

Ours was a sustained routine for nearly three years, until Lily and God indicated that our journey together on this side of life had come to an end. She had been as dependent on me as we are on God. If I had forgotten about her various needs at any point, she would have died. As it was, our lives were intertwined. We were a community of two, with a wider community that helped support our lifestyle. For much of their history, Benedictine monasteries were meant to be self-supporting, yet no one within those walls lived independently. They survived with the help of community and the grace of God. A few weeks after Lily was freed from her failing body, I had the healing dream that I had asked for. Her brother Tiger, whose death three years earlier had broken both my and Lily's hearts, came to me with his sister. They were happy together, playing and exploring as they had since birth. In seeing their happiness, I was able to enter a new stage in my healing process. Having grown restless in my life with God, suddenly God had my undivided attention. Whether I was asking: "What?!" "Why me?" "How long will this continue?" or thanking God for the opportunity to get to know Lily in a new way, my relationship with God was molecularly reconfigured. Lily helped move me from *chronos* into *Kairos*: time as it is meant to be spent. It took an eight-pound cat who was underfoot for nearly two decades to help me get out of my own way. Humor should be a category of dogma.

As the Benedictine pope Gregory the Great said, love itself is a kind of knowledge.[35] Although Lily's story is unusual among nonhuman animals in that her acute care lasted nearly three years, it has much in common with the palliative care settings in which people work with one another. Without romanticizing the experience of parents who care for children with special needs, including difficulty with verbal communication, the circumstances that shape such experiences of the Really Real bear an opportunity for theological reflection. Perhaps their *Kairos* moments can teach people who do not share their struggles, about kenotic love, and the God of laughter and tears. As the inscape hidden in all we encounter, the God of great surprises calls us to mindfulness; to look more closely when we catch a glimmer of divinity on the horizon, or when it catches us. If the devil is in the details, so, too, is God, often hiding in plain sight. New Monasticism has room for eccentricity. It is rooted in the Benedictine life of discipline and community but makes room for the other variables God places in our lives. I hope that with encouragement, people who are led by the intuition to love, and are open to cultivating their sense of humor, will move unconventional manifestations of love from the periphery, sometimes seen as the realm of wishful thinking, to society's collective center of wisdom.

NOTES

1. R. Joseph Owles, *The Didache: The Teaching of the Twelve Apostles* (Create Space Independent Publishing, 2019), 8.3, 15.

2. Ibid.

3. The Roman Forum was the marketplace and civic center in ancient Rome.

4. For *prime* see, for example, Psalms 10, 13; *terce*: 118, 120 for victory and deliverance; *vespers*: Psalms 134 protection during the night; *compline* Psalms 4 recognition of human frailty.

5. Given the interspiritual focus of this book, it is interesting that early Muslims inherited from Christians the practice of prayer at regular intervals throughout the day, which for lay Christians is now uncommon.

6. Peter Damian, "Contra philargyriam et munerum cupiditatem," (ch. 7), *Patrologia Latina*, 145, 540.

7. See also Norman Tanner and Sethina Watson, "Least of the Laity: the Minimum Requirements for a Medieval Christian," *Journal of Medieval History* 32 (2006), 400.

8. Ibid. 400–401.

9. Ibid. 405.

10. J. L. Gonzalez Balado, *The Story of Taizé*, 3rd ed. (Oxford: Mowbray, 1988), 18–19.

11. "The Beginnings," http://www.taize.fr/en_article6526.html (accessed March 29, 2019).

12. Balado, *The Story of Taizé*, 24–25.

13. CELAM (Consejo Episcopal Latinoamericano) is the Roman Catholic Bishops' Conference of Latin America.

14. Balado, *The Story of Taizé*, 40–41.

15. https://www.mercyhousing.org/about (accessed June 1, 2018).

16. Interview with Sister Patsy Harney, RSM. June 11, 2018.

17. Sister Judy Carle, "Sisters and Millennials, Kindred Souls," in *¡Viva Mercy!. Bimonthly Publication for Sisters, Associates and Companions of the Sisters of Mercy of the Americas* (May–June 2018), 13–15.

18. https://www.nytimes.com/2019/05/31/style/milliennial-nuns-spiritual-quest.html.

19. Ibid.

20. This apt description was offered by Dr. Janine Langan in a course called *The Christian Imagination* at the University of St. Michael's College (Toronto) in 1999–2000.

21. https://www.sistersofmercy.org/about-us/mission-values/ (accessed March 29, 2019).

22. Interview with Sister Suzanne Toolan, RSM at Mercy Center, Burlingame CA, April 5, 2018.

23. Retreat: "Inexhaustible Joy." Burlingame, CA: Mercy Center, May 19, 2018.

24. The Celtic Christian Church is historically linked both with the Old Catholics and with the Independent Catholics of South America through Bishop Duarte Costa.

25. In the Episcopal Church a mission differs from a parish. It is a congregation that is no longer able to sustain a full-time priest as rector and is thus placed directly under the auspices of the bishop, who provides support by appointing a vicar to serve the community.

26. The link to the rite of New Skellig can be found on the community's website. https://www.stcolumbasinverness.org/new-skellig.

27. All four of these terms are included in the opening chant. The words are found in the Prayer of Protection, sometimes called *The Deer's Cry* or the *Lorica of Saint Patrick*, who is believed to have lived from 385–461.

28. Boyle, *Barking to the Choir: The Power of Radical Kinship* (New York: Simon and Schuster, 2017), 2.

29. Barbara Brown Taylor, *The Preaching Life* (Rowman & Littlefield Publishers, Inc., 1993), 100.

30. McEntee and Bucko, *The New Monasticism*, 176.

31. Glennon Doyle, *Love Warrior: A Memoir* (New York: Flatiron Books, 2016), 106.

32. Doyle, *Love Warrior*, 107.

33. *Rule of St. Benedict*, line 1 of the "Prologue."

34. I am especially grateful to Judy Dugan, Iulia Istrate and Max Hetherington for their help with Lily during our "time of troubles."

35. Pope Gregory the Great, *Homilia in Evangelium*, 27.4 (PL 76, 1207): *"amor ipse notita est."*

Conclusion

Welcome Home

Most organizations can learn something from the circus. Sharing attributes of both a cavernous cathedral and a circus tent, the temple at Burning Man and the event's many side-show-like camps, provide opportunities for the church to do its holy work, joyfully. Wisdom borne of circus culture includes the fact that everyone is welcome under the big top. Best practices as well as centuries of trial and error in the circus industry can help the church shift its thinking around hospitality. For example, in the early days of U.S. American circuses, fights broke out almost daily but gradually became more civilized. Fortunately, the church no longer tries to justify the violence of the Crusades, yet we have work to do in order to become a more civilized church, one that is welcoming and offers forms of healing that meet the needs of the *polis* (community). As the circus historian Robert Thompson noted, "The emotional physics of the world did not apply under the big top. The circus was a topsy-turvy world. It was about possibility. It was a flip-flop. It was transgressional. And it was loud, and it was colorful, and it was beautiful. It was kind of a pure version of reality. Something that's stripped down to its most elemental parts."[1] Ringmaster Johnathan Lee Iverson described it this way: "There's nothing like a circus. There's nothing in the world like it. You cannot come to a circus and still believe as you previously did. Circus is a peek into what we could be, how great we could be, how beautiful our world could be. It's about making your own miracles, conjuring your own miracles. We're coming for the transcendent."

Some will recoil at the term "conjuring" for its association with sorcery and witchcraft. Since the analogical imagination does not seek one-to-one correlations, perhaps religious people can find in Iverson's description an apt corollary. A substitute for "conjuring your own miracles" might be "praying for the grace needed in order to serve when we would really prefer to sleep, and then doing it." One need only think of the sometimes-exploited performers, whose talents were featured in the early years of the circus, to recognize that, despite what could include a sketchy subculture, circuses were communities that welcomed people who were marginalized. Abused people who had nowhere else to go and were seeking something more literally ran away from home and joined the circus, where they found a sense of place. For the many European circus performers who were at least nominally Christian, the connection to the gospel, if not to the church, must have been apparent.

The ecclesial communities we have explored are legitimate, sponsored ministries. They are also circus-like to greater or lesser extents. Perhaps most importantly, both the church and the circus are human institutions that have been impacted by the tendency toward sin. Wherever sin is pursued, grace is also present. A poetic reminder that the church is an ever-changing institution, St. Peter's Basilica was built on the land that once included the Circus of Nero and a neighboring cemetery. In order to entertain Roman citizens and maintain dominance, Peter and other Christians were tortured and died there upon the order of the government. They were buried on the spot, which became the spiritual and judicial center of what developed into the Roman Catholic Church. The church that was once persecuted became a refuge for many as well as a source of suffering for those who have been marginalized. The purpose of a modern circus is to delight, not through torture as in ancient Rome, but by exposing guests to a world of possibilities. A church that flourished despite tremendous hardship and suffering in the Circus of Nero can use the model of hospitality cultivated by the modern circus to welcome anew those who, like Peter and other Christians in their own day, are treated harshly by contemporary authorities. "Behold I am making all things new" (Rev. 21:5).

The ecclesial communities at Burning Man, The Gubbio Project, the sitcom-in-the-making at St. Columba's in Inverness, and even the theatricality of Taizé Prayer as well as the inspired "foolishness" of the Nuns and Nones experiment hosted by the Sisters of Mercy in Burlingame all make the same point: that the church is an ongoing human performance. It is not a Renaissance painting that should be kept dust-free. In an 1856 review of a circus he attended in Brooklyn, Walt Whitman wrote: "A circus performer is the other half of a college professor."[2] His point was that without reaching beyond our tendencies to learn only from cerebral knowledge, we miss the wisdom received through body and soul. Published in 2006 in *Inside Higher Ed*, Marc Zimmer, a Chemistry professor at Connecticut College wrote an article called "Life in the Circus" about the theatrical environment of the classroom experience.[3] He examines it from various angles: the audience, the lion tamer and the ringmaster, the trapeze artist, the clown, pyrotechnics, the illusionist, and the signature act. He reflects on the importance of knowing one's limits, taking calculated risks, ensuring audience participation and attending to feedback. The church has in its history models, paradigms, enduring doctrines, practices, as well as ample data about what is and is not feeding the people of God. It seems to me that our task in the twenty-first century is to focus on the elements that educate the mind and heart, which requires audience participation, so that seekers might experience the transcendent.

This book was conceived through the spirit of Vatican II, which continues to guide my own faith formation. One goal has been to deepen our understanding of the dignity of and serendipity between the world's great wisdom traditions. The Council introduced this conviction to the Roman Catholic Church in *Nostra Aetate* and *Unitatis Redintegratio.* With their distinct *foci,* these documents signal the still relatively new commitment on the part of the Roman Catholic Church to adjust its centuries-old view of itself as the one true Church outside of which there is no salvation. The participation and leadership of lay ministers in all four of the contemporary movements illustrated in this study are consistent with a key insight offered at Vatican II regarding the centrality of the laity. The council affirmed that laypeople "are called in a special way to make the church present and operative in those places and circumstances where only through them can it become the salt of the earth."[4]

Vatican II did not indicate that the missionary work of the laity moves only from the top, down. Rather, having experienced those hard-to-reach "places and circumstances," the laity can and should return to the ecclesiastical decision makers to share with them the various ways in which the salt that the laypeople offer the world *as church* can make the spiritual food that is regulated by the clergy more interesting and nutritious. Some might argue that the salt provided by the church is also a preservative: of doctrine, traditions, practices, and customs. Surely this is accurate, however, too much salt makes food unpalatable. Also, chefs do not work in isolation: they collaborate in creating recipes that are both healthy and enjoyable. When the food is no longer serving its purpose, they rely on their imaginations and collaborate on new ways to use time-tested ingredients, as well as new ingredients that reflect a new generation of tastes. Celebrating Eucharist beyond the traditional church walls, Christians of different denominations living as if we were in full communion by celebrating the Eucharist together, expanding our understanding of the efficacy of grace through lay ministry are all examples of new recipes that offer thanks to God for beloved ingredients.

As I noted in the Introduction, this book is for graduate students who are just beginning their careers in professional ministry, as well as theologians and pastors who are more established in their fields. By illustrating key doctrinal points from historical perspective, such as enduring, medieval Eucharistic theology and beautifully patinated ancient Christology as well as pastoral approaches to hospitality through visionaries like St. Francis, I have sought to ground contemporary expressions and applications of those historical principles and exemplars.

By illustrating the relationship between the healing work of the priest at the Asclepion, the link between pre-Christian and Christian priesthood, and the priestly work unfolding at Burning Man and The Gubbio Project, I have tried to clear a path for Christians who are willing and prepared to become more hospitable toward those who are painfully alienated from the church. At Burning Man there is a common saying for new arrivals: "Welcome home." While there are rules governing civic responsibility in Black Rock City, everyone is welcome. Since what the church has done before it can do again,[5] I hope to empower decision makers who are custodians of the Christian tradition to throw open the doors and windows, and invite people in who have repeatedly received the message that they are unwelcome, unworthy, misfits, or oddballs, to find rest in the church.

Around the time of the Summer of Love, the award-winning photographer John Marshall captured a bit of graffiti scrawled on a wall in San Francisco's Haight-Ashbury district. Along with an acronym for the word "hippie," the inscription says: "I know you believe you understand what you think I said, but I am not sure you realize that what you heard is not what I meant." I have offered numerous examples of the importance of honoring plurality in interspiritual dialogue. It is important to underscore the need for people of faith to create safeguards that prevent the easy slippage from plurality into the arena of "hyperpluralism." This misstep does not indicate that there are too many people at the table but rather, that those who are present refuse, or do not know how, to listen to one another. In teaching courses that focus on the art of active listening, such as Personal and Interpersonal Skills in Ministry, I am aware that the most important part of understanding is suspending judgment. Humility reminds us that where the experience of another person is concerned, we must assume that we know nothing. The following is an illustration of how easily this can occur even among people in the same degree program who profess a commitment to interspiritual dialogue.

When I was in graduate school, I was enrolled in a roundtable seminar. The class was comprised of a religiously diverse group of students and a facilitator who had no understanding of her role. As I recall, there was one Quaker, one Buddhist, a Jewish convert to Buddhism, one Swedenborgian, one Hindu, as well as three or four Protestants from several mainline denominations. I was the only Roman Catholic. Ironically, the Quaker, whose tradition honors sacred silence, seized the opportunity to rail against Catholicism, as if I represented the whole church. What was even more frustrating was the group's inability to engage in interspiritual dialogue. Everyone was fighting for airtime because no one believed that we *could* be heard by our classmates. The high-speed chase resulted in a pileup. The guidelines for contemplative listening used by the Sisters of Charity of Leavenworth provide an alternative way to share a roundtable. They emphasize a desire to arrive at new understanding by remaining in the present moment, asking for clarification, allowing time for silence and transparency about hidden assumptions. None of this can be accomplished during rush hour.

I interpret the ecclesiological data from Pew, Lilly, and other organizations as indicators that the twenty-first-century church will only thrive if it becomes increasingly prophetic. The choices are to be an agent of change or to be changed from without. In these chapters I have provided a handful of historical case studies and emerging practices in radical hospitality. Not only does Jesus ask all who call on his name to offer unconditional welcome, this is also a good way to ensure the viability of the church. Roman Catholics across all ecclesiastical strata can benefit from ongoing faith formation regarding our nature and mission. If we are truly Catholic (universal), our "Roman-ness" should reflect rather than engulf universality. Despite the cruelty that also marked the Roman Empire, as an extension of that government, the church's longevity, numbers, power, and wealth are potential resources for prophetic action.

I interviewed Sister Patsy Harney, RSM, during the week in 2018 that the federal government had begun to separate children from asylum-seeking parents who were arriving in significant numbers at the U.S.-Mexico border. Within hours of the breaking news, groups of Sisters had boldly declared the illegality of that practice. That is an example of Roman Catholics using their numbers, stability, and voices to do good on behalf of people they will never meet. In other words, their actions implemented the mandate in Matthew 25 to take care of those who are hungry, thirsty, naked, locked out, or imprisoned. Stories like the welcome extended to Rabban Sauma by Pope Nicholas IV, including the Eucharist they shared despite their theological differences also remind us of our generous history. The Gubbio Project, which practices radical hospitality under very challenging circumstances, is a contemporary example of Catholic (universal) generosity that is supported by Roman Catholic decision makers.

The intra- and interspiritual relationships highlighted in this book bear witness to a spirit of generosity. The contemporary ministerial case studies—The Gubbio Project, the Christian camp at Burning Man, New Skellig Contemplative Christian Community, and MercyWorks—provide examples both of street ministries and contemplative communities that practice radical, relevant inclusiveness in the name of Jesus. The story of Lily B. Quantz is an example of God hiding in plain sight. Each uniquely illustrates the harmonious distinctions within two mainline churches: Roman Catholic and Episcopal. The images of the rainbow, the window, and the garden provide invitations both to contemplate and be enriched by the uniqueness of each religious or spiritual expression, and to walk from window to window, house to house and garden to garden so that we might become deeply respectful of our neighbors' vantage point. The image of the neighborhood helps us regard strangers as wisdom figures whom we have yet to meet. Like King Friday in *Mr. Rogers' Neighborhood*, we keep each other honest and discern how to compromise. The focus on interspirituality in chapter 2 distinguishes the new monasticism from the specter of syncretism and offers examples of dual systems, especially what is meant by "multiple belonging." Given that Millennials are 13 percent more likely to reject Christianity than Gen Xers, it behooves the church to work with, rather than against, a generation that is becoming increasingly secular.

The Church has always been an evolving entity yet, unfortunately, we have short historical memories. It is difficult for parents to notice the changes in a child's development because they share daily life as a family, whereas those who see them at longer intervals are struck by the child's changes. In looking at the arc of church history, focusing on what occurred at various intervals such as origins to 300—the Patristic period, the Early Medieval, the High Medieval, the Reformation, Modern, and Postmodern eras—the changes are striking.

In 1970 the American sound designer and archivist Tony Schwartz produced a time lapse recording of the voice of his niece, Nancy, from birth through age 12.[6] The recording is only two minutes thirteen seconds. When the listener focuses first on the changes and then on the continuity in Nancy's voice, two things occur: in leapfrogging from Nancy's voice at one month to twelve years, the similarities are hard to capture. However, in listening to the full recording it is obvious that the voices of the one-month-old and the twelve-year-old belong to the same person. The difference is in whether the listener is focusing on differences or continuity. Each approach provides different insights.

Schwartz's study can help us process the enormous span of church history: two thousand years compared to twelve. Since there are so many pivotal events in the church's mission, and because our historical memories are full of gaps, it is important turn our attention to concrete examples of the church's innate elasticity. Christians who complain about the bygone era of the Latin Mass, one distinct form of solemnity and clear answers to moral issues, suggest a romantic idea that does not accurately represent the church in any era. That idealistic narrative, which appeals to a surprising number of Millennials, none of whom experienced the pre-Vatican II church, is paralyzing and constricting. For example, some look longingly at the church of the 1950s: the years immediately preceding Vatican II. However, as has recently been spotlighted, the sexual abuse problem in the church did not begin with Vatican II. In fact, the egregious conduct of clergy before Vatican II grew in a petri dish from a culture of secrecy among self-protective clergy. A three-year Council could not be expected to resolve long-standing abuses of power. However, the Council's emphasis on lay participation in the mission of Jesus began a conversation about the need for accountability and transparency in church governance. Though it has been fifty-five years since Vatican II, the hierarchy is just now beginning the detoxification process. As a human institution we can expect it to fall of the wagon. As the church, not of second chances, but of 50,000 plus infinity chances, we will support one another in our imperfect commitment to sobriety.

In 1976 I was still young enough to have to hold my mother's hand when we went for a walk. One of our neighbors was an elderly, distinguished-looking Italian whom we knew as "the Life Saver Man." With his hat and overcoat he reminded me of Inspector Clouseau from *The Pink Panther*. The Life Saver Man seemed to me both lonely and kind. I don't think my mother ever knew his name, but he had a grandfatherly smile and we always stopped to greet one another. My brother and I were spellbound by the hat trick that magically produced a pack of five-flavor Life Savers. He was obviously clairvoyant because he knew that I would choose cherry or pineapple and that my brother would go for lime. As he peeled back the paper, whichever of the three emerged first went either to me or my brother. Four decades later I have a warm memory of our neighbor's simple act of generosity. As with most kids, we were taught about the danger of taking candy from strangers. However, thanks to the Life Saver Man, I learned that sometimes the right thing to do is to take the candy.

For whatever reason my mother trusted a man whose name she never knew. She realized that those fleeting encounters were the highlight of the day for two preschool kids and an elderly gentleman. He offered a sign of kinship and my mother reciprocated. Though she had left Catholicism behind by then, that she allowed us to accept a stranger's hospitality taught me about faith. I would describe those encounters as unfiltered moments of spiritual care. We were very young, and the Life Saver Man was very old. The coincidence of opposites was mutually enriching. Many years later this book developed from a deeply rooted belief that strangers are more trustworthy than not. My mother would not have connected her generosity to her Roman Catholic upbringing. However, whether she knew it or not, she had internalized the core message in both Matthew 25 and *Mr. Rogers' Neighborhood*: welcome anyone who turns up and care for them with a generous spirit.

NOTES

1. "The Circus," *PBS American Experience* (2018). Season 1. Part 1. Episode 1, 2018.

2. Walt Whitman, *New York Dissected by Walt Whitman*. A Sheaf of Recently Discovered Newspaper Articles by the Author of Leaves of Grass, ed. Emory Holloway and Ralph Adimari (New York: R. R. Wilson, 1936), 196.

3. https://www.insidehighered.com/views/2006/07/07/life-circus (accessed June 19, 2019).

4. *Lumen Gentium* 4.33. http://www.vatican.va/archive/hist_councils/ii_vatican_council/documents/vat-ii_const_19641121_lumen-gentium_en.html.

5. This expression is often used by Phyllis Zagano in interviews and presentations about the restoration of the Roman Catholic female diaconate.

6. "Nancy Grows Up" from the album *Tony Schwartz Records the Sounds of Children* (Folkways Records, 1970).

Bibliography

Amaladoss, Michael. *Interreligious Encounters: Opportunities and Challenges.* Maryknoll: Orbis Books, 2017.

An-Nawawī's Forty Hadith: An Anthology of the Sayings of the Prophet Muhammad. Translated by Ezzeddin Ibrahim, Denys Johnson-Davies (Abdul Wadoud). Cambridge, UK: Islamic Texts Society, 1997.

Ariarajah, S. Wesley. *Moving Beyond the Impasse: Reorienting Ecumenical and Interfaith Relations.* Minneapolis: Fortress Press, 2018.

Armstrong, Regis et al., eds. "Legend of the Three Companions." In *Francis of Assisi: Early Documents.* Volume 2 *The Founder* (New York: New City Press, 2000), 69–110.

Ash, Steven. *Sacred Drumming.* New York: Sterling Publishing, 2001.

Augustine of Hippo. *Sermon 272.* https://earlychurchtexts.com/public/augustine_sermon_272_eucharist.htm.

Balado, J. L. Gonzalez. *The Story of Taizé*, 3rd edition. Oxford: Mowbray, 1988.

Barone, Giulia. *Enciclopedia dei Papi.* Rome: Treccani, 2000.

Bishop, Bill, and Robert Cushing. *The Big Sort: Why the Clustering of Like-Minded America is Tearing Us Apart.* Boston: First Mariner Books, 2009.

Bonaventure. *Disputed Questions on the Knowledge of Christ.* Translated by Zachary Hayes. Saint Bonaventure, NY: The Franciscan Institute, 1992.

Bouffartigue, Jean, and Anne-Marie Delrius. *Étymologies du Français.* Paris: Éditions Belin, 1996. Volumes: *Les Racines Latines*; *Les Racines Grecques*; *Les Curiosités Étymologiques.*

Boyle, Gregory. *Barking to the Choir: The Power of Radical Kinship.* New York: Simon and Schuster, 2017.

Brock, Sebastian P. "Rabban Ṣauma à Constantinople (1287)." In *Mémorial Mgr Gabriel Khouri-Sarkis (1898–1968), fondateur et directeur de L'Orient Syrien, 1956–1967.* Edited by F. Graffin. Louvain: Imprimerie orientaliste, 1969.

Buber, Martin. *Tales of the Hasidim. The Early Masters.* New York: Schocken Books, Inc. 1975.

Buck, Carl Darling. *A Dictionary of Selected Synonyms in the Principal Indo-European Languages*. Chicago: University of Chicago Press, 1949.

Budge, Wallis E. A., trans. *The Monks of Kûblâi Khân, Emperor of China*. London: Religious Tract Society, 1928.

Burtt, E. A., ed. "Sammanaphala Suttanta." In *The Teachings of the Compassionate Buddha*. New York: New American Library, 1955, 100–107.

Bynner, Witter. *The Way of Life According to Laotzu*. New York: Putnam, 1986.

Carle, Sister Judy. "Sisters and Millennials, Kindred Souls." In *¡Viva Mercy!. Bimonthly Publication for Sisters, Associates and Companions of the Sisters of Mercy of the Americas*. May–June 2018: 12–15.

Chan, Wing-Tsit, trans. and ed. *A Source Book in Chinese Philosophy*. Princeton: Princeton University Press, 1963.

Cho, Adrian. "The Social Life of Quarks." *Science Magazine*, January 14, 2016.

Coakley, John, and Andrea Sterk, eds. "The Lives of Mâr Yahbh-Allâhâ and Rabban Ṣâwmâ." In *Readings in World Christianity*, Vol. 1 Earliest Christianity to 1453. Maryknoll: Orbis, 2004, 373–384.

Conze, Edward, ed. *Buddhist Scriptures*. Baltimore: Penguin Books, 1973.

Dante Alighieri. *The Divine Comedy: Inferno*. Translated by Allen Mandelbaum. New York: Bantam Dell, 1980.

De Chardin, Teilhard. *The Divine Milieu. An Essay on the Interior Life*. New York: Harper and Row, 1968.

———. *Toward the Future*. Translated by René Hague. San Diego: Harcourt Inc., 1975.

De Mello, Anthony. *Heart of the Enlightened: A Book of Story Meditations*. New York: Image Books, 1991.

———. *Taking Flight: A Book of Story Meditations*. New York: Image Books, 1998.

Dorothy Day. *All the Way to Heaven: The Selected Letters of Dorothy Day*. Edited by Robert Ellsberg. NY: Image Books, 2010.

Doyle, Glennon. *Love Warrior: A Memoir*. New York: Flatiron Books, 2016.

Eddington, Sir Arthur. *The Nature of the Physical World*. Cambridge: Cambridge University Press, 1928.

Faber, Heije. "The Circus Clown." In *Images of Pastoral Care*. Edited by Robert C. Dykstra. St. Louis: Chalice Press, 2005, 85–93.

Ferrer, Jorge. "The Future of World Religion: Four Scenarios, One Dream." *Tikkun* 27 (1) (Winter 2012): 14–64.

Franchi, Antonino. *Nicolaus Papa IV: 1288–92: Girolamo d'Ascoli*. Assisi: Edizioni Porziuncola, 1990.

Galen the Physician. *De dignotione ex insomnis libellis. Opera Omnia*. Edited by Karl Gottlob Kühn (1823), 6: 832–835.

Gandhi, Mahatma. *Collected Works of Mahatma Gandhi*. Delhi: Publications Division, Ministry of Publication and Broadcasting, Government of India, 1958.

Garver, Eugene. *Aristotle's Politics: Living Well and Living Together*. Chicago: University of Chicago Press, 2011.

Geanakoplos, Deno John. *Constantinople and the West: Essays on the Late Byzantine (Palaeologan) and Italian Renaissance and the Byzantine and Roman Churches*. Madison: University of Wisconsin Press, 1989.

Geertz, Richard. *The Interpretation of Cultures*. New York: Basic Books, 1973.

Gibran, Kahlil. *Jesus The Son of Man: His Words and His Deeds as Told and Recorded by Those Who Knew Him*. New York: Penguin Books. 1997.

Gilmore, Lee. *Theater in a Crowded Fire: Ritual and Spirituality at Burning Man*. Berkeley: University of California Press, 2010.

Gnuse, R. "The Temple Experience of Jaddus in the Antiquities of Josephus: A Report of Jewish Dream Incubation." *The Jewish Quarterly Review* 83 (3/4) (Jan–April 1993): 349–368.

Gregory the Great. "Homilia in Evangelium" 27 (4). Edited by J. P. Migne, Paris: Garnier, 1857. PL 76, 1207.

Griffiths, Bede. *The Marriage of East and West*. Springfield: Templegate Publishers, 1982.

Haines, C. R., trans. and ed. *The Correspondence of Marcus Cornelius Fronto*. Loeb Classics. Vol. 1. London: William Heinemann, 1919.

Harrisson, Juliette. "The Development of the Practice of Incubation in the Ancient World." In *Medicine and Healing in the Ancient Mediterranean World*. Edited by Demitrios Michaelides. Oxford: Oxbow Books, 2014.

Hicks, Alan, and Rashida Jones. *Quincy*. Netflix documentary (2016).

Hosinski, Thomas. *The Image of the Unseen God: Catholicity, Science and Our Evolving Understanding of God*. Maryknoll, NY: Orbis Books, 2017.

Hubert H. Humphrey Papers. *Dedication of the Hubert H. Humphrey HEW Building*, Washington, DC, November 1, 1977. Speech Text Files. Used with permission from the Minnesota Historical Society.

Hugh of St. Victor. *Libello de quattuor voluntatibus in Christo*. Edited by J. P. Migne. Paris: Garnier, 1854. PL 176, 841.

Israelowich, Ido. "The Authority of Physicians as Dream Interpreters in the Pergamene Asclepion." In *Medicine and Healing in the Ancient Mediterranean*. Edited by Demitrios Michaelides. Oxford: Oxbow Books, 2014.

Jones, Alan. *Soul Making: The Desert Way of Spirituality*. San Francisco: HarperCollins, 1989.

Kennedy, Robert E. *Zen Gifts to Christians*. New York: Continuum, 2000.

Klein, Menachem. *Lives in Common: Arabs and Jews in Jerusalem, Jaffa and Hebron*. Oxford University Press, 2001.

Knitter, Paul. "Interreligious Dialogue: What? Why? How?" In *Interreligious Dialogue: An Anthology of Voices Bridging Cultural and Religious Divides*. Edited by Christoffer H. Grundmann. Winona, MN: Anselm Academic, 2015, 24–44.

Laozi. *Tao Te Ching: A New English Version*. New York: Harper & Row, 1988.

Lewis, Charlton T. and Short, Charles. *A Latin Dictionary*. Oxford University Press, 1969.

Liddell, Henry George and Scott, Robert. *Greek and English Lexicon*. Oxford University Press, 1972.

Lings, Martin. *Muhammad: His Life Based on the Earliest Sources*, 2nd edition. Vermont: Inner Traditions, 2006.

Lumen Gentium 4 (33). http://www.vatican.va/archive/hist_councils/ii_vatican_council/documents/vat-ii_const_19641121_lumen-gentium_en.html.

Macy, Gary. *The Banquet's Wisdom: A Short History of the Theologies of the Lord's Supper*. Akron: OSL Books, 2005.

Manning, Kathleen. "Upstart from Assisi." *U.S. Catholic* 82 (10) (October 2017): 12–17.

McCarty, Robert J., and John M. Vitek. *Going, Going, Gone: The Dynamics of Disaffiliation in Young Catholics.* Winona, MN: A Study by Saint Mary's Press of Minnesota, Inc. Center for Applied Research in the Apostolate (CARA), 2017.

McEntee, Rory, and Adam Bucko. *The New Monasticism: An Interspiritual Manifesto for Contemplative Living.* Maryknoll: Orbis Books, 2015.

McLaren, Brian. *The Great Spiritual Migration: How the World's Largest Religion is Seeking a Better Way to Be Christian.* New York: Convergent, 2016.

Menestò, Enrico, ed. *Niccolò IV: un pontificato tra oriente ed occidente : atti del convegno internazionale di studi in occasione del VII centenario del pontificato di Niccolò IV.* Ascoli Piceno 14–17 dicembre 1989.

Menocal, Maria Rosa. *The Ornament of the World: How Muslims, Jews and Christians Created a Culture of Tolerance in Medieval Spain.* New York: Back Bay Books, 2002.

Miura, Isshū, and Ruth Fuller Sasaki. *The Zen Koan: Its History and Use in Rinzai Zen.* Kyoto, Japan: The First Zen Institute of America in Japan, 1965.

Nouwen, Henri. *Return of the Prodigal Son: A Story of Homecoming.* New York: Image Books, 1992.

———. *The Wounded Healer: Ministry in Contemporary Society.* New York: Doubleday, 1979.

Oakes, Kaya. *The Nones are Alright: A New Generation of Believers, Seekers and Those in Between.* Maryknoll: Orbis Books, 2015.

Owles, R. Joseph, ed. *The Didache: The Teaching of the Twelve Apostles.* Create Space Independent Publishing, 2019.

Panikkar, Raimón. *Christianity: Opera Omnia, vol. III.2, A Christophany.* Edited by Milena Carrara Pavan. Maryknoll, NY: Orbis Books, 2016.

———. *The Intrareligious Dialogue.* New York: Paulist Press, 1978.

———. *The Trinity and the Religious Experience of Man.* Maryknoll: Orbis Books, 1973.

———. *The Unknown Christ of Hinduism.* Maryknoll: Orbis Books, 1964.

Pasquale, Gianluigi, and, Hamad Mahamed. "San Francesco e il Sultano. Un modello per il dialogo." *Città di Vita* 73 (January–February 2018): 63–74.

Patton, Kiberly. "A Great and Strange Correction: Intentionality, Locality, and Epiphany in the Category of Dream Incubation." *History of Religions* 43 (3) (2004): 194–223.

Peter, Damian. 'Contra philargyriam et munerum cupiditatem' (ch. 7), *Patrologia Latina,* vol. 145. Paris: Petit-Montrouge, 1853: 540–542.

Petsalis-Diomidis, Alexia. *Truly Beyond Wonders: Aelius Aristides and the Cult of Asklepios.* New York: Oxford University Press, 2010.

Pope Francis. *Laudato si.* http://w2.vatican.va/content/francesco/en/encyclicals/documents/papa-francesco_20150524_enciclica-laudato-si.html.

Rao, E. Nageswara. *Makers of Indian Literature: Aburri Ramakrishna Rau.* New Delhi: Sahitya Akademi, 2002.

Richo, David. *How to Be an Adult in Faith and Spirituality.* Mahwah, NJ: Paulist Press, 2011.

Rocca, Julius. *Galen on the Brain: Anatomical Knowledge and Physiological Speculation in the Second Century AD. Studies in Ancient Medicine,* volume 26. Edited by John Scarborough. Leiden: Brill, 2003.

Rossabi, Morris. *Voyager from Xanadu: Rabban Sauma and the First Journey from China to the West.* Tokyo: Kodansha International, 1992.

Rumi, Mevlana Jalaluddin. *The Essential Rumi.* Translated by Coleman Barks. New York: HarperCollins, 1995.

Schreiter, Robert. *Constructing Local Theologies.* Maryknoll: Orbis Books, 1985.

Setton, Kenneth. *The Papacy and the Levant, 1204–1271.* Philadelphia: American Philosophical Society, 1976.

Smith, William, ed. *A Dictionary of Greek and Roman Antiquities.* London: John Murray, 1898.

Swami Abhedananda. *The Sayings of Ramakrishna.* New York: The Vedanta Society, 1903.

Tanner, Norman, and Sethina Watson. "Least of the Laity: The Minimum Requirements for a Medieval Christian." *Journal of Medieval History* 32 (2006): 395–423.

Taylor, Barbara Brown. *The Preaching Life.* Rowman & Littlefield Publishers, Inc., 1993.

Tincq, Henri. "Eruption of Truth: An Interview with Raimon Panikkar: On Inter- and Intrareligious Dialogue." Translated by Joseph Cunneen. *The Christian Century* 117 (23) (August 16–23, 2000): 834–836.

Tracy, David. *The Analogical Imagination: Christian Theology and the Culture of Pluralism.* New York: Crossroad Publishing, 1981.

Untener, Bishop Ken. *Preaching Better: Practical Suggestions for Homilists.* Mahwah, NJ: Paulist Press, 1999.

Ware, Timothy. *The Orthodox Church.* London: Penguin Books, 1964.

West, Cornel. "Spiritual Blackout, Imperial Meltdown, Prophetic Fightback." Harvard Divinity School Convocation Address. August 29, 2017.

Index

absolution, 102
advaita, 24, 25
Aelius Aristides, 59, 80n20
Alighieri, Dante, 35, 51n55
Alvarez, Christina, 100
Amaladoss, Michael, 25, 49n27
analogical imagination, xxi, 48n12,
　49n21, 139. *See also* Tracy, David
anamnesis, 33, 63
Arghon, King, 7–9
Ariarajah, Wesley, 49n14
Aristotle, 27, 85, 106n1
Armstrong, Regis, 16n40, 106n17
Asclepius, 58, 59, 60, 61, 79; Temple
　of, 55, 58, 94
Ash Wednesday, 78
augur(s), 57, 77
Ayurvedic, 56

Baal Shem Tov, 39
Barbarosa, Frederick, xxiii
Benedict XVI, Pope, xxi, 112. *See also*
　Ratzinger, Joseph Cardinal
Bertone, Archbishop Tarcisio, xxi
Bishop, Bill, 51n54
Black Rock City, 27, 68, 76, 142. *See
　also* Burning Man
Bolz-Weber, Nadia, 64
Brooks, David, 50n34
Brown, Brené, 28

Buck, Carl Darling, 23, 80n7
Bucko, Adam and Rory McEntee,
　xxvin17, 22, 25, 49n15, 26, 137n30
Burner(s), xx, xxvin18, 51n45, 69, 74,
　75, 77, 82n57, 117
Burning Man, xxvin18, 27, 30–31, 53–
　55, 65, 68–72, 74–79, 80n4, 82nn53,
　57, 63, 103, 104, 105, 112, 139, 140,
　142, 143; Temple of, 69, 70, 76–77,
　79, 139
Byzantine, 15n24, 19, 101

Candomblé, 21
Caveat Magister, 75, 83n65
Chalcedon(ian), 33, 60, 114
chaplain(s), 56, 57, 87, 90, 93, 96, 99,
　106n11, 107n20, 134
Chardin, Teilhard de, 19, 25, 48n10–11,
　49n17, 49n25
Christus vivit, xvii
Chronos, 131, 135
Clinical Pastoral Education, xxiv, 25.
　See also CPE
Concord, Church of, 101
confession(s), sacrament of, 93, 102.
　See also reconciliation
contemplative listening, 23, 142
CPE, 25, 131. *See also* Clinical Pastoral
　Education
Cushing, Robert G., 51n54

About the Author

A native San Franciscan, **Amanda D. Quantz** is Professor of Theology at the University of Saint Mary in Leavenworth, Kansas. She teaches in the areas of historical theology and pastoral ministry. Since 2011 she has been a member of the Bethany Group, an organization that facilitates a faith-sharing opportunity for the men incarcerated at Lansing Correctional Facility in Kansas. Trained as a hospital chaplain and a medievalist, she continues to discover ways to draw on the Christian tradition, both in street ministry and with students whose various careers include care for the soul.

CPSIA information can be obtained
at www.ICGtesting.com
Printed in the USA
LVHW090959090220
646306LV00006B/92

9 781978 702677